Responsible Belief

Responsible Belief

Limitations, Liabilities, and Melioration

ROBERT M. FRAZIER

☙PICKWICK *Publications* · Eugene, Oregon

RESPONSIBLE BELIEF
Limitations, Liabilities, and Melioration

Copyright © 2015 Robert M. Frazier. All rights reserved. Except for brief quotations in critical publications or reviews, no part of this book may be reproduced in any manner without prior written permission from the publisher. Write: Permissions, Wipf and Stock Publishers, 199 W. 8th Ave., Suite 3, Eugene, OR 97401.

Pickwick Publications
An Imprint of Wipf and Stock Publishers
199 W. 8th Ave., Suite 3
Eugene, OR 97401

www.wipfandstock.com

ISBN 13: 978-1-4982-2500-7

Cataloguing-in-Publication Data

Frazier, Robert M.

Responsible belief : limitations, liabilities, and melioration / Robert M. Frazier

xii + 196 p. ; 23 cm. Includes bibliographical references.

ISBN 13: 978-1-4982-2500-7

1. Knowledge, Theory of. 2. Belief and doubt. 3. Critical thinking. 4. Augustine, Saint, Bishop of Hippo. 5. Philo of Alexandria—Criticism and interpretation. I. Title.

BD215 F71 2015

Manufactured in the U.S.A.   10/19/2015

Scripture quotations are from the New Revised Standard Version Bible, copyright © 1989 National Council of the Churches of Christ in the United States of America. Used by permission. All rights reserved.

In memory of our mothers, Mrs. Sarah Fiorillo and Mrs. Clara Frazier

Contents

Preface | ix

Chapter 1
The Waywardness of Belief | 1

Chapter 2
These are the Generations: The Epistemic Dominance of the Critical Thinking Movement | 43

Chapter 3
Psychological Insights on the Formation, Modification, and Holding of Beliefs | 72

Chapter 4
***Gnothi Seauton* and *Quaestro Mihi Factus Sum*: The Problem of Noetic Sin in Augustine** | 99

Chapter 5
Toward a Responsibilist Model of Believing | 129

Chapter 6
Cosmic Beauty and the Ethics of Inquiry: Appropriating Philo of Alexandria | 166

Conclusion
Recapitulation and Prospects | 183

Bibliography | 191

Preface

THIS BOOK ON RESPONSIBLE belief was a long time coming. By that I mean that the ideas behind it and my interests in the question of belief, its formation and revision, and the problems associated with it began back in college in the seventies. In a class on epistemology, I read Dr. Elton Trueblood for the first time and pondered how he understood belief. Soon after I read Dr. Nicholas Wolterstorff's short treatise, first edition, entitled *Reason within the Bounds of Religion*. That small book got me hooked on the problems of belief, the degrees of belief, and the control that some exercise over others. I must say that Nick's book was the catalyst behind my thinking and interests; although familiar with Locke's discussion of the degrees of belief, Wolterstorff's treatise made such sense to me because it carried the discussion beyond the mere strength by which one holds a belief into the deeper terrain of how beliefs relate to each other.

In my first graduate seminar at the University of Buffalo, I took a class entitled "Belief Systems" and in it read Milton Rokeach, whose influence on this book is clear. Rokeach, along with Quine in *Web of Belief*, contended for a structural framework for belief that made great sense to me in light of Wolterstorff's triad of belief. This was followed by work in the ethics of belief and the significant movement identified as "naturalized epistemology," which brought me into contact with a number of other scholars like Hillary Kornblith who seemed to be doing serious work on belief formation. Studying Charles Saunders Peirce's article called the "Fixation of Belief" provided the in-depth analysis of the tenacity of belief that made sense of my other musings and in many ways, with Wolterstorff, became the inspiration behind what I wanted to write about then and in this book. Reading Plato and Aristotle on belief and virtue only deepened my interests in this area. And so I wrote a dissertation applying the insights of these and others to a more practical area called critical thinking or informal logic that was an important topic in the philosophy of education at the time.

Although I benefitted from the work I encountered in the scholars listed above, I was still not satisfied with the account. Wolterstorff's perspective still had much in it that intrigued me, and his formal move into the epistemological perspective known as Reformed Epistemology provided much more by way of a fuller account. Given my theological orientation and my commitment to an Augustinian account of the life of the mind, I realized that some more robust explanation was required for the limitations and liabilities I had come to see in my engagement with belief formation and revision. Augustine's position on the noetic effects of sin supplied an explanation that was respectful of the materials I had previously encountered, but gave so much more in figuring out this thorny issue. Augustine's perspective gave a reason for the intellectual humility I learned about by reading Plato's Socratic dialogues.

I learned firsthand the lesson of intellectual humility from Professor Grady Spires at Gordon College when, in a class on historicism, I raised a question about the application of merkabah (chariot) mysticism to our topic. The question really had nothing to do with historicism, but like many sophomoric college students, I wanted to impress Grady with the little bit of insight I had acquired. Grady did the difficult; he asked me to tell him about merkabah mysticism. He was humble enough and, longing to learn, he placed himself in the position of learning from me. He showed me the virtue that all scholars need: intellectual humility.

My interest in virtue, intellectual virtue primarily as it bears on the interest in belief formation and revision, began in the first ethics class I had in college with Dr. Malcolm Reid, mentor and friend. Malcolm guided the class through the *Nichomachean Ethics*, another area that lives with me in that I offer a course on Aristotle at my college. In graduate school, my work in naturalized epistemology afforded me the chance to look at Aristotle on intellectual virtue before the flurry of books were written on it. I give an account inspired by Aristotle and Ernest Sosa in the pages that follow.

As I worked on this book, the things I learned, taught, and thought about for so many years just did not seem to be complete to me. The account of belief formation and revision coupled with the explanatory power of the notion of the noetic effects of sin and the alternative model of intellectual virtue I offered required something more. I pondered in light of the problems and limitation, and structural confusions I advanced, why anyone would go about revising beliefs. The importance of wonder I had learned from the works of Rabbi Joshua Heschel in my classes with Dr. Marvin Wilson came alive to me again as I gave lectures on wonder at my college in an academic convocation and in my classes in Plato, Aristotle, and the humanities. I discovered middle-Platonism around the same time and this has become a primary area of scholarship and writing for me and a source of interest in beauty. And the study of middle-Platonism has given me the opportunity to marry my interest in classical philosophy with Jewish writers of the middle-Platonist period like Philo of Alexandria and Aristobulus. And so the final turn in this book took shape as I engaged Philo on wonder and beauty.

My concern for beauty was cultivated, one might say, in a class I teach at Geneva College. This class is an invitation to the humanities, and teaching in it with my colleagues is and has been one of the most enriching experiences of my academic career. Through the presence, friendship, and lectures of my colleagues, Dr. Shirley Kilpatrick and Dr. Eric Miller, I have learned what beauty and excellent pedagogy are and how encountering wonder and beauty fosters the kind of disequilibrium needed to see beliefs modified and new beliefs emerge. Our other colleagues in the class coupled with the outstanding TAs we have been blessed to have create for us the loving, learning community of mutual esteem and marvel every semester. Judith Dinsmore, who has assisted me in the mechanics of this treatise and to whom I am deeply grateful, was one of those really bright students who came alongside of us in the journey of humanities. My friend Judith and her fellow TAs have demonstrated time and again the contours of the life we cherish as humanities professors.

There are so many people I wish to thank who have been so instrumental in my own development. Dr. Byron Bitar, who was my colleague in philosophy at Geneva prior to his death in 2003, was a dear friend and conversation partner. My colleague at Geneva in philosophy, Dr. Esther Meek, reminds me of the enthusiasm for learning that must accompany the academic life, and she has been a wonderful support for me in this endeavor and others. For those who have taught with us in humanities, I am deeply indebted and to the others who are my colleagues on the faculty of Geneva that have served as examples. My students in philosophy have been a great blessing to me through the years and have sat through my attempts at clarifying the issues in this book. I have received scholarship grants from the college for many years now and appreciate Geneva's generosity in providing these. I am thankful for the sabbatical the college gave me in the fall of 2014 that allowed me to bring this book to completion. My son Timothy spent countless hours reformatting work from my dissertation and I am grateful to him for this loving expression and the conversations about philosophical issues we enjoy. My son-in-law Brent Weatherly has bailed me out far too many times on the computer issues that have plagued me and so I thank him. Robin Parry, Ian Creeger, Matthew Wimer, and Brian Palmer from Pickwick Publications have been so kind and encouraging in bringing this book to publication.

I had the good fortune to meet a beautiful young woman forty-two years ago, my wife Marina, and her love and grace have sustained me through the years of schooling, child bearing, and child rearing and for her I am truly grateful. Marina has lived through the years supporting me without qualification as I struggled with these problems and as I served in pastoral ministry and in the professoriate. I have four wonderful children, Megan, Abby, Tim, and Daniel, who walked this journey with me and encouraged me along the way. My four precious grandchildren, Chase, Cadence, Emma, and Sophia cause me to continue to wonder and marvel at their brightness and beauty as they reflect the excellence of the God who gives life. These children, my own and my grandchildren, are the joys of my life.

This book is dedicated to the greater glory of God for God's grace. It was that grace that placed my feet on the path of becoming a learner as I sought to understand God's Wisdom/Word, God's eternally begotten Son Jesus Christ. In the last fourteen months, Marina and I both lost our mothers as they passed from this life. I wish to dedicate this book to our moms, Mrs. Sarah Fiorillo and Mrs. Clara Frazier. Ma Fiorillo welcomed me into her family as a young twenty-year-old and always cherished me as more than a son-in-law, but as a son. She and I were very close, and Ma never failed to encourage and support me in the midst of the cares of life. It is hard to capture in words the love, joy, and encouragement my mom, Clara, was to me through the years. We sang musicals together before my baseball games to calm me before I played and she provided the unwavering support I needed through the years both as an adult and a child. Mom was always more concerned with my welfare than her own. I deeply miss both of my mothers and my only sorrow in completing this book is that they are not here to enjoy with us the project they encouraged for so long. In the communion of the saints, I bless the memory of their lives and love.

CHAPTER 1

The Waywardness of Belief

INTRODUCTION

I HAVE LONG BEEN perplexed about the fixation of beliefs. I am afraid that Peirce was correct: once beliefs are established, it is quite difficult to see these revoked. By fixation of beliefs I mean the tendency of humans, once a belief is formed as a part of someone's belief system, to have and hold it tenaciously. Humans form beliefs and pack these away in the reservoir of habit and inclination such that the conscious repudiation of these is quite the formidable task. We humans interpret new experiences in light of whatever beliefs are held by us and find it hard to retreat from our positions.

I am sure my anxiety is two-fold. One reason for such perplexity and anxiety as this is that the Enlightenment taught us that if someone holds a belief in an uncritical fashion, that individual is irresponsible, even unethical. Locke suggested that a proposition ought to be assented to in accordance with the strength of the argument and evidence for it. To do less is a grave error of human judgment. Not only have rational beliefs in education and in the realm of religion been problematic for me, but assenting to beliefs in general as well. I am struck with a sense of insecurity that maybe I am the origin of false belief among persons I instruct and that this false belief led to action that was not altogether right. The ethics of belief, which asks whether one rightfully ought to hold a belief and queries how one in authority ought to communicate it, is most serious for one who feels messianic impulses, like most clergy persons, professors, and social activists. Hence for me, a dark pilgrimage occurs each time I consider my own beliefs and which ones to communicate.

In this book I hope to evaluate and articulate a perspective that wishes to fix the fixation of belief that troubles my soul so intensely. It seems to me that if the fixation of belief is going to be overcome, then one will need to develop the character traits necessary to generate questions that will lead to the revision of these tenaciously held beliefs. And further, as Peirce and Dewey held, the tendency to generate questions will emerge within the confines of inquiry itself. I mean that a model of inquiry needs to be developed that allows for the cultivation of questions that somehow circumvent the problems of the ways in which beliefs are tenaciously held.

Philosophers have long been interested in the issue of the fixation of beliefs. Since Descartes, philosophers have largely addressed belief fixation in the language of epistemology; that is, they sought to develop an epistemic model that would grant certainty in believing. These accounts treat belief fixation as a problem of justification; if one is justified in holding a belief, then fixation will be less of a problem. Even if one holds strongly to a particular belief, the very fact of justification renders it acceptable. They also had great confidence that once a method or model of inquiry was found that would grant certainty of belief, the model would be self-correcting. By this I mean that through application of an epistemological method to belief, the problem of misguided belief would be solved. But, as I will argue later, these accounts provide little by way of establishing the cognitive conditions that make up believing.

The educational application of the issues of justification and the concern for non-fixated beliefs is most clearly seen in what is known as the critical thinking movement. Before I discuss specifically how the critical thinking movement addresses the epistemological problems of fixation, however, the political context of education is in need of mention. There is a great concern over the status of education in the United States. Persons throughout the society wonder about what and how our children are learning and whether their lack of understanding will compromise our intellectual and political stance internally and internationally. Some wonder if this country's children will be able to engage the complexities of modern and future life. There are those who continually denigrate the state of education in the U.S., proposing that unless the educational status quo changes, these children, ours, will not be able to enjoy the privileges and blessings we currently possess.

Michael Scriven, in an article entitled "Critical for Survival," echoes this concern and places it in the context of the need for a renewed emphasis on critical reasoning in our schools. Scriven, as others in the critical thinking movement, is dismayed by the lack of attention given to the development of liberated minds in education. Far too easily education has come to focus on mere memorization and repetition of standard formula. These perpetuate the demise of the liberated mind. Without liberty of thought culture is doomed to failure. Culture and civilization will be undermined without an emphasis and engagement of the conditions that permit the fostering of a liberated mind. The liberated mind is characterized by rationality and the ability to justify one's beliefs. Israel Scheffler passionately appeals to this emphasis as well. He writes, "Whatever we do, I believe we ought to keep uppermost the ideal of rationality and its emphasis on the critical, questioning, responsible free mind."[1]

The continuation of culture and civilization is a primary concern of education. The educational system transmits, socially and epistemically, the culture of its educators. It may do so through indoctrination, through socialization, intimidation, or through providing the conditions for liberty of thought, to hearken back to Scriven. But just how liberty of thought emerges and is sustained is not an easy question to answer. What must a person know or experience to demonstrate liberty of thought? What things ought to be excluded from the curriculum in education given that they may foster indoctrination or socialization is of utmost concern for one who wishes to create the atmosphere for the cultivation of the liberty of thought.

Since at least the time of Descartes, Westerners have thought that if one could find a way of securing true beliefs and then enable persons to generate true beliefs for themselves without dependence on epistemological authorities, then the conditions most likely to produce liberated minds would occur. Not to be overly simplistic but this tradition has advanced epistemology as the queen of philosophical endeavors and the key to fostering and facilitating a free culture. Epistemology has been concerned with discovery and justifying true beliefs. In the twentieth century, epistemology's claim to philosophical preeminence solidified, particularly in the advent of the analytic tradition.

---

1. Scheffler, *Reason and Teaching*, 64.

Epistemological Emphases

In this book, I am going to focus on three epistemological models for critical thinking and will show how these models fail to address some central concerns in overcoming the issue of belief fixation. The first, proposed by Robert Ennis, is an example of an emphasis on achieving rational belief throughout the exercise of right strategies. The second approach is advanced by John McPeck and concentrates on the knowledge that one possesses and how this enables thinkers to manifest free minds.

A third perspective is corrective to both Ennis and McPeck, and its author is thought to be the chief spokesperson of the critical thinking movement, Richard Paul. He wishes to introduce what he calls a strong sense of critical thinking and to formulate a "new theory of knowledge." I am going to explore each model, beginning with Ennis, discussing how each reflects some of the ongoing problems of epistemology. Much of what I see as wanting in these approaches is due to what one might call the "aspychological" dominance of contemporary epistemology. As such, these accounts are inadequate in their treatment of the ways in which beliefs are structured by humankind. Without attending the question of the psychological structure of beliefs and their complexity, the epistemological melioration promised by the critical thinking movement falls fallow.

Historically, epistemologists have focused on "ideal" thinkers; unfortunately none is to be found. Far too often cognitive limitations are ignored and relegated to the field of psychology, assuming that these are epistemologically unimportant. I think one needs to develop much more of an interdisciplinary approach to the question of belief fixation. This approach would take seriously the historic interest of epistemology in providing norms for belief holding and revision and at the same time would consider the effects that cognitive operations actually have on how one believes. The approach that I wish to develop has a healthy respect for the normative aspects of belief formation/revision and yet takes into account the complexity and limitation of belief systems revealed for us by several theorists with a psychological perspective. In particular, we will explore the work of Rokeach, Tversky, and Elster and inquire into how their viewpoints remedy the deficits of theories of belief formation that are primarily epistemic in orientation. But I also see these limitations rooted in a deeper problem that exists in humans, and that is the problem of the noetic effects of sin. The good design structure that one possesses by creation and the norms that govern our cognitive systems has been affected by sin, which from an

Augustinian account such as this, is the vitiation of God's shalomic design. And so I will explore St. Augustine's conception of the noetic effects of sin as a viable explanation for the cognitive failures of humans. My attempted suggestions for melioration are founded in these concerns.

STRATEGIC CRITICAL THINKING AND THE PROBLEMS OF RATIONAL BELIEF IN ROBERT ENNIS

Historically, a major figure in the critical thinking movement has been Robert Ennis, Professor of Education and Philosophy at the University of Illinois. Ennis has primarily attempted to articulate what constitutes a critical thinker and what critical thinking is. His article in 1962, "A Concept of Critical Thinking" was an attempt to identify clearly the features, what Ennis called "aspects" in the 1962 piece, of critical thinking. More recently Ennis has authored two other definitive articles that advance and extend his 1962 position. These articles are "A Conception of Rational Thinking"[2] and "A Taxonomy of Critical Thinking Dispositions and Abilities."[3]

Ennis' conception of critical thinking separates an epistemically, normatively based model from psychological concern by contending that critical thinking is performance. For performance to be judged or assessed good or bad, weak or in need of improvement, Ennis' model requires the projection of an ideally competent thinker. One's critical thinking ability is judged by one's performance in tasks defined by epistemic competence. Subsequent to identifying what stands for performance and competence, I will explore the modifications that he makes from his earlier attempt at definition and argue that although some language has changed, the basic epistemological orientation remains constant. I want to examine some of the ways that belief formation and fixation are developed and how questions are asked, and I will then offer criticism of his perspective.

Ennis' Definition of Critical Thinking: Competence and Performance

Each of the three above-mentioned articles has a particular and distinctive definition of critical thinking. In paper one, Ennis declared that all previous

---

2. Ennis, "Rational Thinking," 3–30.
3. Ennis, "Critical Thinking Dispositions and Abilities," 9–26.

attempts to define critical thinking lacked precision and clarity. He suggests, "There has been a lack of careful attention to the concept of critical thinking,"[4] and that education has simply followed the lead of psychology in its attempts to define critical thinking.[5] Ennis wants to elaborate the "basic notion" of critical thinking through a "classification" and a "logical analysis of the dimensions of critical thinking."[6] In paper one, Ennis assays what constitutes a clear definition of critical thinking.

Ennis defines critical thinking as "the correct assessment of statements."[7] This definition exposes Ennis' central concern; critical thinking is about the performance task. The language of assessment points to a principal component of all of Ennis' work. He envisions critical thinking primarily in terms of logical skill; as one masters the multidimensional skill of assessment, one is identified as a critical thinker. In this first paper, his emphasis on skill and behavior are located in what he calls the twelve aspects of critical thinking. These twelve are all applied skills that one learns and inculcates in one's experience. Education is the vehicle of this inculcation.[8] The word "correct" indicates Ennis' commitment to establishing epistemological norms for true and valid inferences in critical thinking, i.e., the norms of competence. Part of possessing the skill of critical thinking is the ability to identify the validity or invalidity of arguments. Due to the distinction drawn in analytic philosophy between empirical concerns of psychology and language analysis, the province of the philosopher, Ennis' bent toward logic and language is understandable. To engage in systematic analysis of language implies that one's thoughts about reality be translated into statements about it. A statement is the basic stuff of one's analysis. One validates statements and propositions by the way language is used. Ennis' interest in the first article is to advance the notion that critical thinking is actually part of the epistemological branch of philosophy that deals with validation—namely logic. This position identifies the norms necessary for critical thought to be derivative from logic. The norms and principles of logic are a priori and consequently not related to accounts that require experience, such as psychological accounts.

---

4. Ennis, "Concept of Critical Thinking," 157.
5. Ibid., 158.
6. Ibid., 159.
7. Ibid.
8. Ibid.

Another key concept in explicating the meaning of critical thinking is definition. Definition, the searching and extradition of meaning, is the activity of critical thinking. A definition is discovered in usage, and not in essence.[9] Two points from his text demonstrate this. He lists three dimensions of critical thinking that he says are "analytically distinguishable."[10] The first dimension is cited as the logical dimension, which covers "judging the alleged relationships between meanings of words and statements."[11] And then he adds that a person who is "competent in this dimension knows what follows from a statement or a group of statements." Knowing how to define language in use is a central activity of the definitional component of critical thinking.

Ennis suggests that grasping a statement's meaning is an undergirding feature of the logical dimension of the critical thinking enterprise.[12] He states that if one knows the meaning of a statement, he should know what would count as evidence for or against it.[13] He concludes his discussion of the meaning of a sentence by stating, "this aspect is the core of the other logical aspects."[14] One cannot be a critical thinker without knowledge of the usage of a statement and how meaning extraction is central to the logical dimension of the definitional enterprise.

The second dimension of critical thinking he identifies as the criterial dimension. This dimension's task is to know what criteria are utilized in judging statements other than logical criteria. The application of this dimension will be spelled out more clearly when I discuss the twelve aspects of critical thinking later in the book.

Ennis calls the third dimension of analytic distinguishability of the concept critical thinking the pragmatic dimension. This dimension is concerned with whether or not the statement meets norms of evidence in a

---

9. A major source of confusion is found in McPeck's criticism of Ennis at this point. McPeck faults Ennis because Ennis fails to define clearly what critical thinking is. But Ennis is not concerned here with the essence of a definition, its denotation, but with the way in which a definition is used in language. Ennis' focus is on skill in manipulating language. His conception of belief is that it is dispositional. I criticize this notion of belief in chapter 3, where I build on the arguments against a dispositional account of belief from Scheffler.

10. Ennis, "Concept of Critical Thinking," 160.

11. Ibid.

12. Ibid.

13. Ibid.

14. Ibid., 162.

particular field. The pragmatic dimension makes judgments about whether standards have been fulfilled or whether statements are precise enough to fulfill the purpose of a particular endeavor. All three of these dimensions are infused throughout his aforementioned twelve aspects of critical thinking.

In paper two, "A Conception of Rational Thinking," his 1979 presidential address to the Philosophy of Education Society, Ennis alters his 1962 notion of critical thinking. He identifies rational thinking with critical thinking, thus viewing these as one and the same. Ennis claims that rational thinking is an advance over the narrowly defined 1962 article. He argues that the 1962 conception limits the range of activities involved in good thinking to the act of judging.[15] This is far too narrow because other actions are involved as well, like inferring, observing, and offering a well-organized line of reasoning.[16] In the 1962 piece, he identifies his intention as providing a concept of critical thinking. In "Rational Thinking" Ennis extends the notion of "concept" to that of "conception" so that it might include criteria for evaluating whether a given piece of thinking is rational or not.[17] (These criteria for judging were, evidently, absent from the 1962 piece.) If it is, it will lead to both rational action and moral behavior.[18]

The third paper published in 1987 is entitled, "A Taxonomy of Critical Thinking, Dispositions and Abilities." This is Ennis' third attempt to develop a conception of critical thinking. In this paper he goes beyond the earlier papers in defining critical thinking. Ennis suggests in this third piece that "critical thinking is a practical reflective activity that has reasonable belief or action as its goal."[19] He offers this working definition: "Critical thinking is reasonable reflective thinking that is focused on deciding what to believe or do."[20] In this paper the notion earlier cited as tendencies is now termed dispositions, and proficiencies are now called abilities. Judgment, which has fared well in the previous papers, is identified as the ability to form "a decision about a belief or action."[21]

An important distinguishing feature of this paper is that, unlike the previous papers, he wishes to advance a "taxonomy" of critical thinking

15. Ennis, "Conception of Rational Thinking," 3.
16. Ibid.
17. Ibid., 4.
18. Ennis mentions these issues on the last page of the article in one paragraph.
19. Ennis, "Critical Thinking Dispositions and Abilities," 10.
20. Ibid.
21. Ibid., 16.

and this taxonomy has four features to it. The first is called elementary clarification.[22] At this level the critical thinker clarifies what questions to focus on and analyzes arguments. The second level is concerned with inferences the critical thinker makes when evaluating the information which emerges from clarification.[23] The third level is advanced clarification in which terms are defined and assumptions are identified.[24] The last level of critical thinking is identified by interaction with others. Unlike Bloom's taxonomy, which posits some thinking skills as higher order, Ennis argues that these criteria will occur in all good thinking. Good thinking, which is critical thinking, is known by its capacity to clarify meaning, evaluate evidence, and make decisions based on evidence and reflection. The next section will analyze a bit more closely the apparent revisions he proposes.

Continuities in Ennis' Thinking on Thinking

Given my concern with fixation of belief, it is important in this section to demonstrate textually the ways in which, good or bad, Ennis is tenaciously holding his own beliefs about beliefs and to suggest that this results from the assumed differentiation of epistemology from psychology. I will identify parallels among the three papers that illustrate that there are important underlying factors that influence Ennis' position, which he seems to ignore or, at least, not justify. I believe this kind of examination will clarify and illustrate the ways in which one's intentions and beliefs are influenced by other circumstances surrounding the individual thinker as these continue to influence even when one is unaware of their presence.

One might ask what precisely Ennis is attempting in each of these papers and how it is that this concern grows from his first to his third paper. McPeck is not convinced that one can discover Ennis' intention, which, for McPeck, contributes to the ambiguity of Ennis' position. Intention is essential for a rational, critical position, according to McPeck, because he, as the epistemological tradition suggests from Descartes to the present, identifies critical thinking with cognizance of belief. I think that Ennis is driven by a basic intention, which is driven by other beliefs. His intention is to provide a conceptualization of critical thinking that will be testable empirically. He wishes to describe and advance a model for the semantics

22. Ibid., 12.
23. Ibid., 19.
24. Ibid., 23.

of critical thinking that will then evaluate subjects to determine whether they are critical thinkers. This approach to analysis has its roots in the logical positivistic movement, which disassociated the physical sciences (characterized by description) from philosophical analysis (characterized by the pursuit of the conditions necessary for justification). Philosophers in this tradition advanced that epistemology, the theory of justified belief, was their primary province. Hence, philosophers in this tradition devoted their energies to the analysis of the conditions of justification, that is, what are the norms or rules necessary to be satisfied to identify a belief as justified.

To deepen the separation of justification from description, epistemologists have posited a position that became known as the genetic fallacy; one cannot advance norms of justification from the empirical sciences because these describe what is occurring in certain phenomena, not what ought to occur. This is at the heart of Ennis' separation of psychology from epistemology. For example, one may describe the manner in which a child acquires the belief that a certain behavior always elicits certain responses from adults. He internalizes this behavior and conducts himself for the remainder of his life in the childish manner he adopted. The analytic epistemologist suggests that the philosopher and the psychologist look at this information in two different ways. The philosopher wishes to know whether the child reasons correctly, i.e., justifiably according to norms. The psychologist wishes to describe such things as the origin of the phenomenon without making a value judgment, that is, whether it is right or wrong for the child to persist in the belief. The belief in the separation of psychological states from justification determines and controls which questions each will pose in their analyses and also directs even what language is deemed appropriate in their prospective ways of approaching the problems. The philosopher persistently believes that the theories developed by the psychologist are subject to an epistemological evaluation. The philosopher's concern for the evaluation of statements and justification of propositions stand outside the province of psychological experimentation.

I am claiming that despite some important progression in Ennis' articles, the above cited belief in the distinction of description of the psychological processes utilized in coming to believe a proposition from normative, rule-governed justification of a proposition is a legacy of logical positivism, which Ennis assumes and which shapes his model throughout. Ennis writes, "research in thinking has frequently been conducted in the fields of psychology and education, but in both fields there is a significant gap."[25] The focus has been too much on description, far too little on what makes for a conception to be clear. The skills Ennis advances determine the clarity of a proposition, and from that foundation one judges its warrantability.

Ennis continues by suggesting that "education has followed the research concerns of psychology,"[26] and because educators use psychology as their disciplinary base, they fail to provide "a comprehensive and detailed examination of what is involved in making judgments about the worth of statements or answers to problems."[27] They fail to provide a "logical criterion"[28] instead of a psychological criterion for the solution to a problem. In other words, Ennis contends that because educationists have followed the lead of psychologists rather than philosophers in evaluating the products of thinking, they have failed to identify what constitutes the rules and norms of good thinking, critical thinking. This again is established by articulating the conditions of justification or validity.

Ennis claims to provide a simplified and a comprehensive view of the conception of critical thinking which had not been attempted prior to 1962. He identifies his concept of critical thinking as a "desirable basis for research."[29] He contends that the "main task of this paper is to present a clear and detailed account of the concept of critical thinking."[30] That is, he wishes to draw out the logical implications of the concept of critical thinking and then use it for a research base. In other words, what research should test with regard to critical thinking should be derived mainly from the clear analysis of the concept of critical thinking. He believes the best way of proceeding is by supplying a "classification" of the aspects of critical thinking. Ennis' attachment to the epistemological tradition/belief that description of the origin and use and substance of one's beliefs is unrelated to how one justifies those beliefs is not questioned. One might wonder why he believes that such a separation is necessary. My suggestion is that there are beliefs, the origin of which and the occurrences of which control one's interpretation of the world and how to navigate in it. Some of these beliefs are historically held and tacitly utilized in one's analysis of the world.

25. Ennis, "Concept of Critical Thinking," 157.
26. Ibid., 158.
27. Ibid.
28. Ibid.
29. Ibid.
30. Ibid., 159.

By claiming distance from the influences of one's psychological states and from the more general influence of the past, Ennis fails to recognize the potential for cognitive melioration connected with a broader perspective that considers these descriptive elements that go into believing.

Analytic epistemology, the offspring of logical positivism and the dominant conduit for the separation of the description of psychological states from the epistemological ones of justification and validity, advanced the idea that the domain of philosophy is to provide a semantic model of conceptualization unrelated to the growth of ideas. A semantic model is a classification, a taxonomy, a system of rules and usages of language that govern a particular concept. In each of the three articles cited in this chapter by Ennis, he attempts a classification of the concept of critical thinking. My argument at this point is to underscore the notion (developed most fully by Gadamer in *Truth and Method*) that one's historicity is inescapable; one will interpret the world in concert with one's places in the sequence of time. Logical classification allows one to stand outside time in judging and evaluating experience. It is one of the conditions that permit the rational thinker to be identified as a transcendental ego, a concept that pervades all three epistemological concepts of critical thinking and a concept that I will criticize in chapter 2. Ennis manifests this attachment to concepts of justification and validity in his logical categorization schemes found in all three articles. In the 1962 piece, he called it classification, in the 1979, he identifies it as characterization, and in the 1987 piece, it is called a taxonomy.

A Textual Examination of the 1962 Article

I want now to use Ennis as an example of how continuities of position are deeply embedded in the way we approach so-called new positions. I want to emphasize that the continuities that we find in Ennis result from a pretheoretical commitment to the analytic epistemological tradition, which divorces psychology from epistemological concern and which seeks primarily the establishment of norms for justification and validity.

Ennis contends in paper two that he has made significant changes in his position. In this paper, Ennis detects a weakness in his earlier article. He states that this is so because paper one focused on "judging statements" not on "observing, inferring, conceiving alternatives, and offering a well organized line of reasoning."[31] Another fault in the earlier position is that

31. Ennis, "Conception of Rational Thinking," 3.

it provided a "concept of critical thinking" now a "conception." A concept is equivalent to a basic definition while a conception is supplied when "criteria are established for determining whether a given piece of thinking is rational."[32] These two revisions provide the grounds for articulating a conception of critical thinking.

Textually, Ennis' claim for the aforementioned revisions is confusing. Ennis defends the notion throughout that a critical thinker is one who clearly defines positions and avoids ambiguity in language. The critical thinker straight-forwardly and competently utilizes language. If Ennis means what he says in article two about article one, then one would expect to find little reference to the ideas of observing or inferring in article one. But as one examines his first piece, this is simply not the case. He actually discusses quite extensively these ideas and posits them as crucial components of critical thinking. Twelve aspects identify the critical thinker in article one. Aspect 7 is all about observing, inference is a dominant feature of 6 and 8. Ennis has indeed talked about these earlier in the context of clarifying and validating statements. In paper two Ennis suggests that conception is articulated when in the context of clarifying and validating statements as well.

But, one might suggest, Ennis discusses these things differently in the two papers. Maybe he means something different when he discusses observation in the first paper and observing in the second. In paper two, Ennis states, "Rational thinkers are proficient at observing."[33] To be so, such a thinker will manifest the following traits:

1. observing in an area of his experience,

2. be careful,

3. be in full possession of his faculties,

4. have no conflict of interest in making the observation,

5. be skilled at observing the thing observed,

6. have sensory equipment in sufficiently good condition,

7. be precise,

8. avoid being influenced by preconceived notion.[34]

---

32. Ibid., 5.
33. Ennis, "Conception of Rational Thinking," 6.
34. Ibid., 6–7.

Now in paper one, one discovers the following items that all pertain to the observer and demonstrate the constancy of Ennis' position. On page 166 of "Concept," number [7.13] is identified as having sensory equipment which is in good condition. This seems to be essentially what is said in 6 above. In [7.12] the observer is "skilled at observing the sort of thing observed," reminiscent of 5 above. In fact, when comparing the list of features on the observer in section [7.1] of article one, one discovers their presence in the list above. Interestingly, by the third paper Ennis uses the language of "observing and judging observation," thus retaining the emphasis of the first paper, which tacitly informed paper two. And in paper three, he defines observing and judging by utilizing the characterization of observation in paper one, [7.2]–[7.4].

It seems to me that the key to understanding Ennis' constancy is that he, like all of us, is directed by what Nicholas Wolterstorff calls control beliefs, and these determine the interpretation of subject matter for the interpreter. Historically, justification occurs when a rational agent sufficiently clarifies competently the substance of a belief such that he/she can make a judgment about it. Since Kant the notion that an ideal rational agent, one who manifests what right thinking is and who is divorced from self-interest and preconceived ideas, as per above, is posited so that other thinkers might be judged by the ideal agent. In chapter 2 of this book I will identify the history of this concept and in chapter 3 I will argue that this notion is unhelpful because no such agents exist. To improve thinking and to provide an epistemological framework, the theorist ought to consider how persons *actually* go about thinking and framing decisions and then develop ways of improving the activity and habits of thinking.

Textually, the autonomous subject, what Kant called the transcendental ego, is identifiable in each of Ennis' papers. The critical/rational thinker is "unemotional, alert, and disinterested." Also, he/she must have "no preconceptions about the way the observation would turn out."[35] His/her selection of instances of a subject matter must be "unbiased." There must be "no conflict of interests" present in the observation made.[36] He/she must be able to "avoid being influenced by preconceived notions." In paper three, the critical thinker must be "open-minded," refrain from making judgments until all appropriate evidence is in place and must have a

---

35. Ibid., 7.
36. Ibid., 6.

"lack of conflict of interest."[37] Ennis' thinker is ahistorical and unconnected to previous psychological and sociological states. To the extent that one is bound to these constructs, one is not a critical thinker, according to Ennis. In fact, for the ideal rational/critical thinker, revision of belief is unnecessary because he/she got it right the first time around when judgment about it was made.

Ennis' analysis misses the complexity of belief and belief systems when contending for such an ahistorical autonomy. One's preconceptions govern the ways in which one interprets reality. These direct the information that one attends to in the interpretation of the world, and persons readily look for evidence that confirms beliefs already possessed.

In fairness to Ennis, one must admit he does not address problems of belief revision directly. The way one holds beliefs, even the way beliefs within a belief system interact with other belief, is not his concern. He is much more interested in how beliefs are justified and the logic employed to settle the question of which ones to assent to. But this supports my earlier contention that the epistemologically dominated theorist is one who believes the right model of justification protects one from the problem of fixation; one fixes the believing process before it needs fixing. Unfortunately, without some engagement of the ways in which belief holding and manufacturing influences belief validation, Ennis' position remains truncated.

As Ennis has confessed and my examination has shown, he is primarily interested in the issue of justification, that is, what goes into deciding whether assertion x is to be adopted by believer S in such a way that the belief is warranted. He is interested in the grounds of establishing or withholding belief. In this he holds a position that might be called "the on-the-paper-thesis-of-epistemology."[38] This entails being able to lay out on paper the assertions that pertain and influence the particular proposition under inspection. Once one determines how other beliefs one holds support or do not support the proposition under examination, the statement may be accepted or rejected. This supposes the believer capable of seeing and identifying all relevant beliefs and which ones support or interconnect with others. This notion conjectures an agent intelligent enough to identify all applicable beliefs, but this clearly does not occur in any believing. In fact,

---

37. Ennis, "Critical Thinking Dispositions and Abilities," 12.

38. Throughout the remainder of this manuscript, I will identify the common features of the dominant view of epistemology by this title. I borrow this phrase from Hilary Kornblith.

hundreds of beliefs have changed in both the reader and myself as we have read or written this chapter. Given the earlier argument that preconceptions govern interpretation of reality and determine which information is deemed appropriate for the statement under inspection, this position by Ennis is untenable.

To recapitulate, Ennis' position is incomplete due to its inability to address how beliefs originate and how these interact with other beliefs held. He fails to understand how there is more to evaluation than simply a formula that advances logical skills. The necessary surfacing of all pertinent beliefs, which is required for clarity to be realized, just does not occur. Agents are not autonomous and "the-on-the-paper-thesis-of-epistemology" does not hold.

A final comment about Ennis. He mentions the notion of reflection. In paper two Ennis defines critical thinking as reasonable reflective thinking that is focused on deciding what to believe or do.[39] He fails, however, to describe what reflection is. Reflection is the basis for one to access other beliefs that one holds. Reflection by all counts must be included in critical thinking, but we find far clearer and engaging descriptions and analyses of reflection, however, in the work of the next authors. I now turn to John McPeck's attempt to improve on the notion of critical thinking.

MCPECK'S CONCEPTION OF CRITICAL THINKING

The critical thinking movement is universally concerned with developing persons who form and revise beliefs rationally. In fact, persons involved in the movement would suggest that if one is a critical thinker, he or she will be less likely to hold beliefs tenaciously. There will be embedded in the critical thinker a propensity toward revisability and carefulness in belief formation. Unfortunately, participants in the discussion of what constitutes a critical thinker seem to have erred on one or the other side of the epistemology/psychology debate. The perspective that I think will clear up the confusion of belief fixation must be one broad enough to account *both* for norms in belief formation *and* for cognitive limitations.

This is to contend that persons involved in the critical thinking movement share a concern for cognitive melioration, for intellectual perfection, and cultivation. They wish to develop models of thought that enable students to critically engage problems, circumstances, and situations as these

39. Ennis, "Conception of Rational Thinking," 4.

emerge in everyday experience. In a real sense, critical thinking theorists share the burden of equipping students with rigorous intellectual skills and frames of mind such that the education of their vassals will affect the vassal's ability to satisfy problems and dilemmas outside the institution. Critical thinking theorists claim to unlock the conditions necessary to get on well in the world beyond time shared in the classroom.

John McPeck avers that the way to satisfy the burden of educating critical thinkers is to be more assiduous in articulating an epistemological perspective for critical thinking. Unlike Ennis, whose focus is on the competent analysis of statements, McPeck envisions critical thinking as the educational enterprise that acknowledges and articulates a connection with the theory of knowledge. The limitation of Ennis' position for McPeck is in its exclusive concern with validity of arguments. Critical thinking must be concerned with truth: is one justified in holding and assenting to beliefs and what evidence does one possess for holding beliefs? These are the kinds of question that fancy the interest of McPeck.

McPeck suggests that the public outcry against the absence of critical thinking has fostered a myriad of naive proposals and that it is "generally inclined to accept proposals for formal courses in logic or critical thinking."[40] Although the general public responds this way, McPeck argues that,

> The real problem with uncritical students is not a deficiency in a general skill such as logical ability, but rather a more general lack of education in the traditional sense. Courses in logic fail to accomplish the goal of critical thinkers and the epistemology of various subjects is the most reasonable route to that end.[41]

He claims that, "the epistemological approach to critical thinking involves little more that providing what has always been a necessary condition of education, namely understanding what constitutes good reasons for various beliefs."[42] McPeck advances a reformation, a return to an epistemic base to delineate the essence of critical thinking. This return to an epistemological foundation with its emphasis on truth, evidence, and good reasons is a profitable twist in the critical thinking movement. In what follows, I will first cite some issues that McPeck identifies as crucial in critical thinking contra Ennis. Secondly, I will examine and expound McPeck's position to determine what his epistemological model portends. Lastly, I will offer

40. McPeck, *Critical Thinking and Education*, 22.
41. Ibid.
42. Ibid.

some criticisms of McPeck—referring to the limitations of his theory with respect to the fixation of beliefs.

McPeck's Advance

To establish critical thinking on an epistemological base, McPeck first considers why Ennis' model of critical thinking does not provide students with the initiation into the canons of rationality necessary for the successful engagement of everyday problems. McPeck defines Ennis' most basic problem, and that of the informal logic movement as well, as the identification of critical thinking with what has been called argument analysis. McPeck contends that critical thinking cannot be reduced to a generalizable skill but must take into account the complexity of information involved in a particular piece of critical thinking. Ennis' concentration on logical validation is, according to McPeck, a distortion and incomplete as a theory of critical thought.

Arguments do not appear in isolation, McPeck contends. They cannot be extracted from the consideration of how evidence and the truth of an argument's premises determine the acceptance of a statement. According to McPeck, one must know or possess background information regarding a statement to analyze correctly any argument. It is not enough to syllogize an argument, unless one first knows what makes an argument good or bad, right or wrong, in a given discipline to assess the truthfulness of a proposition. He writes, "In making rational judgments one does not need to know more about the validity of arguments, one needs to know more about the complex ways in which information is provided."[43] The emphasis on understanding and evidence in McPeck introduces a new focus, an improvement to critical thinking. This focus is on determining the epistemological foundation of critical thinking. Unlike the unarticulated but actual dependence of Ennis on the transcendental ego and autonomy of theoretical thought, McPeck envisions our beliefs about different affairs and our justification of those beliefs to be tied to beliefs and positions taken prior to the analysis of those beliefs. The autonomous determination of belief present in Ennis has no place in McPeck. Beliefs come to persons because of the way these have been constructed in a social environment. There are forms of thought, i.e., disciplines, and learning and knowing the beliefs contained within these forms is necessary if one is to form new beliefs in that field.

43. Ibid., 22.

McPeck is advancing both a social epistemology (that knowledge is held in a particular way due to the structure given it by a social group) and a coherence notion of knowledge (that beliefs, to be justified, are connected internally in a consistent and coherent fashion with other beliefs held in a particular discipline). Individual believers form and frame beliefs in relationship to other beliefs held by one in a field of thought. Consequently, no belief stands alone for assessment. Each belief is justified in terms of its association with other beliefs in a field or discipline.

Further, McPeck argues for the importance of knowing background information in a discipline and that one must know the canons of truth and epistemology within that discipline. This suggests that if one is to understand a belief, one must know how it relates to previously held beliefs in that area and how these were arrived at. The critical thinker applies the criteria of evidence to a given belief to determine its status with other beliefs in that field. The claim that beliefs are judged in relationship with other beliefs that one holds is an important advance in McPeck. His scheme suggests that one must always consider a more complete evaluation of beliefs in determining which ones stand as knowledge in a given field. Now I will provide a fuller exposition of McPeck's perspective.

Reflective Skepticism and the Generation of Questions

John McPeck is concerned with developing persons with the propensity and skill to think critically about beliefs that they possess or are in the process of forming. McPeck contends that although there are many texts on critical thinking, few engage in the process of telling, defining, and justifying what critical thinking is. In his book *Critical Thinking and Education*, McPeck seeks to provide an analysis of the concept, critical thinking, which insures its usability and applicability in education. Further, McPeck wishes to create thinkers who will be able to question rationally the worlds they have received and who will be able to assess the belief systems they possess with the goal of altering, revising, and forming new beliefs. This kind of thinker he identifies as a reflective skeptic.

McPeck describes a person as a critical thinker "about x if he has the propensity and skill to engage in x with reflective skepticism."[44] This definition captures the essence of McPeck's concerns. There are three components of a critical thinker in this definition that need to be explored:

44. Ibid., 7.

1. Critical thinking is about x, i.e., critical thinking engages some subject matter or field of inquiry and can only be carried on in the context of a subject matter.
2. A critical thinker uses the skills necessary to engage x. To know a subject matter x means that one is able to utilize the rules, procedures, and assessment techniques of that subject area.
3. One and two above are necessary conditions for a person to be a reflective skeptic, i.e. one who suspends beliefs, raises questions, and justifies propositions in the field in question.[45]

I will explore McPeck's idea of the reflective skeptic with these categories in mind to determine whether his conception of critical thinking will produce the propensity to question one's currently held beliefs.

About X

McPeck argues that critical thinking is always about some subject matter. He writes, "it is important to note that thinking is always about something."[46] That something is the field of inquiry—discipline, mind you—in which a person is engaged. To talk about thinking without an object, he writes, is vacuous, "for to think about nothing in particular is equivalent to not thinking at all."[47] It is a necessary condition of critical thought that a person be thinking in some previously standardized and framed discipline.

The field of study is important, essential, because it provides, prior to an evaluation of the belief under examination, the norms, rules, procedures, method of inquiry of that field. Fields of study or disciplines contain the epistemic foundation of critical thinking.[48] Without these foundations, one is incapable of articulating questions to challenge or alter currently held beliefs. Questions emergent from the discipline in question require, first and foremost, the skills of an historian. Similarly, critical thinking about a scientific question requires the knowledge and skills of a scientist. He writes "there is no set of supervening skills that can replace basic

---

45. Ibid., 7–9.
46. Ibid., 3.
47. Ibid.
48. Ibid., 156.

knowledge of the field in question."⁴⁹ Hence, each field of inquiry generates questions when faced with new data in the process of thought.

This kind of approach guarantees the sovereignty and autonomy of fields of research because no one who has not been initiated into the field at hand is able to make sense of the issues, problems, and procedures that are under evaluation. Just how much one needs to understand and know to qualify as initiated leads to our discussion of skill to engage the subject area.

Skills to engage subject x

Critical thinking is always about a subject matter or activity. And the quality of that thought is what determines whether one is a critical thinker or not. The quality of one's thought in a subject area does not result from possessing information about it alone, but from one's ability to utilize and manipulate the rules, standards, and procedures embedded in the discipline. It entails knowing the "criteria" that belong to a field in making a judgment. Quality "must be determined by the norms and standard of the subject area in question."[50]

The skill McPeck has in mind is "learning to know when to question something, and what sorts of questions to ask. Not just any question will do."[51] He calls critical thinking a task and achievement concept. The skill includes the "assessment of statements," but is not limited to it as Ennis would contend. Critical thinking involves the "methods, procedures and techniques" of a field that have "identifiable intellectual qualities."[52] In contrast to Michael Polanyi, who views skills as "the observance of a set of rules which are not known as such to the person following them, the critical thinker is able to scrutinize"[53] the intellection that occurs in the use of the skill by identifying the benefits or deficiencies of said skill.[54]

In sum, critical thinking is coming to know what constitutes evidence in a given area, using its procedures to evaluate a problem at hand; it is

---

49. Ibid., 9.
50. Ibid., 7.
51. Ibid., 8.
52. Ibid., 10.
53. Ibid., 11.
54. On page 11, McPeck also distances himself from G. Ryle's emphasis on knowing how. This is an unhealthy distinction, according to McPeck, because it makes critical thinking a part of practical reasoning and not epistemology.

"the intelligent use of all available evidence" in determining a solution to a problem.[55] The intelligent use of evidence leads us to query what this phrase means, hence the object of our third section.

Reflective Skepticism and Epistemology

McPeck argues for an epistemic base for critical thinking. The summation of the epistemic orientation of critical thinking is found on page 23 of *Critical Thinking and Education*:

> When we say of some one that he has learned to understand a particular discipline or field of study, we are saying that he appreciates what constitutes a good reason in that area. And further the critical thinker has an understanding of the concepts and peculiarities of the nature of evidence as they are understood by the practitioners in the field in which they emanate.

When McPeck speaks of understanding, he is referring to the awareness of how evidence functions, the ways that one uses evidence, the manner in which one finds evidence, and the meaning of the words employed in a given field. Initiation of one into a field supplies this basic understanding. The critical thinker is one who is able to use this understanding in the process of justifying beliefs.

Justification, according to McPeck, begins with the suspension of a judgment about a proposition which may or may not become a part of one's belief system. Suspension is important so that the critical thinker can evaluate a proposition in terms of the methods, procedures and evidence-gathering processes of the discipline in question. This suspension of propositions allows one the opportunity to question it, to impose questions based on its field, and to determine whether it is coherent with other beliefs within that field. Presumably, lack of coherence is a ground for dismissing the proposition. But McPeck does not suggest how the belief system itself might change or be revised during this process. Coherence, though, is a necessary condition of rationality, i.e., to be a critical thinker one is rational, coherence must be a component of it as well.

The epistemological process involves suspension of belief, evaluation of this belief, questions framed from the discipline in which the belief is found, and assessments of the internal coherence of the belief with the

---

55. McPeck, *Critical Thinking and Education*, 12.

evidential structure and belief system held by the practitioners of a field of study. McPeck writes, "A temporary suspension of judgment is required for justifying one's belief is simply saying that one must be self-critical or possess a critical mind."[56] Furthermore, once the evidence is evaluated, this must constitute the reason that the critical thinker has for holding the belief in question. We must notice the importance of the evidence constituting the person's reason for believing the proposition under investigation. A critical thinker will judge that the evidence at hand is sufficient to determine the acceptability of the belief. And, the critical thinker will be able to give an account of why it is that the evidence points to accepting or rejecting the belief under evaluation.

To summarize, to raise a question about a belief one must understand the field in which the belief emanates and know the procedures utilized in inquiry by the practitioners of that field. McPeck suggests that one will develop questions regarding beliefs as one applies the epistemic model he proposes in *Critical Thinking and Education*. It is his contention that this model is essential for critical thought and the critical self.

Is McPeck Pecking Up the Wrong Tree?

McPeck has placed great emphasis on the models, methods, procedures, and standards of evidence in generating questions that hope to lead one to belief formation and revision. In McPeck's view, one cannot raise a question about a belief save in accordance with the discipline in which the belief emerges. McPeck's epistemic foundation supposedly assures one of the on-going questioning of beliefs as they filter into the spectrum of judgment. The method of justification of belief is that which guarantees perpetual inquiry.

I see as essential to McPeck's position the desire to develop a model of critical thinking that encourages the suspension of a belief so that questions about the belief may be developed, evidence evaluated, and coherence within one's current belief system assessed. The place of generating questions is an essential component of the entire process of justifying a belief. The question emerges because the critical thinker has learned and understands the structure of the discipline in which a belief is found. Knowing a discipline allows one to cultivate questions about a belief and encourages the evaluation of it. Further, this means that each discipline has certain

56. Ibid., 37.

questions that are appropriate for it to ask. A question then emanates from the discipline and the beliefs one holds within that discipline.

There are several problems that I have with the contention that questions emerge solely within the discipline in which one practices. First of all, the isolation of beliefs within specific field sides does not account for the complexity of belief systems. Belief systems are not simply propositions that one views as the case, that one is aware of, but beliefs in one field are dependent upon and intertwined with beliefs in other fields. We simply cannot teach people to think critically about x without taking into account how the person's view of x relates to y and z. Secondly, beliefs are habits, disposition, propositions—a highly ambiguous set. One's belief system more resembles a spider's web than a constitution which the rule-governed model of McPeck advances. Rokeach discusses the problem of belief fragmentation and isolation in his model of belief organization, an account that I will discuss later.

There are beliefs within one's belief apparatus that direct or control the interpretation of data as it comes to a believer. These beliefs are not always occurrent in the mind of a believer but, nonetheless, are the controlling factors in what may account for acceptable evidence within a given field. For example, in the last 150 years a much-heated debate has surrounded those who believe in creation science and those who believe in some kind of evolutionary process. One can readily cite numerous examples of how passionate this debate is. There have been attempts to legislate creation science in high school biology classes, for example, which have led to numerous court appearances throughout the country. Both the creationist and the evolutionist share a common assumption, a control belief: facts are gathered through empirical procedures and only those that allow for empirical demonstrability are true. The anxiety of the creationist is that Genesis 1 will not meet this criterion. But the creationist has confidence in the notion that empirical research assures truthfulness. The evolutionist offers counter evidence of the empirical variety because the structure of the discipline of biology directs it so. Both creationist and evolutionist believe themselves to be a part of the scientific community, and both share similar assumptions about how that might work.

The creationist contends that if Genesis 1 meets the standard of the scientific community, then it is appropriate material to be studied in classroom situations. Interestingly, the controlling assumption for both creationist and evolutionist is that facts are found and justified through empirical procedures and methods. For the creationist, this might seem odd, for one would imagine that belief in God would be the directing principle. The inculcation of the empiricist assumption, however, allows for the control of interpretation of data (in this case, Genesis 1) in the language of the scientist and not the author of the text, which of course is difficult to establish. My point is that although at times we articulate a belief as directive for the establishment of other beliefs, in actuality certain beliefs function to control the new data with which we are faced.

It is important to appreciate that persons have the propensity to interpret a new datum in terms of the way in which it resembles or represents previously adopted beliefs, even if these are abeyant. The point is that new material or evidence tends to look like beliefs already embedded in our belief systems. Representational schemes are transdisciplinary; they are not isolated within the confines of a particular structure or "question" one might advance. In McPeck's case, to assume the isolation of one discipline from another does not seem to guard against the way in which beliefs actually function. I think the kind of model needed is one that opens up the barriers sustained and created by the structure of the discipline model. One must realize the framers of these structures, whoever they are, were influenced by controlling representational beliefs. They did not experiment in a vacuum, but in accord with a complete belief system, much of which one is not aware of.

Further, it seems to me that the confidence McPeck has in the structure of a discipline providing the questions of that discipline fails to do justice to the data in a discipline. If one accepts certain kinds of questions as legitimate for a subject area and then imposes these on information, texts in that field, it supposes the supremacy of the discipline's question over that of the situation in which the data emerges. It assumes a kind of autonomy of questions that are framed within a discipline.

Let me illustrate by discussing an historical text. According to McPeck there are certain questions that the discipline supplies and these direct one's understanding of the text. So one might propose to look at Thomas Hobbes' *Leviathan*. Now what kind of text is this? Is it historical? Is it political? Is it philosophical? Is it anthropological or psychological? Is it theological, given that over half of the text discusses the kingdom of God? If one imposes questions from these disciplines onto the text itself and suggests that the questions the discipline has evoked are the key to understanding it, one would certainly miss the obvious intention of Hobbes, for he sees these issues as highly *integrated*. More so, it aborts the question(s) that Hobbes possessed as the reason for writing the book. McPeck's approach castrates the source of life in Hobbes' thinking that gave birth to his tome. Hobbes' question(s) is the important matter in studying this text for it reveals the priority of the situation in which it was written. McPeck's approach does not engage primarily the understanding of the historical text. It minimalizes the intention of the person who wrote it by suggesting that his question is secondary to a discipline. I echo the concern of Dewey, who suggested that philosophy destroys itself when it thinks that there are a number of standard questions that it imposes on a philosophical text because it divorces that text from the life situation that gave it birth.

In summary, McPeck's notion that the discipline evokes the appropriate questions that one may ask, does not deal adequately with the problem of the complexity of one's belief system and the control that some beliefs have over others. Furthermore such a truncated view tends to dismiss the importance of the situation in which something arises. A critical thinker trained to see things in the way McPeck advances will not allow for questions to be raised that may lead to a radical revision of belief and the formation of new beliefs because of the inadequacy of his model in dealing with the complexity of belief. His fragmented thinker will enhance the already-insulated beliefs one possesses.

RICHARD PAUL'S DIALECTICAL THINKING AND INTELLECTUAL PASSION

Richard Paul is undoubtedly one of the key forces stimulating the present-day critical thinking movement with its epistemological framework. To endeavor a thorough and exhaustive exegesis of his writing would take us far beyond the scope of this book. I can only hope to deal with some of the major issues in Paul's writing and apply these to the discussion of this book. Paul adds richly to the discussion of the fixation, holding, and forming of beliefs, and my attempt will be to extrapolate some of the features of his program that advance the discussion. I intend my comments to be a clarification and, hopefully, an extension of some of what he claims, rather than a repudiation of his point of view.

THE WAYWARDNESS OF BELIEF

Weak Sense Critical Thinking

Early in the 1980s, during what was the initial period of the informal logic movement, Paul published an article in the journal *Informal Logic* entitled, "Teaching Critical Thinking in the Strong Sense: A Focus on Self-Deception, Worldviews and a Dialectical Mode of Analysis." In this article, Paul identifies some of the major issues and problems of critical thinking that had been ignored by those writing on the topic. For one, he emphasizes the role of self-interest in the formation and holding of beliefs. Self-interest directs and guards long-cherished beliefs and positions hindering a person's capacity to think critically about her or his own belief system. He offers an analysis of the inadequacy of critical thinking programs that focus on logical skills, arguing that these can unwittingly benefit the long-cherished beliefs a person holds uncritically. Paul identifies ego-centrism and sociocentrism as limitations to belief formation and revision. These issues demonstrate the pellucidness of Paul's perspective in that he identifies obstacles in the challenge for cognitive melioration. He suggests ways of overcoming the deep-seated nature of these obstacles with a rigorous program of thought and education. Paul advances the notion that many teaching strategies hinder belief revision by not providing ways of challenging beliefs which are entrenched in one's worldview.

The role of self-interest in believing

A first level improvement in Paul's analysis of critical thinking over McPeck's is his emphasis on the plurality of things involved in believing and cognitive melioration. Critical thinking is more than simply rationally assessing statements and propositions. An on-the-paper-thesis-of-epistemology seriously misses the other cognitive states such as attitudes, interests, and voluntary and involuntary assessments which are involved in the formation, holding and modifying of beliefs. Attitudes, habits, interests, and desires, all contribute to the process of thinking and ought to be considered in all discussions of intellectual advancement. Of the three theorists discussed in this chapter, Paul is the first and only one who frames his discussion around the value-centered obstacles to belief formation and revision.

Paul contends that many critical thinking programs foster, unwittingly, a "weak sense" of thinking.[57] The weak sense of critical thinking Paul calls

---

57. Paul, "Teaching Critical Thinking in the Strong Sense," 171.

"sophistry," reminiscent of the antagonists in Plato's Socratic dialogues. The simple inculcation of a "battery of technical skills which are mastered" does not challenge the deeply held egoistic tendencies of persons.[58] The weak sense of critical thinking only tends to support the biases, egocentricities, and sociocentricities of one's uncritical state.

The weak sense of critical thinking is only a slight improvement over what Paul believes to be the common plight of humankind. Humankind naturally is inclined toward "simpleminded answers," "nationalistic myopia," "a functionalist interpretation of life," and not the pursuit of truth.[59] To date, Paul has not discovered, historically, any critical society. For him, "uncritical societies" encourage "the maintenance of routine life," which is pseudo-knowledge.[60] Humans are "not truth seekers by nature but functional knowledge seekers."[61] A functionalist approach maintains the status quo by applying the "de facto test of knowledge, personal desire or social conformity."[62]

Self-deception and social conformity pose major obstacles for critical thinking. Paul believes that persons do not seek truth, knowledge, and understanding because of their nature as human beings. Persons interpret the world egocentrically, as if they are the center of things and are not easily persuaded otherwise. Paul suggests egocentric interpretations of the world result largely from self-interests, whatever those may be, and these go into establishing a person's "worldview." A worldview is a point of reference; the point of view that an individual holds because of the experiences which he has had. Worldviews are largely "unarticulated" and represent "what a person is."[63] The substance of a person's worldview is comprised of those things, beliefs, attitudes, and desires that the person actually holds to be true, even when unconscious of them.

In addition to the egocentric, unarticulated attitudes and beliefs that Paul is proposing as comprising what a person is, a person has sociocentric biases and worldviews. These worldviews are articulated points of view that demonstrate what a person "thinks" he is. National interest, class prejudices, family, religious and economic ways of identifying oneself make up

58. Ibid.
59. Paul, "Critical Thinking in North America," 29.
60. Ibid., 28.
61. Ibid., 29.
62. Ibid.
63. Paul, "Teaching Critical Thinking," 374.

The Waywardness of Belief

sociocentric worldviews. One's sociocentric worldview directs one's interaction and interpretations of reality and results from a person's overly functionalist interpretation and orientation. Paul thus introduces two contributing factors in all epistemological schemas: a view from the person and his or her place in social structures.

Paul's contribution demonstrates the complexity of believing. Interests shape beliefs, egocentrically and sociocentrically. As these interact, they further muddle the already complex status of believing. Paul attempts to elucidate the interfacing of these concepts.

A person, according to Paul, exercises bad faith and self-deception to the extent that there are inconsistencies and contradictions between the egocentric and sociocentric views that one holds. This is due to the unarticulated nature of the egocentric view, which identifies what one believes, and the articulated, sociocentric view, in which a person states what he thinks he is. The relationship between sociocentric and egocentric beliefs indeed poses a messy situation. It is not altogether clear how these interact. Paul identifies the inconsistencies as bad faith. Bad faith is the existence of an inconsistency between what one actually believes egocentrically and what one articulates as belief sociocentrically.

Paul's account of the struggle between egocentric/sociocentric beliefs and critical thinking is helpful and enlightening. There are contradictions and inconsistencies in our belief systems/worldviews that hinder our thinking. Paul argues, pertinently, about how these interact with one another. At its initial stage, Paul suggests three things that characterize the intellectual life. He calls this stage "uncritical thinking."[64] The three aspects of this level of thinking are:

1. Thought captive to one's ego, desires, social conditioning, prejudices, or irrational impressions.

2. Thinking that is egocentric, careless, heedless of assumptions, relevant evidence, implications, or inconsistency.

3. Thinking that habitually ignores epistemological demands in virtue of egocentric commitments.[65]

Sociocentric thinking supports, adds to, but does not challenge, this kind of thinking. Paul outlines some of the features of this support which illustrates the fixation of belief motif.

64. Paul, "Critical Thinking in North America," 213.
65. Ibid.

Paul claims that basically our thinking is "monological." Problems exposed to monological thinking "are settled within one frame of reference with a definite set of logical moves. The proposed answer or solution can be shown to be the right answer or solution by standards implicit in the frame of reference."[66] Monological thinking helps one to view "the world as we define it in relation to our interests, perspective, and point of view. We shape our interests and point of view in light of our sense of what significant others think, and so live in a world that is exceedingly narrow, static and closed."[67]

Factors contributing to egocentricity

Egocentricity is the initial problem that must be overcome if one is to be a rational/critical thinker. There must be a re-organization, reconstruction, of the manner in which one revises beliefs already held. Paul suggests pedagogical and psychological reasons for the perpetuation of the problem of egocentricity.

Paul calls traditional learning the didactic model of learning, and this model supports deeply ingrained egocentricity. Didactic learning treats the student as a passive, apathetic learner. He writes:

> Most instructional practice, in most academic institutions around the globe, presupposes a didactic theory of knowledge, learning and literacy ill suited to the development of critical minds and persons. After a superficial exposure to reading, writing and arithmetic, schooling is typically fragmented into more or less technical domains, each characterized by an extensive technical vocabulary and an extensive content or propositional base. . . . [S]tudents memorize and reiterate domain-specific details. Teachers lecture and drill; active integration of the students daily non-academic experiences are rare. Students are not typically encouraged to doubt . . . [and] students' personal points of view are considered largely irrelevant to education.[68]

The kind of learning/teaching Paul is describing isolates the egocentric beliefs persons possess from other points of view that might challenge the egocentricity. This pedagogical method encourages the irrelevance of one's

---

66. Paul, "Dialogical Thinking," 205.
67. Ibid.
68. Paul, "Critical Thinking in North America," 199.

own point of view, egocentristic beliefs are removed from the province of examination and challenge. Obviously, this serves the human propensity of students to hold, tenaciously, their beliefs. Egocentric beliefs persist without opposition in didactic learning situations because of the monological, non-questioning, non-truth-seeking inclination of humankind mentioned earlier. Didactic instruction conceals the fact that for a person to develop a critically rational mind, he must come to know his "need" to overcome egocentrism. Students are not presented with the opportunity to see or understand that their positions have been arrived at in an irrational fashion.

In the article, "A New Theory of Knowledge, Learning, and Literacy," Paul outlines twenty aspects of the didactic model. I list below, in outline, the features of this model of pedagogy.

1. Students are taught what to think.
2. Knowledge is independent of the thinker.
3. An educated person stores away great amounts of information as true.
4. Lecture is the way to transfer knowledge from one person to another.
5. Students learn by paying attention to the instructor.
6. Reading and writing are taught without emphasis on higher order skills.
7. Doubt and questioning weaken belief.
8. Quiet classes are good classes.
9. Knowledge is best learned in small bits and pieces.
10. Values are not a part of education.
11. How the mind actually works is not epistemically interesting for a student.
12. Prejudice will be overcome with more information.
13 Students do not need to understand the deeper logic of what they learn.
14. Covers great amount of information.
15. Teachers teach, learners learn, and they each should maintain their positions.
16. Teaching corrects ignorance.
17. The teacher is fundamentally responsible for the student's learning.

18. Students naturally transfer knowledge to real life situations.

19. Personal experience plays no role in education.

20. Learning is monological.[69]

This model of pedagogy preserves students as passive, non-thinking agents who do not sense their need to become critical thinkers.

The pedagogical problems cited above are encouraged by the way in which people, cognitively, gain knowledge. Paul claims that persons utilize what he calls an "associationist" model of learning. This conception "is based on a rather simple fact: what we find tied together in experience, we associate together in our thoughts."[70] The associationist model attaches simple concepts with others that appear similar but does so without understanding. The didactic pedagogy, as it perpetuates the passivity of the learner, unwittingly capitalizes on this cognitive deficiency.

Paul criticizes cognitive psychology because of its propensity to emulate associationist thinking in its experiments. In his view, critical thinking is best developed by philosophers given their epistemological concerns and dialectical bent. Paul contrasts dialectical thinkers from cognitive psychologists in the following areas:

1. Cognitive psychologists play down the importance of dialogue.

2. They underestimate the affective obstacles to rational thinking.

3. They view teaching as a step by step procedure.

4. They discourage the ethical or value-centered dimension of all critical thought.[71]

This is troublesome to Paul given cognitive psychology's dominance in education and the development of programs in critical thinking. These features parallel the inadequacies of the didactic model, and in partnership foster the continuation of egocentric thinking.

Sociocentric beliefs/sophistical critical thinking

Paul identifies a second level of thinking (higher of course than the uncritical thinking about which I have been exploring), which he calls sophistical

---

69. Paul, "Critical Thinking in North America," 200–209.
70. Paul, "Critical Thinking and the Challenge of Modern Education," 20.
71. Paul, "Critical Thinking: Fundamental for a Free Society," 94–95.

thinking. Sophistical critical thinking is called weak sense critical thinking, and it is the topic of the "Informal Logic" article I discussed earlier. Persons who are taught to view critical thinking as the acquisition of logical skills exemplify this type of thinking. A sophist is one who inculcates skills for the purpose of defending his own position, the sociocentrism and egocentrism cited above. He writes, "sophistic critical thinking can be described as thinking which meets epistemological demands only in so far as they accommodate the vested interests of the thinker,"[72] and such thinking, skilled as it may be, is "motivated by vested interest, egocentrism, or ethnocentrism rather than by truth or objective reasonability."[73] Sophistic thinking never challenges the inert knowledge one possesses, but allows for the continuation of prejudiced beliefs.

Sophistic thinkers are represented in all points of view. Remembering that there can be Marxist sophists or republican sophists or religious sophists, Paul cites the work of C. Wright Mills in confirmation of sophistical thinking. Mills writes that sophistical thinkers are those prone to read books and articles for the purpose of refuting another's position but not for understanding.[74] Sophistical thinking always enhances the belief that there is one right perspective, one's own. Now I will turn to an examination of what Paul identifies as the strong sense of critical thinking.

Strong Sense Critical Thinking

At the beginning of this chapter, I suggested that the dominant models of critical thinking with which I was to deal in this paper shared a common concern to provide an epistemological orientation to the field of cognitive melioration. Richard Paul is the most articulate among the epistemologists we have discussed and he creatively ties in most forcefully questions pertaining to pedagogy. In doing so, he advances the notion that knowledge, the province of epistemology, is inextricably bound to how one gets it, the models and procedures one utilizes to achieve it, and the methods for its accomplishment. These are all tied to pedagogy, that is, how one has been taught procedures for acquiring knowledge. Epistemology concerns more than the true propositions that one believes. It is bound to all the particular beliefs that one holds to be true and by which one identifies one's life.

72. Paul, "Critical Thinking in North America," 32.
73. Ibid.
74. Paul, "Dialogical Thinking," 215.

Responsible Belief

According to Paul, this gives it a much more "holistic" orientation.[75] It is this, Paul's epistemology, that I intend now to examine.

I have already discussed the issues of egocentric and sociocentric worldviews and how these define uncritical and sophistic thinking. These habits of mind are so deeply entrenched in one's way of going about the world, that it requires great effort and "courage" to revise and reconstruct one's belief system. Paul warns the reader that truth-seeking does not come naturally to humans. Persons have the latent potential to engage in rational thought, but most do not. At best, humans remain sophistic thinkers, ones who perpetuate their nationalistic prejudices through rationalization.

A constructionist perspective

Although persons are not truth seekers, nonetheless, they construct worldviews that situate them in the world of self-interest and social interest. What is natural to all three types of thinkers discussed by Paul is their constructionist direction. All persons, no matter how illogically done, for ill or good, cultivate, construct, manufacture a perspective for getting on in the world. Persons naturally fabricate perspectives in terms of their interests, attitudes, and desires. He suggests:

> Our primary nature is spontaneous, egocentric, and strongly prone to irrational belief formation. It is the basis for instinctual thought. People need no training to believe what they want to believe, what serves their immediate interests, what preserves their sense of personal comfort and righteousness, what minimizes their sense of inconsistency, and what presupposes their correctness. . . . People need no training to assume that their own most fundamental beliefs are self-evidently true or easily justified by evidence.[76]

It is interesting that even though our primary nature moves us to construct the world selfishly, we are still in possession of the condition necessary for rational reconstruction of the world. For Paul, to the extent that a person remains egocentric, he/she will not engage in critical thinking, i.e., rationality. Persons construct worldviews and then "identify with their own beliefs and experience, view most disagreements as personal attack,

---

75. Paul, "Critical Thinking and the Critical Person," 109.
76. Paul, "Dialogical Thinking," 207.

adopting as a result a defensiveness that minimizes their capacity to empathize with or enter into points of view other than their own."[77]

Paul acknowledges the vast influence of social construction of reality on personal points of view. In many ways, the social constructions support and give evidence for the individual worldviews one holds to and, consequently, is bound by. Paul contends, "one manifestation of the irrational mind is to uncritically and affectively absorb common frames of reference from the social setting in which we live. Our interests and purposes find a place within a socially absorbed picture of the world."[78] Therefore, it is the interaction of self interests with social construction that define the person.

I take this constructionist epistemology as an improvement over McPeck's idea of persons constructed by disciplines or fields. Paul's perspective, while acknowledging a social bent or influence, does not restrict selfhood to social constraints. Social constraints are, for Paul, just one of several obstacles that must be conquered en route to critical thinking. Knowing how to engage these constructs in dialogue is the outcome of critical thinking.

Paul's constructionist epistemology is infused into his pedagogy. Metamorphizing the state of egocentricity is a primary focus of education and Paul claims his model of epistemology pedagogized will actualize this metamorphosis. To secure this change, pedagogy will have to be altered so that it reflects a challenge to monological thinking. Although the didactic instruction perpetuates constructions that are irrational, Paul contends that his new theory of knowledge, learning, and literacy, will overcome the long-entrenched egocentric beliefs persons hold.

The new theory and its pedagogy have the following characteristics, which distinguish it from the didactic model of pedagogy. Its features are:

1. Students should focus on content through live issues that stimulate students to gather, analyze, and assess that content.
2. All knowledge is generated, organized by thinking.
3. "An educated, literate person is fundamentally a repository of strategies, principles, concepts and insights."
4. Persons possess knowledge by thinking things throughout, not by the transmission of propositions.

---

77. Ibid.
78. Paul, "Dialogical Thinking," 207.

5. Students must learn to listen critically, challenging, doubting, withholding belief until evidence is assessed.

6. Reading and writing are inferential skills that require the student to question the origin of belief.

7. Students, to learn, must be questioners.

8. Knowledge is holistic, its justificatory status depends on its relationship to other beliefs.

9. Values are crucial in the acquisition of all beliefs.

10. One must be aware of the learning processes.

11. Students must actively reason their way through and out of their prejudicial points of view.

12. Rational assent is "essential to all genuine learning."

13. Students are responsible for their learning.

14. Authoritative answers ought to be replaced by authoritative standards of rationality.[79]

The principles listed above are learned as second nature by extensive practice and an unlearning of beliefs presently held. Learners as critical thinkers must cultivate the potential of this second nature. He writes, "people need extensive and systematic practice to develop their secondary nature, their implicit capacity to function rationally."[80] In essence, persons need to reconstruct their point of view in light of this pedagogy, which surfaces in the process of dialectical thinking.

Reconstructing worldviews

A constructionist epistemology identifies the facilitators of egocentrism and sociocentrism in one's belief system. To get out of this dilemma, one must use multi-logical thinking, and thinking that suggests the plurality of worldviews contesting for the honor of rational beliefs. The remedy for the irrational construct one possesses entails a reconstruction of one's beliefs. There are several basic features of Paul's deconstructionism that should be discussed.

---

79. Paul, "Critical Thinking in North America," 200–209
80. Ibid., 208.

The Problem of Self-Interest

I have already discussed the problem of egocentricity and the contribution Paul makes in his analysis of self-interest in uncritical thought. Paul contends that self-interest is detrimental to right belief. To the extent that one's beliefs remain a product of self-interest, dogma and monological thinking will characterize it.

The dominance of self-interest is surmounted by engaging in an analysis of other points of view. But analysis is incomplete; one must enter "empathetically" the view of the other.[81] The critical thinker does not caricature opposing views, but advances the strongest arguments of the opposition honestly and thinks through its perspective. This necessitates that one put aside his/her perspective so that the other views can be presented in the most positive light.

Enter reciprocity

Paul's work is highly committed to one of the central ideas espoused by Jean Piaget, the concept of reciprocity.[82] Piaget identifies reciprocity as the cooperation that occurs between one's own view and that of the social constructions environing him/her. Reciprocity contributes to the mutual support of both orientations of thought without challenging or addressing potential contradictions and inconsistencies in either of these. Persons adapt to and adopt from the social constructions features that solidify egocentric beliefs.

Reciprocity facilitates the program of uncritical, deep-seated beliefs, ones entrenched so strongly in one's worldview that it takes great effort to unsettle them. But even as reciprocity fosters the tenacity of beliefs, so also it potentially serves to overcome these. As the critical thinker enters empathetically into the mindset and position of another, reciprocity identifies some of the connections between one's egocentrism and other possible models of understanding the world. But this occurs only in the context of applying dialogical and dialectical thinking.

---

81. Paul, "Dialogical Thinking," 206.
82. Ibid.

Dialogical/dialectical thinking

Multilogical thinking must address head on the challenge and myopia of monological thought. The two features of monological thought—egocentrism and sociocentrism—must be openly confronted if reconstruction is to be realized. These aspects must be divested of their embeddedness with methods of thought directly aimed at their sources. Dialogical and dialectical thinking are two multilogical strategies that invest thinkers with the capacity to handle and execute the necessary challenge. Throughout the uncritical and sophistic stages of one's experience, the conditions of egocentrism and sociocentrism have reinforced one another's dominance; models of thought necessary to diffuse the deep-seatedness of these worldviews must be advanced and empowered in pedagogical situations.

Dialogical thinking addresses the problem of egocentrism by divesting egocentrism of its power. Dialogical thinking requires that the critical thinker "enter sympathetically into the thinking of others," whereas in monological, egocentric thinking, one does not expose his/her own perspective for examination and criticism in light of other points of view. Egocentricity is characterized by quickly formed, spontaneous, superficial beliefs. But it is also informed by attitude and desires. Dialogical thinking engages one in a clarification of one's beliefs by empathetic identification of another's position by placing the two in conversation with one another. Dialogical thinking supplants the self-centered passions, which motivate egocentricity with rational passions. Following Hume, Paul believes that thought does not motivate itself, but can only be advanced and stimulated by passions.

Paul claims that students leave school "with unreconstructed personal, social, moral, historical, economic, and political views. Students leave school not knowing what they really, that is deeply believe."[83] Dialogical thinking must be experienced "because such thinking is essential for rationally approaching the most significant and pervasive everyday human problems, and without it they will not develop the intellectual tools essential for confronting their own instinctual egocentric thought."[84] The schooling of critical thinking is called "purgatory" because it takes time to understand one's point of view.[85] He calls it the strategy for breaking down egocentric identification and mindsets.

83. Paul, "Dialogical Thinking," 214.
84. Ibid.
85. Ibid., 216.

The Waywardness of Belief

Dialectical thinking replaces self-centered interests and passions with rational ones. Paul summarizes this contention in the following quotation:

> Only the development of rational passions can prevent our intelligence from becoming the tool of our egocentric motions and the point of view embedded in them. A passionate drive for clarity, accuracy and fair-mindedness, a fervor for getting to the bottom of things, to the deepest root issues, for listening sympathetically to oppositional points of view, a compelling drive to seek out evidence, and intensive aversion to contradiction, sloppy thinking, inconsistent application of standards, a devotion to truth as against self-interest.[86]

Earlier on, I suggested a major contribution of Paul was his identification of interests and beliefs in overcoming the problem of uncritical thought. He writes that "emotions and beliefs are always inseparably wedded together. When we describe ourselves as driven by irrational emotions, we are also driven by the irrational beliefs that structure and support them."[87]

Paul lists a number of rational passions that must be cultivated so that reconstruction can advance. The two primary passions are fair-mindedness and impartiality. Fair-mindedness keeps one sympathetic to others in dialogue with other viewpoints, and impartiality allows one the distance necessary for criticism of one's own beliefs. Reflective self-criticism demands the presence of impartiality because one must take a step away from one's position if it is to be critiqued and if one is to reflect on its truthfulness. These passions are learned by pedagogical exposure and practice.

Dialectical thinking occurs when opposing viewpoints are evaluated by and with the principle of rationality so that one might discover what is more reasonable to believe. Reasoned judgment is the end of the process of dialectical thinking. There are examples of dialectical thinking such as debate in the courts of law, and these culminate in a decision about which position is better and more accurate. Dialectical thinking relies on dialogical thinking for its substance.

---

86. Ibid., 218.
87. Paul, "Dialogical Thinking," 218.

An Holistic Epistemology

Unlike McPeck who conceives of epistemology as reflective skepticism about a belief in a given field of thought, Paul advances what he calls an "holistic" approach to epistemology. By holistic he means that one evaluates a particular belief in light of its relationship with other beliefs. A critical thinker is one who attains "coherence" in his/her worldview. An holistic account considers interdisciplinary questions and issues to clarify beliefs. It strives for consistency among beliefs and is repulsed by any lack of coherence. An holistic approach addresses both the beliefs and attitudes of a believer.

Paul is opposed to what he calls the atomic view of knowledge, which views knowledge as the accumulation of small amounts of information justified independently. He has in mind the traditional foundationalist epistemology, which contends that a belief is justified to the extent that it is based on a small foundation of indubitable basic beliefs. Paul believes that McPeck advances an atomistic perspective with his identification of beliefs with closely defined forms of thought that do not interact due to the unshared questions of the varying fields of thought. Global and holistic are the factors one must consider in examining beliefs.

It is important to note that in an holistic approach to belief justification and revision there is an element of conservatism; the believer holds onto beliefs until they are demonstrably inconsistent with other beliefs. Persons simply cannot give up all their beliefs at once, a person cannot even carry on inquiry in a complete state of skepticism, so one conserves the greatest number of them to help critique other beliefs.

The concept of "worldview" used extensively by Paul illustrates his holistic approach. A worldview is the way in which a person interprets the world. The issue of worldviews found its way into philosophical discussion via the debate over what constitutes *verstehen*, understanding, in the writing of Wilhelm Dilthey, a late nineteenth-, early twentieth-century German philosopher. In an attempt to articulate *verstehen*, Dilthey advanced the notion that one's entire *weltanshauugen* (worldview) affects the understanding of anything, in his case, another's writing or text. According to Dilthey, persons structure the world in similar fashions because minds are structured alike. What allows one to understand another is that minds construct the world according to certain a priori categories that all persons share. An interpreter enters the experience of the writer and reconstructs the intention of the writer based on the commonly shared categories of human understanding, a view adopted from Kant's categories. Paul proposes the same sort of constructionist model for understanding another's point of view in dialogue.

There are two things that I find problematic with this account. One is that Paul supposes a version of the on-the-paper-thesis-of-epistemology because he assumes that one can evaluate briefs and their connections with other beliefs in total. One can identify all the pertinent beliefs that bear on a given topic. Given the complexity of belief, the subject for the remainder of the book, I find this position untenable. Beliefs cause other beliefs in ways that the on-the-paper-thesis-of-epistemology cannot explain.

The second concern I have with Paul's position is his unwarranted confidence in a person's ability to transcend psychological, historical, and sociological constraints in belief formation and revision. This account assumes that all beliefs are volitional. This seems to contradict his earlier account of persons as weak willed in terms of interests and irrational in the formation of beliefs. This account by Paul is much in the tradition of post-Kantian epistemology, which posits that ideal cognizers exist and that one's epistemological endeavors ought to emulate them. I find this perspective unrealistic and simply contrary to what happens in cognition. As such, it provides a limited perspective on cognitive amelioration.

In summary, Paul, in a more sophistical fashion, retains two of the major complaints I offered against Ennis and McPeck. Following Ennis, he advances the notion of an impartial, objective, self-directed cognizing as a necessary condition of an epistemological approach to critical thinking. For reasons I will elaborate in chapter 2, I find this to be a limiting conception. Although differing in its emphasis from Ennis, Paul still retains the on-the-paper-thesis-of-epistemology, which claims that an ideal cognizer can list all the pertinent beliefs in the evaluation of a new belief for its justification. But beliefs direct, control, hide, and hinder the inspection of other beliefs. Beliefs are compartmentalized, isolated, and in most cases nonvolitional and abeyant. The on-the-paper-thesis-of-epistemology, which all three accounts have adopted, fails to adequately address the epistemology of belief itself. Although Paul has introduced some important new issues into the discussion of an epistemological orientation to critical thinking, his account is limited in its approach to how beliefs are held and utilized in the formation and modification of beliefs.

CLARIFYING SOME EMERGENT PROBLEMS

As I stated at the beginning of section 3, Paul addresses some of the major issues needed in defining critical thought as a remedy for the complexity of belief. He discussed the relationship of attitudes to beliefs, and suggested that one must develop a method of inquiry that unearths beliefs so that they might be reviewed, revised, rejected, or retained. He discusses justification, clarification of beliefs, and intellectual passions and their role in the formation of beliefs. Those are all helpful directives, but I find his position neither extensive nor rigorous enough to capture the problematics of the complexity of belief. These complexities of belief suggest a limited, minimal agent of rationality, and it is to that kind of individual that the direction of amelioration must proceed.

For cognitive melioration to be achieved in a society that hopes for rational (even if minimally rational) agents, the issues of how cognition proceeds in both psychological and philosophical ways need to be explored. In chapter 2, I will discuss the philosophical issues surrounding an epistemology of belief for critical thinking. I will analyze the on-the-paper-thesis-of-epistemology and the notion of the ideal rational cognizer. I will discuss the sources and structures of belief and whether a universal logic is necessary for critical thinking. Against the position advanced by McPeck and Paul, I will suggest that doubt is but one of the intellectual passions involved in initiating inquiry. This too has been the historic position of epistemologists. And I will discuss the ethics of belief and how this topic informs the passion expressed primarily by Paul regarding an uncritical society.

Some of the questions that help frame the preceding issues are:
- What is justification and what are the major expressions of the on-the-paper-thesis-of-epistemology?
- Does one have to be impartial and autonomous to be a critical thinker? Is it at all a possibility? What does the autonomous thinker possess?
- Why is rationality conceived as the only source of justified belief? Is it ethically permissible to hold a belief without having enough evidence and without impartiality?
- Is doubt the only stable stimulus to belief revision? Is belief intentional? How do beliefs and attitudes function in a belief system? How do our beliefs about our beliefs help define justification?

These kinds of questions inform the substance of chapter 2.

CHAPTER 2

These are the Generations
The Epistemic Dominance of the Critical Thinking Movement

ADDRESSING AND SOLVING THE issue of the fixation of belief is central to the agenda of critical thinking. To be a critical thinker one must possess the skills and capacities necessary to engage one's beliefs in analysis and revision. Beliefs should be revisable and modifiable lest we become so absolutely attached to them that we deem them infallible. Beliefs should be subject to provisions that make for their alteration and updating, and the models of critical thinking we engaged in the first chapter suggest how this might be accomplished.

Philosophers have long been concerned that persons do not commit themselves to versions of infallibility in believing. These appear as a form of dogmatism. Critical thinkers are those who understand that intense commitment to a belief may result in illusions of infallibility. Critical thinking theorists suggest that when one considers a belief as not subject to alteration, the believer manifests illusions of infallibility. They warn against not allowing for change, of holding beliefs too dogmatically, of not facilitating revision. The claim of infallibility obstructs the flow of new evidence and contrary reasons that might challenge the beliefs one holds. Deeply embedded in the historical conversation of what makes some kind of thinking critical is its ability to modify some beliefs. Since the Enlightenment, scholars have had a phobia about not being critical enough, of not being governed by rationality, and have made it a transgression to believe or hold beliefs without sufficient evidence. Error was attached to the lack of pervasiveness of one's rationality and, God forbid, that one carry a belief without rationality's credentiality.

The strength of the claim of iniquitous believing emerges in the work of nineteenth-century philosopher W. K. Clifford, who reacted to beliefs that were held from a religious perspective. Religious belief was deemed by many of the day, and especially those imbued with the scientific spirit, as Clifford and his colleagues were, as an irrational way of forming beliefs. One might make the claim that one may be religious, but clearly not for rational reasons. And further, in England at the time, the issue of whether religion could at all contribute to an open and rational society was hotly contested. Clifford argued that a belief was rational only if it was established on the grounds of adequate evidence. He wrote, "It is wrong always and everywhere to believe something on insufficient evidence." To believe without such sufficiency was considered a grave transgression that affected negatively the lives of others, for belief was thought to be the origin of action.

In this chapter, I discuss several salient issues and subjects as they pertain to the way in which the critical thinking advocates (discussed in chapter 1) remain committed to the dominant epistemological assumptions of the post/Cartesian tradition in epistemology. I will evaluate how this point of view pertains to the discussion of holding and modifying beliefs. These assumptions advance a particular historicity, an apsychologism, and a limited notion of belief that hinder the discussion of critical thinking. Without a more complete analysis of the topic of belief and the role of cognitive structure and historical influence on belief, there is little chance for developing a complete picture of critical thought.

Twentieth-century epistemology has echoed some of the fundamental concerns that we find in the tradition of philosophy dating to Descartes. Although there have been those who have entertained anti-Descartes sentiments, Descartes (particularly his version of an internalist model of the justification of beliefs) has dominated epistemology into the twentieth century.

C. S. Peirce summarized the Cartesian perspective in epistemology: "Descartes is the father of modern philosophy, and the spirit of Cartesianism may be compendiously stated as follows:"[1]

1. It teaches that epistemology must begin with universal doubt.

---

1. Peirce, "Some Consequences of Four Incapacities," in *Philosophical Writings*, 228.

2. It teaches that the ultimate test of certainty is to be found in the individual consciousness. (I will later identify this as internalism).

3. This form of argument is a single thread of inference depending upon inconspicuous premises. This is foundationalism, which is one variety of internalism.

4. Absolutism in terms of justification. That is once one finds an infallible method and engages it perfectly, one is construed as a critical thinker.

I might add that Descartes advanced the notion that belief is a clear and distinct idea/representation of reality that is conscious to the mind.[2] Hence, there is always some exercise of the will in believing; the strength of that exercise has been of interest to philosophers concerned with belief change.

The models of critical thinking discussed in chapter 1 followed the lead of epistemologists in not only advancing an ahistorical/aspsychological dimension to the discussion of critical thinking but make critical thinking dependent on the internalist conception of justification found initially in Descartes. Along with this commitment is the notion that the status of a belief critically held results from its inferential relationships to other beliefs possessed by the believer.

The issue of the relevance of psychology to critical belief has been denied by the three representatives of the critical thinking movement. I take this to indicate the dominance of traditional epistemology and twentieth-century analytic epistemology over the critical thinking landscape. One reason proposed for the separation of epistemology from psychology is that epistemology is concerned with conceptual analysis while psychology is concerned with description (Hamlyn). A second reason is that epistemology is concerned with justification and psychology with discovery (Popper). I will offer a more historical account of the separation and suggest that the heritage of critical thinking can be outlined by two questions. Epistemological oriented critical theorists like Ennis, McPeck, and Paul believe that critical believing is concerned with:

---

2. Descartes advances this conception of belief and assumes it when discussing epistemic concerns. David Hume, though, was the first of the modern philosophers who deals extensively with the concept. I will discuss Hume's contribution later in the chapter.

1. How *ought* a person form or revise her beliefs? What are the *normative* constraints that ought to identify a person's appraisal of her beliefs?

    Epistemology is concerned with evaluation, appraisal, and norms of justification. The epistemologist, dominant in the critical thinking movement, suggests, with the history of twentieth-century philosophy, that the psychologist is concerned with *how* a person arrives at a belief, not with the normativity of this process. The second question is concerned with the ways in which one describes how belief formation occurs.

2. How *do* persons develop beliefs? How does one describe the ways in which someone arrives at a belief?

    This is the province of the psychologist, according to the epistemological tradition. The procedure/process utilized when a person actually arrives at belief does not satisfy the condition of normatively for fear of transgressing what has been called the "naturalistic fallacy."

It is my contention that the first question cannot be answered without recourse to the second question if one is interested in belief melioration. Questions about how one actually acquires a belief and how one sustains a belief acquisition fill out and complete our understanding of how one ought to arrive at belief.

In the rest of this chapter I am going to expound on how these Cartesian assumptions identified by Peirce have dominated the ways in which philosophers have thought of the formation/holding and modifying of beliefs. I will also claim that the idealized model of an epistemic agent proposed by philosophers is a misinformed way of approaching the subject of critical thinking, and finally, I will be alluding to and examining some examples of illusory believing.

THE STATE OF THE ON-PAPER-CONCEPTION-OF-BELIEF-JUSTIFICATION

It is the claim of this book that the apsychological orientation of epistemology stems from the perfectionism embedded in Cartesianism, with its emphasis on finding an absolute method or structure for critical believing. The twentieth century's fragmentation of epistemologically associated disciplines, each with their own normative structure, has further cultivated the apsychological attitude in epistemology and fostered what I call the on-the-paper-thesis-of-epistemology. The on-the-paper-thesis-of-epistemology holds that beliefs are identifiable in the believer by a verbal acknowledgment (I believe that such and such is the case) or by the behavior/actions of the individual. For instance, one posits that person A has belief B at time 1 *if* she behaves as if she has the belief. In each case, belief is construed as a propositional account of the world, a representation of something in the mind of the believer. Both of these perspectives suggest that there must be some consciousness in believing and that the criticalness of a belief resides in one's level of consciousness, one's reflectiveness and capacity for appraisal. When we apply this to the issue of belief revision, a belief to be revisable must be consciously present to the believer and he/she must *intentionally* modify it. The on-the-paper-thesis-of-epistemology advances that a belief must be placed on the table for analysis and one must be able to evaluate the logical construction of a belief's association with other beliefs that the believer holds. As Descartes indicated, one must know the fit of one belief with another. To doubt the truthfulness of a belief presumes that it must be analyzable in some occurrent mental state, i.e., some mental state of which the critical thinker has access and of which he is aware. The reason to hold or reject a belief rests with its conforming to what constitutes a good argument.

The quest for perfectionism in critical thought manifests itself in two dominant internalist epistemologies. One stresses the importance of the justification of a belief as that which determines whether a belief is critically held. This focus is on the conditions of whether a belief is actually knowledge or not. This position argues that a belief is critical if one is justified personally in holding it. Care in holding only those beliefs for which one has justification is a strategy for belief revision because it advances the notion that the critical believer will be one who is cautious in appraising beliefs. This cautiousness will preclude beliefs for which one had little or no evidence. This position equates justification with knowledge, and critical thinking with justification.

The other position focuses on the methodology employed in the holding and forming of a belief. This methodism stresses that one will achieve perfection in belief regulations as one acquires and employs the right methodology for thinking and the inclination and discipline to use these. I take

McPeck to advance the former position and Paul and Ennis to advance the latter.

Critical thinking theorists have mimicked their epistemological cousins in the on-the-paper-thesis-of-epistemology by treating belief as a proposition. In both Paul and McPeck the view of belief as proposition is simply assumed and no discussion is given for belief. The dogma of belief as proposition finds its clearest and most exhaustive exposition in David Hume's account of belief in the *Treatise on Human Nature*, Book 1, part 3, section 7. This account states that a person's believing something is equivalent to that person having before his consciousness a vivid or lively impression of the proposition. He writes, "[a] belief may most accurately be defined as a lively idea related to or associated with a present impression." Assuming belief to be a vivid, occurrent idea before one's consciousness implies that to revise or modify one's belief, it must be brought into consciousness for evaluation. This notion of belief has grave consequences for any theory of belief revision. As with the Cartesians, this perspective requires introspection/internal access to be the means of revision. The problematics of this perspective will be discussed later in the book.

In McPeck, the notion of belief as conscious idea comes to the fore when he discusses the status of a belief becoming a part of one's belief system. He writes,

> The process of integrating a belief or new piece of evidence into one's overall belief system is part of the justificatory process; one must perceive the appropriate connections between the available evidence and the belief system. But most important from the point of view of knowledge, the connection(s) between the evidence and the belief must constitute one's reason for believing it.[3]

To perceive the connections that he is talking about presumes one's ability to bring to mind, into consciousness, the beliefs, all of them, appropriate to the belief being appraised. One must formulate statements about the world that must represent the world in a definitive sort of way. For McPeck, the critical thinker possesses the right/correct theory of justification and that theory establishes the criticalness of the conscious belief.

Paul holds to the propositional account of belief as well. In the discussion above, it was argued that McPeck's notion of belief was identified by his conception of justification; justification advanced by him as the necessary feature of critical thought. Likewise in Paul belief revision occurs in

---

3. McPeck, *Critical Thinking and Education*, 36.

the context of justification/rationality with rationality seen as the right use of argumentation. It is through the conversation of different perspectives about the world that one's bigoted positions are refuted. Once these surface, one is enabled to reject them and form new, more tolerant beliefs. Unlike the traditional epistemological approach of McPeck with its emphasis on evidential justification, Paul's emphasis is on methodism; when one possesses the correct method of inquiry, questionable beliefs will surface and one will then be able to reject them. But together they share the conception of belief as present to consciousness and as a propositional representation of the world.

Justification Equated with Knowledge

The equation of rational belief with justification has dominated the twentieth century's quest in epistemology. C. I. Lewis stated that "Knowledge is belief which not only is true but also is justified in its believing attitude."[4] In this tradition, belief revision is not a problem because one does not think critically without having a belief which is knowledge. Given that, in this tradition, the believer ought "to be sure"[5] of a belief and that one does not have a "right to believe anything on insufficient evidence," it follows that only those beliefs that meet these conditions are counted as critical.

To support the claim that concern for justification has dominated twentieth-century accounts of knowledge, I cite below several statements from leading epistemologists. According to Roderick Firth: "To decide whether Watson knows that the coachman did it we must decide whether or not Watson is justified in believing that the coachman did it, we must decide whether his conclusion is based rationally on the evidence."[6] Knowledge equals, as it did in McPeck, belief grounded in the evidence one possesses and of which one is conscious.

Lawrence Bonjour echoes this concern:

> We cannot, in most cases at least, bring it about that our beliefs are true, but we can presumably bring it about directly that they are epistemically justified. It follows that one's cognitive endeavors are epistemically justified only if and to the extent that they are aimed at this goal which means roughly that one accepts all and

---

4. Lewis, *Analysis*, 9.
5. Ayer, *Problem of Knowledge*, 28.
6. Firth, "Are Epistemic Concepts Reducible?" 219.

only those beliefs which one has good reason to think are true. To accept a belief in the absence of such a reason . . . is to neglect the pursuit of truth; such acceptance is epistemically irresponsible. My contention here is that the idea of avoiding such irresponsibility is the core of notion of epistemic justification.[7]

And finally, Earl Conee:

A person has a justified belief only if the person has reflective access to evidence that the belief is true. . . . Such examples make it reasonable to conclude that there is epistemic justification for a belief only where the person has cognitive access to evidence that supports the truth of the belief. Justifying evidence must be internally available.[8]

In what follows I will clarify the notion of justification and discuss the issue of internal states of conscious justification so central to the hegemonies epistemological position.

Justification

What is meant by the language of justification? What have philosophers and others to say about this concept? Justification pertains to what one *ought* or *ought not* to believe. It is concerned with what is *permissible* to believe. Justification attempts to maximize truth over error, veracity over falsehood. To be epistemically justified, one will adhere to certain norms appropriate to and derivative from the intellectual life. Programs to describe and defend justification are interested in articulating what belief-guiding principle(s), norms, and rules one should follow.

Plato identified justification as a state one found oneself in: when a belief corresponds to reality and the believer knows why, he is justified in believing it. Once one is justified in this manner, the justified belief does not depart from the believer. To know something means to know it absolutely. Justification is a static notion, i.e., a completed state, in which one finds oneself. Plato calls this justified state a *dynamis*, a power, a faculty.

Aristotle views justification as an activity, in contrast to Plato's staticity. His emphasis is on what cognitive faculties are employed in evaluating or appraising a belief. In the *Nicomachean Ethics*, Aristotle wrote:

---

7. Bonjour, *Structure of Empirical Knowledge*, 8.
8. Conee, "Evidentialism," 398.

The life of the rational element can be used in two senses, we must make it clear that we mean a life determined by *energia* as opposed to the mere possession of the rational element. For the activity, it seems, has a greater claim to be the activity of man.[9]

Whereas Plato calls the state of justification a kind of culmination, a state of affairs which then is identified as *dynamis*, Aristotle identifies *dynamis* as a potential, a capacity, a latent ability that remains dormant until *energia* (i.e., activity) invigorates the potential. In Book Two of the *Ethics*, Aristotle wrote, "the virtues are implanted in us neither by nature nor contrary to nature: we are by nature equipped with the ability to receive them, and habit brings this ability to completion and fulfillment." This passage is clearly an answer to the question posed by Plato in the *Meno*, (70a): Is knowledge acquired by teaching, by practice, or by nature? Doxastic justification is called *dynamis* in Plato and refers to the estate of a believer when he has achieved acquaintance with the forms. *Dynamis* for Aristotle is merely latent until it is accompanied by *energia*. Justification for Plato is an irrevocable state, whereas Aristotle sets out to clarify what takes place in justifying beliefs. In Plato, intellectual virtue is the presence of knowledge, of justified true belief, whereas Aristotle views intellectual virtue as an activity of the soul that judges, evaluates, and generates beliefs and skills.

From this discussion of Aristotle and Plato we find that justification is a concept that implies either a state in which one finds oneself or the processes in which one engages in acquiring belief. The history of philosophy reminds us that this basic distinction has emerged again and again in discussions of justification. Descartes advanced that no belief could be justified unless somehow anchored in an incorrigible belief as we saw earlier in Peirce's discussion. Justification only occurs when at least one belief associated with the belief in question is certain, thus harkening back to the Platonic notion of staticity in justification. Thomas Reid, the eighteenth-century common-sense realist, reacted against this model of justification by emphasizing that justification is dependent on the mental powers one engages in evaluating a belief. In the twentieth century, the analytic tradition takes the more static account by suggesting that justification occurs when one's epistemic duties are fulfilled, that is, when one achieves a state of justification because the right rule of reason is applied to an issue. This is McPeck's emphasis. Justification is a function of language analysis and not of some psychological condition of an individual. As of late, a number of

---

9. Aristotle, *Nicomachean Ethics*, 1098a line 5.

philosophers have attempted to approach the question of justification in a more psychologistic manner. These philosophers are identified as naturalistic epistemologists (Quine, for instance). I will refer to this set of issues as the cognitive aspect of justification; that is, whether justification is a static state in which one finds oneself or a set of processes of the mental life. It is my contention that the focus of critical thought needs to be placed on those processes that bring about beliefs and that these processes have much to say about the concept of justification.

A second component of justification is a motivational aspect. There are several accounts of this aspect of justification that seek to discover what duties are involved in warranting a belief. A nice overview of this concern is found in the *Nicomachean Ethics* Book 2. For a belief to be virtuous the believer "must know what he is doing," he must choose to believe the way he does, and the belief must spring from a firm and unchangeable character. The motivational aspect complements and completes the language of justification.

In "The Concept of Epistemic Justification," William Alston identifies the dominant model of motivation as deontological. One is motivated deontologically when one fulfills one's epistemic duties. These duties provide a framework that must be satisfied prior to identifying a belief as justified. In the analytic tradition, we find the following duties expressed: (1) prescriptivism; there are right principles of assessment that must be employed if a belief is to be justified, (2) coherentism, beliefs must cohere with and be consistent to beliefs already in the believer's belief system, and (3) volunteerism, the believer must freely accept and assent to the belief after evaluation for justification. Persons like McPeck, Ennis, and Paul advocate a deontological theory of justification. Two accounts of the deontological theory of justification claim to supply the ingredients required to appraise beliefs. These are evidentialism and methodism, which I mentioned earlier. In what follows I will provide a discussion and evaluation of these perspectives.

Evidentialist Theory of Internal Justification

To flesh out my discussion of justification, I will now discuss the interworkings of belief within the on-the-paper-thesis-of-epistemology. The strategy of justification, the dominant model presented in the last section, argues that the justification of a belief depends upon its relationship to other beliefs and how their linkage is established with the awareness of these connections by the believer. Historically, there are two positions that take the deontological orientation to critical thought as their guide. The first of these is called by epistemologists "evidentialism" because it focuses on the idea that one must somehow establish a foundation of certitude, *evidentially* supported and incorrigible, for the critical acceptance of other beliefs. The second epistemological strategy identifies logic with rationality, (that is, one is rational to the extent that one's system of beliefs cohere with one another and that they stand in logical relationship with one another consistently and without fallacy). Both strategies argue that epistemology is not dependent on (in fact, is dependent of) one's commitments and values, past beliefs, and psychological structures. I will examine these models more completely in the paragraphs which follow.

The evidentialist model of justification advances that there are beliefs that are foundational for other beliefs. A foundational belief is one that, in the Cartesian tradition, is indubitable. The critical thinker in this model takes the justification of belief presently under inspection as critical to the extent that he/she understands the relationship of it to foundational beliefs. Justified beliefs function like the structure of a pyramid inverted, to use Sosa's metaphor. Certain basic beliefs, foundational ones, serve to support the rest of the edifice. The strength of a belief depends upon its connection to the incorrigible base structure. These beliefs have somewhat of a life of their own, not needing support of the rest of one's believing. Beliefs are structured so as to support other beliefs.

I want to consider what is entailed in this model. For a belief to be justified presumes that one has the capacity to bring into consciousness all those beliefs that support the belief under inspection. To do so implies that one currently understands and remembers the grounds of justification for each of those beliefs. And to make sure that the evidential grounding of those beliefs is supportive of the current belief, one would also need to have available to the believer all the potential aberrations of those beliefs held in the past. Beliefs produce a whole range of beliefs that may not be directly related to the belief under inspection but may well serve to support other beliefs that one holds to be the case. For instance, my believing that the Gulf War was not justified on the basis of the just war theory might have a ripple effect causing me to believe more firmly that the administration has no real interest in peace, or alternatively, that the just war theory of war justification has no legitimacy in discussions of war in the nuclear age. Beliefs create the atmosphere for a number of other beliefs to emerge or find support that have not a wit of justificatory relevance for the belief under inspection.

The structure of belief in the foundational system of thought is quite complex, which its advocates fail to realize. G. Harman describes what would have to occur when the foundationalist/evidentialist model of justification is faced with the revision of belief. He writes, "The basic principle of the foundations theory is that one must keep track of one's original reasons for one's belief so that one's ongoing beliefs may have a justification for others. These beliefs are more basic or fundamental for justification than the beliefs they justify."[10] Because of the evidential structure of believing in foundationalist theory, when a belief, theoretically, is known to be wrong, this position requires that every associated belief ought to be rethought and rejustified, given the new information. As Harman has pointed out, this is because the beliefs in one's system, allegedly justified, serve as reasons for other beliefs, ad infinitum. Harman argues further, "if one comes not to be justified in continuing to believe p in this way, then not only is it true that one must abandon belief in p, but justifications one has for other beliefs are also affected if these justifications appeal to one's belief in p. Justification appealing to p must be abandoned when p is abandoned."[11] The kind of cognitive mess and overload that this would provoke is descriptively beyond the pale of our mind's capacity to funnel overload into more comfortable units, scripts, and schemata. The dogma that suggests that it must, presumes the existence of an ideal, unconditioned theorist. This projection is rejected in this book.

Cherniak in *Minimal Rationality* calls the above the "ideal rationality condition" and suggests that:

> [An] ideal rationality condition requires an agent not only not to be sloppy but to have a peculiarly idealized deductive ability. The most important unsatisfactoriness of the ideal general rationality condition arises from its denial of a fundamental feature of human existence that human beings are in a finitely predicament of having fixed limits on their cognitive capacities and the time available to them. Unlike Turing machines, actual human beings

---

10. Harman, *Change in View*, 30.
11. Ibid.

in everyday situations or even in scientific inquiry do not have potentially infinite memory and computing time.[12]

Cherniak is arguing that human beings simply do not possess the capacity to revise beliefs in this fashion by having present to their minds all the interrelationships of the briefs that they possess in their belief system.

The evidentialist perspective, although it claims to be apsychological, requires a cognitive/psychological process to secure change. To engage the kind of absolute revision that this perspective requires, necessitates the use of the cognitive apparatus we call memory. The evidentialist perspective requires that justification is established by only normative components, not historical, traditional, or psychological ones or inactive ones which cannot derive from these. To utilize memory requires historical, sociological, and psychological components. The exercise of memory requires a sharpness of historical consciousness and psychological analysis that is precluded by the on-the-paper-thesis-of-epistemology. The ahistorical and apsychological accounts of foundationalism advance a theoretical autonomy for critical thinking that disregards the descriptive insights of cognitive studies and historical analysis. Memory is a crucial cognitive faculty, and it functions in establishing belief and in evaluating the acceptability of a belief. This suggests that in establishing normative conditions one must go beyond the idealized cognizer and look to how people *actually* treat evidence

Methodism

Thus far I have suggested that the critical thinking theorists discussed in chapter 1 hold to an on-the-paper-thesis-of-epistemology. This tradition finds its roots in Descartes and has been the dominant strategy for epistemologists since the seventeenth century. The Cartesian model advances the dogma that a belief, to be critically held, must be presented to the mind occurrently as a clear and distinct idea. I identified this as a propositional account of belief. This tradition equates knowledge with justification, stresses the normative element of justification (i.e., where one has fulfilled one's epistemic duties one is justified in believing something), and argues that the motivation of fulfilling these duties is an essential component of the process of justifying a belief. Critical thinking theorists accept these Cartesian presuppositions without justification, an odd claim in light of

---

12. Cherniak, *Minimal Rationality*, 8.

the eminence of justification in their schema. In the last section I explored one of the two epistemological strategies, evidentialism, which posits the kind of justification of belief deemed necessary for critical thought. In this section, I want to discuss another strategy, which I call methodism.

Methodism has several salient features presumed by epistemologists that contribute to obscuring the on-the-paper-thesis-of-epistemology. Superficially, the methodist claims that a transcendental method, i.e., one that surpasses history and circumstances and, as such, is not confined by history, needs to be postulated as the bounds of critical thought. The transcendental method is not limited by the vicissitudes of history and culture. It, then, is a fundamentally ahistorical conception. Persons who have advocated the discovery of such a transcendental methodology are Descartes, Kant, Mill, the logical positivists, and those in the critical thinking movement inclined toward argument analysis, an outgrowth of analytic epistemology.

Descartes suggests four methodological "rules" that oversee the directions of an enquiry. In his *Discourse on Method* he resolves to:

> 1. Accept nothing as true which I did not clearly recognize to be so: that is to say, to avoid carefully precipitation and prejudice, and to accept nothing in my judgments beyond what presented itself so clearly and distinctly to my mind, that I should have no occasion to doubt it. 2. Divide each of the difficulties which I examined into as many parts as possible, and as might be necessary in order best to resolve them. 3. Carry on my reflections in order, starting with simple and easy to understand ideas. 4. Finally, in all cases make enumerations so complete and reviews so general that I should leave nothing out.[13]

Descartes established these rules of enquiry to overcome the possibility of skepticism, of not having the grounds for claiming to have knowledge.

Clearly, though, these four points are not the sum of Descartes' method of enquiry. A fifth passage suggests a deeper orientation of Descartes' thought. He writes:

> For a long time I had remarked that so far as practical life is concerned, it is sometimes necessary to follow opinions which one knows to be very uncertain, just as though they were indubitable; but because I wanted to devote myself solely to the search for truth, I thought that it was necessary that I should do just the opposite, and that I should reject, just as though it were absolutely

---

13. Descartes, *Discourse on Method*, in *Philosophical Writing*, VI 18–19.

false, everything in which I would imagine the slightest doubt, so as to see whether after that anything remained in my belief which was entirely indubitable.[14]

Similarly, in his *Meditations* Descartes writes, "Reason persuades me already, that I should withhold assent no less carefully from things which are not clearly certain and indubitable, as from things which are evidently false; so if I find some reason for doubt in each of them, this will be enough to reject them all."[15]

Descartes' method of doubt has an interesting twist to it, an assumption deeply embedded that has informed epistemology in the methodological tradition ever since. This feature is purification. Descartes believed, and epistemologists have concurred at least implicitly, that the adoption of the right method will discipline one in such a fashion that purification of one's intention in believing will occur. The right method sanctifies the beliefs one has so that only those which will stand the purifying methodology are held.

Purification of intention and will is necessary, in this tradition, for critical belief. Methodists assume that the initial formation of beliefs is tainted, immature, may be even compulsive. In Paul's methodism, the believer believes in a biased fashion. Persons are not "truth seekers," rather, they are more concerned with fitting functionally into social life. He writes, "The human mind and social life being what it is, we generate a good deal of pseudo-knowledge.... We avoid producing knowledge that might undermine our social engagements and vested interests."[16] In Paul, the dialectical method is that which purifies these interests in our believings.

Methodism also suggests that through the process of purification one rationally assents to propositions. Only those beliefs that are gotten by the method are those critically held. These statements raise a number of questions: Are beliefs adopted by a person solely on the basis of an exercise of the will? Are human beings constituted so that they intentionally accept those beliefs in their belief systems? Are there degrees to our beliefs? That is, do we hold some beliefs more firmly than others and does that firmness have something to do with rational assent? Do we really decide to believe? Why is a belief accepted by authority any less critical?

The methodist tradition advances that belief purification results from the application of the right method to beliefs that one possess. In the

---

14. Ibid., 32–33.
15. Descartes, *Meditations*, 13.
16. Paul, "Critical Thinking in North America," 29.

tradition represented by Paul, this presumes that the right method (disputation/dialectics) will cleanse believers of bias, prejudice, and bigotry. Purification of one's believings, then, results from application of the right method in our believings. The "method" stands outside the canons of history, and is, hence, applicable to every place and time.

I will pursue the questions raised in the previous paragraph after I illustrate how, at least in Descartes, this tradition has been informed by the context of a particular period of history, the late sixteenth century.

A Genealogy of Methodism

Methodism, historically in Descartes, had the particular feature of emerging in a time of both skepticism and religious turmoil. His methodism resulted from the particular historical milieu in which he lived. And the perfection/purification that characterizes his thought resulted from the context of these struggles.

I want to illustrate the struggle over perfectionism in method, theologically. To account for this, I must recast some of the history surrounding the Reformation and, in particular, the dogma of the Reformation called justification by faith alone. The reformers, Luther, Calvin, Zwingli, and Melanchthon shared in common the belief that for one to stand justified before God, one must first express faith in God. As excellent biblicists, these reformers discovered the roots of this dogma in Holy Scripture. They cited the prophet Habakkuk: "The righteous shall live by their faith" (Hab 2:4) and the apostle Paul, "We are justified by faith" (Rom 5:1). Justification had its origin in a faith sustaining and generating a relationship with God.

One might ask what the Reformation has to do with philosophical thought and especially an epistemically oriented tradition. I suggest chiefly two. Firstly Descartes, a Catholic, wanted to ground our knowledge of the world in terms of a rational knowledge of God. The Reformers had rejected the notion that one can arrive at the knowledge of the Creator through rationality. For Calvin, the effects of the fall were noetic as well as ethical. Intellectually, one could not arrive at an understanding of God's nature. Descartes, though, wanted to establish the possibility of the human mind achieving the knowledge of God by suggesting that the human mind was like the mind of God. If it were like the mind of God, it had the capacity for perfection. God was perfect thought. Mankind emulated that thought by becoming more and more rational.

Perfectionism, theologically, suggested that through the application of the method of rationality, one would become justified in one's believings. Since Descartes followed Plato in believing that sin was the result of ignorance, the perfection of thought would overcome the tenacity of noetic transgressions. The idea that that thinker was justified before God and peers, from the earliest period of church history onward was grounded in the notion of human perfectibility as the foundation of a right relationship to God. The new twist with Descartes, again as a student of Plato, resulted from his claim that the perfection of being came through knowledge, not by perfection of being through impeccable morality. Method and discipline in method secures the acquisition of knowledge, which, in turn, guarantees perfectionism.

Descartes' concern for grounding of knowledge in method had a second antagonist, the revival of Pryhhonism in the philosophy of Montaigne. (It is interesting to note that Calvin and Montaigne are both Frenchmen, like Descartes.) According to Copleston,

> Montaigne revived the ancient arguments in favor of skepticism; the relativity and unreliable character of sense experience, the minds dependence on sense experience and it consequent incapacity for attaining absolute truth, and our inability to solve the problems which arise out of the conflicting claims of the senses and the reason. To exalt the powers of the human mind like the humanists did is absurd; rather, we should confess our ignorance and the weakness of our mental capacities.[17]

In a revealing passage from Montaigne, he argues that knowledge depends upon the right method/instrument for its procurement. Montaigne writes in his "Apology for Raimond Sebond," "To judge the appearances that we receive of objects, we would need a judicatory instrument, to verify the demonstration, an instrument; there we are in a circle. . . . Since the senses cannot decide our dispute, being themselves full of uncertainty, it must be reason that does so. No reason can be established without another reason: there we go retreating back to infinity."[18] In Montaigne we find, then, two things that the Cartesian method seeks to overcome. One is the problem of circularity which needs an instrument or method in which to

---

17. Copleston, *History of Philosophy*, 31.
18. Montaigne, *Apology*, 80.

be grounded. This grounding solves the second problem, that of infinite regress of reasons; the method secures an end to the regress, a justified true and certain belief. Montaigne lays the problem that epistemologists in the post-reformation period must address; a way of overcoming the enigma of circularity and infinite regress. Discovering the right method of inquiry would result in justification, that is, perfectionism in thought, purification of will, and the overcoming of skepticism. The complementary figures of Calvin and Montaigne create the anxiety out of which Descartes works.

Descartes' epistemology stems from a desire to solve this problem. To do so, he posits that the source of his model of justification is beyond experience. The source of his methodism, he claims, is intuition. For all of the methodists in epistemology, intuition is the non-experiential source of their model of justification.

THE EPISTEMOLOGY OF BELIEF FORMATION

In the opening section and subsections of this chapter, I have emphasized that the on-the-paper-thesis-of-epistemology has, as one of its features, the historic epistemological pre-occupation with doxastic justification. I have suggested this orientation to epistemology is internalist; that is, the believer must be consciously aware that the reason for a belief is that person's reason for belief. In other words, where true belief is not sufficient for a belief to be held critically, one must fulfill one's epistemic duties and obligation, and this fulfillment will be done occurrently by the believer such that he will voluntarily assent to his beliefs rationally. This is identified by epistemologists as Doxastic voluntarism. In this section I want to further the discussion of the on-the-paper-thesis-of-epistemology by exploring the foundational conception of rational assent shared by both the methodists and evidentialists discussed in the last section.

In the previous section, my focus was on the status of a belief, that is, what constitutes rationality in holding a belief. In this section, I want to concentrate on how the on-the-paper-thesis-of-epistemology views the formation of belief itself. Although we found errors in the formulation of justification, we didn't address the deeper concern of how persons form beliefs. As with justification, the dogma of rational assent limits other contributing factors in the discussion of the formation of belief, for instance psychological or historical considerations. The strength of bias against psychological and historical considerations limits the deeper evaluation of what occurs when in fact someone assents to a belief. Actually, without the consideration of the psychological effects of beliefs, one has a dwarfed and in fact limited notion of doxastic states.

Locke's Conception of Rational Assent

The critical thinking theorists explored in chapter 1 of this book share a common tradition in accepting the epistemological dominance of the on-the-paper-thesis-of-epistemology. In that concern, they focused primarily on the issue of how one ought to hold one's beliefs. The strategies suggested in section one of this chapter from the historic conversation of epistemologists guard, so they contend, one from the improper holding of belief. Embedded in the dogma that there is something wrong morally with believing erroneously, is the presupposition of rational assent; that is, a believer has the capacity to assent to beliefs and then somehow errors are the consequence of doxastic irresponsibility assentually. The assumption of rational assent establishes the condition that must be fulfilled in critical believing; a belief is critically held to the extent that it is rationally assented to.

An exploration of the notion of rational assent as formulated by John Locke will focus our attention on the historic origins of the dogma. Locke recognized that indeed there was a difference between the doxastic state of knowledge and others such as belief or opinion. He proposed that persons in their everyday lives hold to varied positions concerning opinion. He claimed that these opinions were not always subject to persuasive, deductive demonstrations and yet persons still held them. He sought to discover just how the forming of these beliefs concurred with the view that one nonetheless was culpable for holding them. The forming of beliefs nondemonstrably deductively are, in fact, the kinds of belief states with which the critical thinking movement is most enchanted.

In Book 4 of *An Essay Concerning Human Understanding*, Locke is concerned with knowledge or belief that is not demonstrable within the confines of formal logic. That is, belief that is not held/formed on the basis of logical deduction, which he, like most logicians, conceived as irrefutable. Locke was interested in establishing some condition whereby one could form a belief, hold it without its certainty, and yet be seen as a morally and intellectually responsible agent. He was keenly concerned with establishing an ethic of belief, beliefs that it is morally permitted to hold. Much of his interests developed as a response to what he called "enthusiasm."

Enthusiasm developed because of the historic disregard for "reason and revelation" in holding belief, according to Locke. Evidently, there were those in seventeenth-century post-Cromwellian era who formed beliefs on the appeal to revelation—not revelation of the sacred text, but "ungrounded fancies of man's own brain." He calls these fancies self-constructed "illuminations," ones that, in fact, were illusions. John Locke's reaction to the enthusiasts gave rise to his concern for adopting only those beliefs for which one had at least some support. Unlike the enthusiasts who subjectively accepted beliefs because of authority or fear, Locke sought to establish some stronger grounds for the acceptance of belief. When one could not establish a belief certainly, one needed some other method for accepting it.

On the surface, this sounds like a good thing. One ought to teach people a formula that governs the acceptance or rejection of a belief. Historically, it is an important point to make so as to guard against the excesses of individualism, that is, when everyone subjectively accepts whatever belief suites his fancy. Locke was trying to establish some normative principles to give direction to believers as they formed beliefs.

The principle that governed Locke's thought was probability; one could justifiably accept a belief if there was a great deal of probability that it was true. To believe only on the basis of high probability was an epistemic duty. Locke in his essay writes: "For he governs his assent right and places it as he should. Who, in any case or matter whatever, believes or disbelieves according as reason directs him. He that does otherwise, transgresses against his own light, and misuses those faculties which were given him to no other end, but to search and follow the clearer evidence and greater probability."[19] One accepts a belief on the basis of the probability of its veracity. The firmness of belief, and consequently one's commitment to it, is established by its probableness.

The perspective on belief mentioned above illustrates the voluntary character of believing in both Locke and the later critical thinking theorists. One had the capacity to not form a belief until the probable evidence emerged and was appraised. I find this view contrary to much information about the formation of belief.

The dogma of assent is closely connected to the development of the idea of probability as an account of rationality. The notion of probability as

---

19. Locke, *Essay*, XVII 24.

an account of rationality emerges within the discussion of assent in Locke. To engage in a complete discussion of probability would require a rather exhaustive historical sketch, which, I am afraid, would take us far beyond the scope of this book. But its emergence within Locke is greatly illustrative of the kind of reasoning that occurs in our day with respect to belief formation. Locke's model is advanced as a way to strengthen the firmness of one's formation in believing.

Locke's discussion of probability occurs in his essay in Book 4 chapter 15, and is simply entitled "Of Probability." Unlike Descartes—who wished only to discuss certain knowledge, which was discovered by an infallible method inferentially demonstrated—Locke acknowledges the existence of beliefs that one holds or formed that did not conform to the standard of absolute inference. Although this kind of discussion was in no wise absolutely new (for instance, in the "tropics" Aristotle discusses the phenomena of non-demonstrable belief), Locke's interest in the issue of how one can be morally justified in holding a non-demonstrable belief stimulated the continued discussion of an ethics of belief. The issue of an ethics of belief persists to this day in the context of philosophers influenced by the British analytic tradition. In the contemporary analysis of belief forming, one must acknowledge its indebtedness to this tradition.

Locke's discussion of probability has as its purpose the supplying of information so that one can make a judgment, i.e., assent or dissent to a proposition that culminates in belief. Belief for Locke is assent to a proposition. The state of a proposition's probability to be true provides the "Want" of demonstration that discussions of belief are subject to. Locke writes:

> Our knowledge, as has been shown, being very narrow, and we are not happy enough to find certain truth in everything which we have occasion to consider, most of the propositions we think, reason, discourse, nay, act upon, are such as we cannot have undoubted knowledge of their truth; yet some of them border so near upon certainty that we make no doubt at all about them, but assent to them firmly, and act, according to that assent, as resolutely as if they were infallibly demonstrated and that our knowledge of them was perfect and certain.[20]

Locke, like most of the critical thinking movement, contends that a proposition's acceptability results from one fulfilling some normative condition. In this case, if one finds a certain level of probability for the belief,

20. Ibid., XV 2.

then one is justified in holding it. It is important to keep in mind that "certain" beliefs are true just as Descartes earlier indicated. Certainty in believing was established because of the inferential structure of belief. That is, as I previously discussed in the foundationalist account of justification, a belief was inferentially related to an indubitable foundational belief. Here Locke is not so convinced that each belief or proposition has such a grounding. He, then, must establish another normative account from his forming a belief that does not requires absolute certainty.

Probability, as a normative strategy, supplies the ground in uncertain situations so that one might make a judgment regarding a belief. Because knowledge requires intuition on the part of the believers, and belief not so, Locke sees probability as a guarantee of the condition of normativity in believing. He writes:

> Probability wanting [lacking] that intuitive evidence which infallibility determines the understanding and produces certain knowledge, the mind, if it will proceed rationally, ought to examine all the grounds of probability and see how they make more or less for or against any proposition before it assents or dissents from it; and upon a due balancing the whole, reject or receive it, with a more or less firm assent, proportionately to the greater preponderance of the greater found of probability on one side or the other.[21]

For one to assent (i.e., form a belief) on grounds lacking probability is to believe irrationally and, in Locke's view, to believe immorally. This concern for guarding our believing influences the later speculation about ethics and belief.

WEAKNESSES IN THE EPISTEMOLOGICAL DOMINANCE OF BELIEF FORMATION AND REVISIONS

In this last section I will explore the weaknesses of the internalist perspective discussed earlier. To summarize, the dominant perspective in epistemology is internalist. Internalism suggests that for belief to be critically held one must have conscious access to it. The internalist contends that a correct epistemological theory ushers our belief into the court room of examination for analysis, which either exonerates or condemns the belief. The method of epistemology one holds grants justificatory status to the belief

---

21. Ibid., 3.

that has been placed on the table for inspection. The internalist perspective suggests that in critical believing, one's *assent* to a *belief* must be rational to fulfill one's intellectual obligation. Critical thinking theory ascribes to internalist epistemology. Hence I now turn to a critique of it.

In "Justification in the Twentieth Century" Alvin Plantinga suggests three motifs that define internalism. The first motif is that the internalist asserts that "epistemic justification is entirely up to one and within my power." An individual to have critical and epistemic blamelessness must fulfill her duties, which, because of the liberty of will, she has the capacity to fulfill. Error originates when one misuses that liberty.

> But if I abstain from giving my judgment on anything when I do not perceive it without sufficient clearness and distinctness, it is plain that I act rightly. . . . But if I determine to deny or affirm, I no longer make use as I should of my free will, and if I affirm what is not true it is evident that I deceive myself; even though I judge according to truth, this comes about only by chance, and I do not escape the blame of misusing my freedom; for the light of nature teaches us that the knowledge of the understanding should always precede the determination of the will. It is in the misuse of the free will that the privation which constitutes the characteristic nature of error is met with.[22]

The internalist position suggests that misbelief and all critical belief is up to me.

A second motif of internalism is that when someone does not fulfill his duty, he is violating his own nature as a human being. Locke wrote that to disregard one's total evidence one "transgresses against his own light, and misuses those faculties which are given him." This implies that a person will know when and if he has applied the norms of critical belief to a particular belief.

The third motif of internalism is that one must have some sort of guaranteed access to past beliefs if one is going to critically revise them. In other words, one must have the cognitive resources to evoke and bring into a present, occurrent state beliefs for evaluation. Internalism suggests that this can, in fact, be accomplished.

Present in all three positions discussed in chapter 1 is the notion that as our critical believing matures, there is more of a chance for us to exhibit volunteerism in belief. But several objections can be made against this

---

22. Descartes, *Meditations*, 4.

conception. Our beliefs change all the time without our noticing the change and without noticing the facts that encourage and cause the change. All the while the changes can be truly and rightly advanced, but be causally or perceptually gotten. For instance, when in nursery school, my son Timothy, aged five at the time, made a small poster with four figures on it indicating the weather. One was a sun, another a cloud, etc. When he got up the next day, it was still dark. He declared it was cloudy outside. Now he assumed that since it was cloudy the day before, when he could see, it was still cloudy the next morning. When light finally arrived, it was in fact still cloudy. (Confirmation of one's theories furthers the difficulty in revising beliefs.) Several hours later, the clouds had disappeared. When I returned home, he had changed the poster to indicate a sunny day. He did not voluntarily believe it to be a sunny day now; he was correctly perceiving the situation as changed. The causal connection of changed perception rightly determined his belief. Humans do not have to *voluntarily* accept or assent to a belief for it to be correctly held. Many such beliefs are the result of causal activities of which one has little recall or need to recall.

There are several limitations as well for a person to know the historic ancestry of all her beliefs and to ascertain the supporting roles for a belief. Some would maintain that this is because belief is dispositional. Others would contend that humans merely do not possess the cognitive capacity to engage in total recall. I will contend in the next chapter that it is a function of our cognitive system to hide beliefs and to isolate them from one another so that one has difficulty ascertaining their relevance in our present noetic circumstance.

Internalist perspectives do not answer adequately the issue of belief perseverance. We all have the experience in which we wonder why a person continues to believe certain things when the evidence seems so strongly against it. Belief perseverance is explained in terms of the immature will. They've been indoctrinated; they believe on account of authority; they believe that way because their family always has. The thought again is that if one can strengthen the method whereby one arrives at belief, one will strengthen the resolve not to hold belief uncritically.

Illusory Believing

The models of critical thinking and epistemology that have occupied this book assume that a correct epistemology will yield inferential clarity. The two dominant models of epistemology discussed in this chapter share this confidence. The internal evidentialist believes that once a person has adequate evidence, she will change her beliefs to fit the evidence. The internal methodologist believes that as perfection is realized in a believer, and as the thinker engages other perspectives on an issue, the critical thinker will revise her beliefs. But the burgeoning literature in experimental psychology suggests that beliefs persevere even in the face of evidence and also persevere in those who have been exposed to a variety of positions. The narrow view of belief and its anti-psychologism have contributed to the epistemologically dominated milieu of critical thinking, which cannot deal with the complexity of these situations without their epistemically dominant models being revoked or modified.

Long ago, Lord Bacon decried the human propensity to maintain preconceived beliefs even though evidence suggested their invalidity. And as Paul points out, we stand aghast at the ways in which persons retain beliefs when good thinking and empirical evidence seem to indicate clearly that they ought to believe otherwise. Blind faith, credulity, bigotry, bias, and self-deception are all obstacles to revising beliefs. The critical thinking theorists maintain that persons who are delivered from the shadowy caves of irrationality will be able to revise their beliefs. But there is a mountain of evidence that does not support this claim. I will discuss the inferential obstacles to belief in the paragraphs that follow.

In the face of evidence, a person's beliefs persevere because of the control these have on our memories and interpretations of reality. Craig Anderson and Lee Ross explored the ways in which the biasing power of currently held beliefs serve to limit the evidential potency of new information. Their experiment focused on two groups and wanted to determine the power of implanting beliefs, true or false, into these groups. The experiment had each of the groups view a set of films and engage literature that supported one of two claims: that risk-taking fire fighters are more effective than non-risk-taking fire fighters or vice versa. With one group Anderson/Ross supplied information that supported the claim that risk takers were better fire fighters, cautious fire-fighting information was supplied to the other. After the subjects of the experiment developed beliefs in support of one of the two hypotheses, they were given a new piece of evidence; the confirming evidence for their perspectives was a fabrication, a lie. Interestingly they found that even though the subjects of the experiment were supplied this information, they retained their beliefs about whether cautious or brave fire fighters are better than the others. Beliefs persevere because a framework of one's believing is deeply a part of one's overall cognitive structure.[23]

A second experiment conducted by Lord, Lepper, and Ross sketch a similar portrait. Two supposedly authentic studies on the deterrent effect of capital punishment were presented to persons who had indicated a strong preference either in favor of capital punishment as a deterrent or against it. Subjects who believed in the deterrent value of capital punishment read papers and were provided with data that supported their beliefs. After this, both groups were given the data that opposed their beliefs and supported the opposite claim. Everyone was supplied with a panel design, which compared murder rates before and after the legalization or elimination of the death penalty. They also had the opportunity to view a concurrent design, comparing homicides in those states with and without capital punishment status during the same period. The panel's design provided confirming evidence to one group and disconfirming evidence and vice versa, the concurrent design provided the same. There were three main results to exposing the subjects to the contradicting sets of evidence.[24]

First, the study that supported the belief of a person's initial position was deemed more convincing or better conducted. There was a greater tendency to look for and find the flaws in the argument of the other than in one's position.

Second, the overall attitude and beliefs held by the subjects were more influenced by exposure to evidence that supported their position than to exposure to opposing viewpoints. Ross summarizes this in this fashion:

> Descriptions of methodological details and possible critiques of the research further enhanced these effects. Reading the details of supporting studies did little if anything to attenuate their initial impact on the subjects' attitudes; reading the details of opposing studies markedly reduced their already evident impact sometimes

---

23. Anderson et al., "Perseverance of Social Theories," 1037–49.
24. Lord et al., "Biased Assimilation," 2098–2109.

even producing a boomerang effect, whereby the subjects beliefs were actually strengthened by an opposing study, once the details of methodology and resulting possibilities for artifact and misinterpretation in that study were explicated.[25]

The third consequence was that once a person read studies that supported and opposed their initial positions, subjects became more convinced and assured in their views than they were even before reading the data. Persons look for evidence that confirms their beliefs, and when confronted with alternative positions have mechanisms for rejecting the claims. This experiment has a dismal impact on positions from Mill to Paul, which maintain that exposure to different positions enhances one's ability in exposing the inferential maladies of one's perspective. Our preconceived beliefs have definite impact on the ways in which we analyze and view alternative positions.

A person sustains his erroneous beliefs by his tendency to recreate memories according to the present power of one's beliefs. Loftus and Palmer illustrate this in an experiment designed to ascertain how past memories are influenced by the language of belief in the present. Their experiment ran as follows: A group of subjects viewed a series of films that displayed automobile accidents. The subjects were told to note the features of the accidents and later they would be tested on their recall. Several weeks later the subjects were divided into two groups with the experimenters verbally reviewing the films. To one group an accident was described as a wreck, as a crash. The other group heard of this accident in milder terms such as mishap. The subjects were then instructed to answer a question that identified the amount of glass broken in the accident. The persons who heard the accident described in terms of wreck/crash imposed the belief of harshness on the actual accident, describing it as having a lot of broken glass. The others, who had it described in softer terms, remember it as such. There was no broken glass in the accident at all. In this case, the experimenters capitalized on the cultural usage of language and descriptions of situations to define a memorial belief possessed by their subjects.[26]

People tend to overestimate the precision of their beliefs, regardless of whether they are logicians or merely common folk. Once someone forms a belief, he strongly holds it as a way of interpreting the world. He tends to believe and feel more confident than he ought to regarding his beliefs.

---

25. Lepper and Ross, "The Perseverance of Beliefs," 20.
26. Loftus and Palmer, "Automobile Destruction," 585–89.

People who answer questions correctly 60% of the time usually feel 75% sure they have gotten the right answer. For example, P. C. Wason conducted an experiment in which he gave its subjects a simple number sequence, 2–4–6 and asked them to find a rule that would help determine a series of three numbers which conformed to the rule and to present them to the experimenter. Some assumed that the rule was three numbers in sequence. They continually provided the researcher with examples of three even numbers in sequence such as 8–10–12 without suggesting alternative rules to disconfirm their projection. They continued to cite confirming numbers instead of offering an alternative. The rule was any three ascending numbers; 5, 99, 102 would conform to the rule.[27]

I have altered the above experiment and have used the alternative in "Introduction to Philosophy" and "Epistemology" classes through my years of teaching. Instead of giving three numbers, I have only provided the student with two, 2–4, and have asked by students to provide the next number in sequence. I did this because there are, intuitively, more possible responses and rules. For instance, a person might believe that I am looking for all even numbers so they respond 6. Others might believe I am looking for numbers that are doubled and so they would respond 8. I then gave the students an opportunity to show me the next number etc. Invariably, the students who believed that I was after even numbers continued to provide even numbers. And those who thought I was interested in doubled numbers did the same. This simple example in class experimentation confirmed the experiment done by Wason, but more, it lent support to the claim that even when one gives another person vast amounts of information that ought to make them look for disconfirming evidence, they fail to do so. In each case in which I have used this simple experiment, it followed an extended class discussion/lecture on how persons do not try to disconfirm beliefs. In the face of instruction about how people function in their believing and how they look for rules to define it, these students failed to create alternatives. I believe this is an important experimental insight that suggests that the mere learning of the rules of fallacious argumentation does not guarantee that someone will attempt to re-evaluate what she has cited as fallacious.

I have provided three examples of inferential obstacles to belief that have their source in how people hold and form beliefs. Some philosophers, such as Stephen Stich, use this kind of information to argue that human

---

27. Wason, "Failure," 129–40. Wason and Johnson-Laird illustrate this and other inferential errors in their classic text, *Psychology of Reasoning*.

beings are basically irrational. Others, like Donald Campbell and John Pollock, argue that people follow internally embedded normative codes and that this is simply the way people develop beliefs at this particular point of evolution. To attempt an evaluation of these answers to the obstacles I have cited would take me too far afield from my intention, which is to show how experimental insights into the holding and modifying of beliefs (the psychological perspective) provide us with normative suggestions to meliorate our believings. In the next chapter I will examine and illustrate how this might occur.

CHAPTER 3

Psychological Insights on the Formation, Modification, and Holding of Beliefs

WHAT IS BELIEF?

THE KIND OF DOMINANT tradition in epistemology that focuses on internal states of justification has been rejected in the previous chapter. There are inherent difficulties in the conceptions of justification in this tradition which limit the ways in which critical theorists assist in the melioration of belief, a central task of critical thinking. The internalist suggestion that one can be conscious of all the grounds of justification, morally and intellectually, has been discarded in favor of a more realistic notion of the cognitive capabilities of human beings. The discussion up to this point has focused on justification, but this is only a part of the epistemological dominance. Included in the on-the-paper-thesis-of-epistemology is a particular conception of belief. I alluded to this earlier in terms of a propositional representation of the world. However, I think a broader discussion of what a belief is as a prelude to the rest of this chapter needs to be developed. I argue for a more complex account of belief; it is more like a map by which one's life is directed than exclusively a representational account of the world. I will now explore how this affects the formation and obstinate retention of our beliefs.

Charles Sanders Peirce, in many ways the inspiration behind this chapter, was quite concerned about belief and its fixation. As we observed in chapter 2, Peirce was rather dubious about the internalist Cartesian prospect. Much of his disdain for the project cuts at the soul of the project itself. The volunteerist assumption, the volitionist faith of Descartes, just did not seem to depict the intellectual goings on of human beings. Humans were creatures of habit, and their beliefs were dispositions that caused them to respond in certain circumstances eliciting belief. Descartes' account was strictly propositional, a mental representation of reality that could be altered at any time by rigorous introspection and methodological sanctification.

Peirce was imminently concerned with the sources of belief as these contributed to their fixation. The epistemologically dominant model had little regard for the activities of appraising it. In this section I want to give an account of Peirce's "Fixation of belief," emphasizing the obstinacy with which we cling to our doxastic condition.

Peirce on the Source of Belief

For the critical thinking theorist R. Paul, the genesis of a belief is valued only in so far as it suggests what state of mind (bigoted, biased, or sophist) an individual was in when forming a belief. Paul contends for the notion that beliefs initially acquired may have the quality of bigotry or bias. The immature soul in believing is the one who invokes the outlook of his group when forming a belief. In his view, persons manifest social group bias, and in the individual believer this needs to be overcome if one is to be a critical thinker.

Although Paul's view of bias is too limited, he does open the door for a more intense conversation about the origin of a belief as crucial in developing models of revision of belief. He, in a sense, is attempting to break away from the analytic tradition by suggesting sociological factors as components in the believing process.

Peirce, in the "Fixation of Belief," suggests that to understand the problem of fixation one must wrestle with the issue of what constitutes a belief and how the definition of a belief leads to a concern over what sources a belief has, i.e., what has brought it into existence, what is its genesis.

There are some fundamental insights in Peirce's "Fixation of Belief" that, when pursued in light of some of the findings in contemporary cognitive psychology, direct one to understand more clearly how the obstinacy of

Responsible Belief

belief might find melioration. Peirce contends, rightly, that the genesis of a belief is of fundamental importance to its revocability. The origin of a belief carries weight as to its accessibility and modifiability. Peirce's notion of the origin of belief influences the way in which one holds a belief. The causal connection between a belief and its inputs, genesis, ensures, the strength with which a belief is held. Pierce argues that the nature of belief is crucial to its revocability. I will pursue these issues by showing how Peirce raised these important issues and how his analysis might get us closer to a critical theory of belief revision which is cognitively informed. I will begin with the last of these issues.

What is a belief? is a question that ought to be at the center of the discussion of what constitutes belief melioration. It is helpful to know what a belief is as a condition for knowing how to improve and better it. Peirce strayed from the notion of belief as a clear distinct propositional account of something in the real world which was accessible by consciousness and introspection. He asked what a belief is in order to clarify how some of the models of belief origin might be criticized. Peirce acknowledges that one passes from the state of doubt into a state of belief. This is, up to this point, exactly what the internalist could contend. The internalist identifies this as a passage of accepting an argument of the support of a belief because it represents more accurately the nature of the world. But Peirce rejects the sentential account of beliefs; I have a clear, distinct representation of the object under inquiry and this sentence describes it. He argues the transition is from doubt into belief, both of which are psychological states. He writes:

> The feeling of believing is a more or less sure indication of there being established in our nature some habit which will determine our actions. Doubt is an uneasy and dissatisfied state from which we struggle to free ourselves and pass into the state of belief. Belief does not make us act at once but pursues into such a condition that we shall behave in some certain ways when the occasion arises. The irritation of doubt causes a struggle to attain a state of belief.[1]

Belief is a psychological state, a disposition to act in a way that corresponds to the state. One's beliefs places one in the position of acting on that belief when a situation calls for it. A belief predisposes one to act in concert with that belief when put into a circumstance that merits its output. A belief is a habit, but one is not necessarily conscious of it when one is engaged

---

1. Peirce, "The Fixation of Belief" in *Philosophical Writings*, 10.

in it. Its habituatedness lends to its difficulty in revision. A situation that troubles the mind seeks for satisfaction resulting in belief.

How one gets, though, from the state of doubt into the state of belief is of utmost importance to Peirce. If belief is a settled disposition, how one goes about getting in that state requires attention. He warns, "we cling tenaciously, not merely to believing but to believing just what we do believe."[2]

Because belief is a passage from one psychological state to another, Peirce is equally concerned to keep alive the option of doubting. If arriving at a belief requires this passage, then one would assume the importance of creating the condition in which the doubting attitude might emerge. Prior to suggesting the conditions, he suggests several inhibiting ways in which beliefs are developed and formed that do not place one in a position to inquire about what one doubts. In other words, the presence of doubt does not require that one inquires, only that one passes from unsettledness. One seeks to settle the disturbed condition of doubt.

He cites several procedures for arriving at belief that is escaping the unsettled state of doubt. One of these origins of belief is "authority." He suggests that much belief comes from a reliance on authority. He is leery of an authority being a valued source of belief because of its propensity to preserve itself. This is a reasonable concern. The one who is the authority inculcates beliefs that lead to the strengthening of that authority. Peirce suggests that this kind of origin of belief does not generate the intensive inquiry that needs to follow the presence of doubt. The kind of attitude that Peirce seeks to cultivate anticipates Dewey's contention that persons are scientific-like problem solvers. Dewey, like Peirce, sees the development of doubt as an opportunity to engage in an inquiry that will alter the belief held. In doing so, both Dewey and Pierce tacitly presume the dogma of Cartesian doubt.

How one acquires a belief secures its potential for revision. Peirce advocates what he calls the "scientific attitude of fallibilism." This attitude suggests that one should always be ready to give up his beliefs. He writes: "the scientific spirit requires a man to be at all times ready to dump his whole carload of beliefs the moment experience is against them. The desire to learn forbids him to be perfectly cocksure that he knows already."[3] The point here is that the scientific attitude requires one to get for oneself through the

---

2. Ibid.
3. Peirce, "The Scientific Attitude and Fallibilism," in *Philosophical Writings*, 47.

practice of inquiry the beliefs one has. And if that attitude characterizes a person, he will place himself in the position to enquire further.

Peirce's notion of belief is a beginning, but it does not satisfy the larger complexity of belief. He has raised the issue of viewing belief as a psychological attitude and state, and we need to pursue this conception a bit more. Though Peirce has not exhausted the nature of belief, he does shed light on how we hold them. In order to deepen the analysis, I suggest a distinction between an occurrent belief and a memorial belief offered by Plato in his work, *Theaetetus*.

Plato's Psychology of Belief

Although Plato's early account of belief is that belief is a mental state with propositional content, a representation of the world, he broadens this conception in this later dialogue. The propositional account, he suggests, does not account for false belief. Wanting to solve the problem of falsity, Plato introduces an account of belief that he associates with the metaphor of an aviary from *Theaetetus*. I quote the dialogue, 197a-202a:

> Soc.: Think of the analogy of someone who has tracked down some wild birds and keeps them at home in a pigeonary he constructed. Surely we would say that in a sense he always has them, because he possesses them, wouldn't we?
>
> Theaetetus: Yes
>
> Soc.: But in another sense he has none of them, except potentially. Because they are under his control in his own enclosure, he has given himself the ability to track them, get hold of and have any one of them he wants, and to let it go again.
>
> 198d Now we can employ the analogy of the acquisition and tracking down of pigeons to point out that there are two kinds of tracking: one takes place before acquisition and as a means to acquisition; the other takes place after acquisition as a means of getting hold of and having in one's grasp what one possessed for a while.

Psychological Insights

This section of the dialogue suggests that to discover the source of false belief one must be aware of the kind of belief it constitutes. Plato's kinds of belief are what one might call occurrent and memorial. An occurrent belief is one that has the feature of being present to the awareness of an inquirer. For instance, the phenomenon of believing that currently I am writing on a sheet of white, lined paper with an American #2 pencil is present to my consciousness. If I pick up and use the Velvet #2 lying next to me, my occurrent state of belief will alter. An occurrent belief seems to have propositional content: I believe that I have an American pencil and that I believe my present state of consciousness is unimpaired to make such a judgment. I am not under the influence of mind-altering drugs nor has anyone brainwashed me to believe it. There is simply the conscious presence of belief about this pencil caused not because of any operation of introspection but by the correct operation of my perceptual apparatus.

Memorial beliefs, though they exist in one's belief system, can remain dormant. There are times when one's circumstances provoke a belief to emerge consciously. For instance, a man finds himself at a party or some social event when someone whom he met two days ago walks in. The man finds himself searching for the person's name because he is coming his way. The person does have a memory of the person's name being James or John, but he does not know for sure. We acknowledge that this belief was present in the belief system prior to the event of recognizing this person. The efficient function of the man's memory will serve to guide and direct the greetings he offers. Plato interestingly calls the emergence into a conscious state, a relearning of the belief. The search through the aviary of one's belief system is an activity of the cognitive process of memory.

Plato raises an all-important question in belief revising: how can one's belief become accessible to the believer?

Scheffler's Account of Belief Accessibility

Israel Scheffler in *Conditions of Knowledge* takes issue with the dispositional account by asking how one attributes belief A to person B in this model. If belief is mere disposition, how does one gain cognitive access to it? He writes "Belief is, then, let us suppose, an abstract thing, in the nature of a habit on readiness, a disposition to act in certain ways under certain circumstances. But—and here is our problem—what ways and what circumstances?"[4] Scheffler is concerned with how one might attribute a belief to another such that one can identify the belief as an instance of actual belief on the part of the subject.

Scheffler criticizes several accounts of dispositional belief in his *Conditions of Knowledge*. He criticizes the simplistic model of belief that attributes an action (verbal or behavioral) to a belief. The one-to-one correspondence between disposition to action and action does not give a full enough account of the complexity of belief. Belief as disposition to respond in certain circumstances does not give range enough for there to be extensive interaction among the beliefs which one possesses. The mere one-to-one correspondence between belief and reality does not do justice to the "delicate interaction with his (a believer's) unusual attitudes" which give rise to belief. Scheffler suggests, "More important is the recognition that a man's beliefs hang together and exercise mutual influence upon one another."[5] He writes,

> A single belief cannot be attributed to a person simply on the basis of his response dispositions under given overt circumstances, no matter how varied these dispositions are taken to be. For the single belief is judged in part by reference to the other beliefs and goals which we assume the person to have. Relative to overt circumstances arose, therefore, we typically need to consider attributing complex of beliefs and goals to the person.[6]

People have and hold beliefs in units that are connected within the system of beliefs. A person might behave differently and verbally acknowledge briefs variedly because of the circumstances that call for their recall on action. Without acknowledging the varied ways that circumstances present themselves to believers, one is at a loss to identify a particular belief.

This leads Scheffler to argue for a "theoretical character of belief attribution." He suggests that, "We tentatively ascribe to persons clusters of beliefs and objectives in a way that is governed by general assumptions."[7] These clusters of belief suggest that "belief is a 'Theoretical' state characterizing, in subtle ways, the orientation of one in the world." One's beliefs position one to interpret the world in ways that accord with that belief system.

4. Scheffler, *Conditions*, 76.
5. Scheffler, *Conditions*, 86.
6. Ibid.
7. Ibid., 89.

In other places this belief system is called *weltanshauggen*, one's worldview. Scheffler rightly points out that these worldviews orient one in the world of experience and offer ways of situating and receiving data about the world. It is because of this complexity and the contribution of the plurality of ways in which we orient ourselves in the world that one needs to consider the apparati in which we hold our beliefs.

Scheffler has introduced the term "state" to describe or define what a belief is. I think he is correct, but the distinctness of belief as a psychological state needs to be spelled out more fully.

Belief as a State

I want now to build on Scheffler's discussion by explicating the notion that belief is a state and suggest what kind of state belief in fact is. A state is a condition of one's being, specifically for belief, one's cognitive structure and attitudinal apparatus, which endures and is continuous until it is replaced by some other state of being. For instance, one can be in a state of running and until that person stops, trips, falls over, that state is continuous.

The continuousness of a state does not need to be something of which one is aware. A state can be automatic, an habitual affair in which one conducts oneself. Humans function in states irrespective of their consciousness of those states. One might be writing with pen or pencil and give no thought to the action of where the instrument falls on one's fingers. A writer habitually writes in a particular way until something disturbs the state of writing.

A disposition is a kind of state, but is not coextensive with all kinds of states. A person's belief that p is the case is a continuous condition, a state that endures for the entire time that the person hold the belief. A belief state is different from a dispositional state in that a dispositional state requires some manifestation of itself. A dispositional state is a stimulus-dependent concept; one that requires an external force to cause it to manifest itself. For instance, for a glass to break it must have the state of brittleness. But for that state to be actualized,[8] it requires some sort of stimulus to cause its brittleness to be manifested, a drop on the floor, a rock thrown at it, a person to sit on it, to manifest its state requires an external force. This is not the case with the state of belief. A belief may continue in a person latently without it ever needing to emerge. It might also exist as a series of inter-

---

8. The language of possibility/actuality is common from Aristotle on; it is that context I had in mind.

connectional beliefs without external stimulus. Beliefs are manifested in an infinite variety of ways, whereas dispositions are manifested in a particular way, like brittleness.

In the *Theaetetus,* Plato provides a metaphor of the notion of belief as a state that I find helpful. He is discussing the problem of error in believing and wants to know to what one should attribute its origin. He suggests that one might liken a belief to an imprint on a wax tablet, a representation which is stored on it. The imprint remains upon the tablet and even muddles the perception one might have of it. But as an imprint that remains, it has become a state, a reminder not consciously or occurrently of the presence of a belief to the believer, but one that creates the environment and conditions for other beliefs to exist.

More specifically, one might think of the state of belief as a cognitive map. According to the mathematician Frank Ramsey, a belief is a "map of neighboring space by which we steer." It is a map that defines reality for the believer and its function is to steer, guide, and direct one in one's experiences in life. The metaphor of a map by which one steers suggests that one's beliefs define for them reality; it is an interpretive scheme to help make sense out of new experiences.

A map only defines the areas which are covered by its creation. If one is taking a trip to Boston's North End and the local AAA provides a 1960 map of Boston when it is 1990, the map will interpret the way inadequately, or at least incompletely. There are too few roads on it to make sense of the vast development that has gone into the area since that time. One might find oneself confused in trying to get from point A to B with the older map. The roads listed serve as a sign for how to get from Boston to Woburn; the efficiency of the way depends on the quality of the map.

A map structures the routes for us in traveling from one location to another. In some cases, a map divides up the terrain from one by highlighting a different region. For instance, when one goes to a large city like Boston, most maps will have an enlarged view of the city itself separated from the more general ways of proceeding. The general map one might have of Boston suggests that route 3 south is also interstate 93. The more specific map of Boston would suggest that one is on the Southeastern Expressway and significant places like the location of the Boston Tea Party, the Aquarium, and Quincy Market are all immediately off of that route. A map by which we steer identifies those things that are important to one along the routes of life, of areas of which one will and ought to take notice of. I simply mean that our beliefs place us in a position to respond to certain data and not others. This map is internal, state-like, and it does not necessarily emerge into consciousness. It is one's own interpretation of reality.

I suggest that one views beliefs in terms of the strength with which one holds them. Part of the analysis of belief needs to focus on the notion of strength. There are some beliefs that are very easy to give up, to alter and change. One's experience creates the context in which superficial beliefs can be altered immediately. Quine in *Web of Belief* suggests that superficial beliefs change immediately in one's experience.

Beliefs have a causal relationship with other beliefs. To flesh this out a bit, we consider some beliefs as more basic than others. Those beliefs that are most basic are identified as control beliefs by Wolterstorff, or "terminal beliefs" by Hilary Kornblith. A control belief guides the complex structure of beliefs that Scheffler identified in *Condition of Knowledge*. A control belief is one that puts a person in a position to see new information in reference to the control belief. A control belief determines and directs one to consider some things as plausible and others as not. The function of a control belief is to limit the field of expectation of what might be considered at the time or what might be the case. Control beliefs shape data, allowing some aspects of an experience to be noticed, but not all of it. A control belief turns a deaf ear to information that might challenge its perpetuity. These insights from Wolterstorff provide a clear explanation for William James' insightful distinction between "live" and "dead" options in believing that impede inquiry and belief revision. In the next section I will discuss literature that supports the claim of belief perseverance. Beliefs persevere because of the ways in which one structures one's beliefs, with control belief paving the way.

STRUCTURE OF BELIEF

In this section I will explore the terrain marked out by Milton Rokeach in his theory of open and closed belief systems. Given the plausibility of the notion of belief depicted in the previous section, the manner in which our belief states are structured, or not structured, would seem to have great potential for advancing the topic of belief melioration. The complexity of belief, or believing, is further complicated by the ways in which one holds beliefs. But there are those who advocate the idea that one's belief system is a "theoretical" construct. The presumption is that beliefs are accessed as one evolves as a rational agent. The more theoretically inclined or proficient one becomes, the more that one is empowered to realize the logic and connections between one's beliefs. This kind of model assumes that belief systems are logical constructs, but this is an inadequate conception of belief holding, according to Rokeach.

Rokeach's model of the organization of belief systems concentrates on the psychological structure of our beliefs. Part of the assumption of a logical explanation of a belief system is that its parts (beliefs) communicate with one another. In identifying the psychological structure, he and his colleagues, have proposed that a belief system may have logical connections within it, but not necessarily so, and certainly not in communication within its diverse segments. The way beliefs are structured by individual believers will potentially and realistically survive the communication that exists among its component parts. The depth of maturity of a given belief system, in his view, fosters communication among the parts/compartments of one's belief system. Let me proceed to explain Rokeach's model of belief system and how it furthers my discussion of beliefs in the previous section.

How Then Does One Organize One's Belief System?

Rokeach lays great emphasis on the holding of belief as illuminative for an understanding of a belief system. The first issue brought to bear on the topic is that one's belief system is comprised of positive affirmations, those beliefs that one possesses and hold to be true, and one's disbeliefs, those conscious and unconscious negative positions and assumptions. Rokeach contends that all of one's beliefs have disbeliefs associated with the adoption of the belief.[9] When someone believes positively a proposition, it creates responses in that person's belief system that are negative. For instance, if I say I believe in the God of Israel, that implies a disbelief in the gods of Canaanite peoples, presuming I live in the first millennium BCE in Palestine. To identify belief as a map whereby we steer, when one proceeds down a particular route identified by the map that precludes a number of other potential routes. The precluding might be conscious, (I prefer route 3 over interstate 93), or it may be an unconscious state produced by the presence of the belief. If I believe that the Qur'an is the word of the prophet, this

---

9. Rokeach, *Open and Closed Mind*, 35.

precludes me from even entertaining the possibility of the Scripture of the Mormons as the word of God.

Rokeach's position complements and expands the notion of belief developed earlier. It gives credence to the position advanced by persons concerned with what is called hidden curriculum in education. Those things which are excluded are important, negatively, for a believer. Our disbeliefs serve to limit information that might be explored in the process of developing new beliefs, and disbeliefs also hinder us from seeing, understanding, and exploring some of the beliefs that we hold. The organizational model advanced by Rokeach explains this phenomenon.

Rokeach argues for two dimensions of the belief/disbelief systems. The first dimension is organized into the two interdependent parts of belief and disbelief and focuses specifically on the degree of similarity or dissimilarity of belief and disbelief. The similarities/dissimilarities have certain properties. The first he identifies as isolation. He defines isolation: "to the extent that we are reluctant to see them (belief/disbelief) as interrelated, the two beliefs are said to be isolated from each other."

The isolation manifests itself in the following summary ways. There is the "coexistence of logically contradictory beliefs" within the belief system. This is the well-known psychoanalytic mechanism of compartmentalization. It is designed to satisfy the person's need to see them as consistent. There are many examples of this kind of property. Historically for Christians to believe that Jesus was the Jewish Messiah and to see themselves grafted into the tree of Israel by faith, and yet to engage in twenty centuries of pogroms against Jews results from the mental isolation of their belief states. Other examples of the coexistence of contradictory beliefs are (1) to believe that humankind bears God's image and yet to defame one another verbally and physically, (2) to believe in democracy and yet advocate governance by intellectual elite. Isolation explains how this phenomenon is possible.

A second aspect of isolation is found in the "accentuation of differences and minimalizations of similarities between beliefs and disbelief systems." Persons fail to recognize the similarity between their beliefs and disbeliefs. It would be highly likely that a Protestant who appreciates the emergence of the Reformation would disdain the communist revolution, although the feature of radical revolt against an oppressor emerges in each. Or a contemporary multiculturalist would have a fundamental abhorrence of the Puritan renewal, although Puritanism was a radical movement in the sixteenth and seventeenth century. The accentuation of differences impedes the resolution of divergent beliefs from communication with each other.

Rokeach calls the third component of isolation "the perception of irrelevance." Persons identify opponents as advocating irrelevant arguments and deny the very accusation of one's opponents. And a further component is the "denial of contradiction." He writes, "A final indication of isolation is the outright denial of contradiction. Contradictory facts can be denied in several ways: on grounds of face absurdity, chance, the exception that proves the rule, the true facts are not accessible, and the only available sources of information are biased."[10]

Rokeach cites two other properties of the organization of one's belief/disbelief system. He calls one property the differentiation between one's beliefs and disbeliefs. This property is enhanced or deprived by the "relative amount of knowledge" of the believer and by the similarity that the believer envisions between parts of the belief system. For example, religious believers, especially fundamentalists, often see capitalism and Christianity as coextensive and complementary. The last property of the first dimension he calls the comprehensiveness or narrowness of the system.

A Second Dimension

Rokeach identifies the second dimension of a belief system as the central-peripheral dimension. He argues that there is a "central region" of one's belief system, in which one's most fundamental beliefs are stored. Rokeach suggests that these belief states are most often acquired during one's early development in life. Although this is probably the case, I would extend this analysis to include all those beliefs that I earlier called pre-theoretical control/core beliefs. Because these belief states give direction to the very entertainment of data or information, these beliefs are quite difficult to identify and get at. The storing of beliefs in a core region explains the isolation and differentiation mentioned in the last section. A belief system is comprised of core/central region beliefs that, as compartmentalized, perpetuate fixation. The problem here is that core beliefs are not only isolated and compartmentalized but also insulated from external challenge.

---

10. Ibid., 37.

In addition to the central region of one's belief system, there is the "intermediate area." The intermediate level of a belief system houses those beliefs that one possesses due to authority. He writes,

> These beliefs are concerned with the nature of the positive and negative authority to be depended on to fill out a map of our world. For no person can hope to form such a picture all by himself. Authorities are the intermediaries to whom we turn for information to supplement what we can obtain for ourselves.[11]

Authority and reason are not rival ways of believing, contrary to the teaching of the Enlightenment tradition. According to Rokeach, authority and reason are complementary cognitive features for arriving at belief. He quotes from the Quaker philosopher Elton Trueblood to support this contention. Trueblood argues,

> Popular error about authority which calls for correction is the notion that authority and reason are somehow rival ways of coming to know the truth. . . . [T]he point is that when we rely on authority we are not guilty of credulity. There is a reason for our reliance. We trust the men and institutions presenting the most reason for being trusted. We must use reason to determine which authority to follow, just as we use reason to determine which faith to adopt.[12]

Rokeach contends that one looks to authorities for information and to check information one already is evaluating, affirming the value of epistemic authority. In this region of our belief system, one searches out authorities to clarify and influence the adoption of a belief that then becomes a part of the whole system of beliefs. The search for authorities has positive and negative aspects to it; one accepts the authority of some while rejecting outright the authority of other positions. One does not necessarily have to know much about the negative authority's positions; one simply identifies that one as one from which one should not acquire clarity or definition. In fact, at times one clarifies one's position by juxtaposing it with that of a negative authority. Suppose one, for instance, has inculcated the belief that a Marxist concept of economic activity is fundamentally wrong. There might be those, let's say of a religious background, who have learned of Marx's antagonism toward religion or belief in God. For example, Latin American liberation theology fuses a Marxist analysis of capitalism's effect

---

11. Ibid., 40.
12. Ibid., 43.

on perpetuating the condition of poverty in Third World nations. The religionist will identify the connection with the negative authority, Marxism, to reject the totality of liberation theology. At other times, negative authority is used as a kind of straw man to bolster one's position. One characterizes a Marxist perspective as advocating such and such positions and it must be absolutely wrong because our position of such and such are these.

A philosopher from an earlier period recognized authority wholly as a cognitive capacity, an intellectual power. I am thinking of Thomas Reid in his work *An Inquiry into the Human Mind on the Principles of Common Sense*. Reid points to authority, what he calls "testimony," as a cognitive process and function, the utilization of which can be improved. He writes,

> The objects of human knowledge are innumerable, but the channels by which it is conveyed to the mind are few. Among these, the perception of external things by our senses, and the information which we receive upon human testimony, are not the least considerable; and so remarkable is the analogy between these two, and the analogy between the principles of the mind which are subservient to the one and those which are subservient to the other, that, without further apology . . . in the testimony of Nature given by the senses, as well as in the human testimony given by language things are signified to us by signs: and in one as well as the other, the mind, either by original principles or by custom, passes from the sign to the conception and belief of the things signified.[13]

Reid is arguing that the use of testimony in arriving at belief is as natural to one's mental states as perception is. The argument, again, by both Rokeach and Thomas Reid is that this mechanism in belief formation is natural to the human species, provable, albeit, by practice and use, but not perfectible nor worthy of outright rejection, as the critical thinking theorists claim.

In a wonderfully illuminating discussion of the authority of tacit knowledge, Michael Polanyi, in his book *Meaning*, argues that one cannot know, or understand, or find meaning in present day discussions of intellectual freedom because of the autonomy of persons from authority and tradition. Authority and tradition, he contends, shape the very debates, tacitly, about freedom of the intellectual life in which intellectuals engage. Without accepting the authority of traditions as shaping current belief structures, one suffers from an "eclipse of thought." This eclipse separates one from

---

13. Reid, *An Inquiry Into the Human Mind*, 194.

finding meaning in contemporary discussions of intellectual freedom, stifling the very intellection the intellectual freedom fighters wish to attain. The disinclination to acknowledge this as a natural cognitive mechanism impoverishes the critical thinking theorists conceptualization of believing.

Peripheral Region of Belief

The final region of the believing system in Rokeach's perspective he calls the "peripheral region." The peripheral region of one's believing is identified less by the content of those beliefs but more by the "structural interconnections" it manifests with the two other regions. Because this region is on the periphery, the beliefs held are more readily identified as possible candidates for revisions in one's belief system. For instance, a Protestant Christian, when confessing the Apostles Creed, cites acceptance of the dogma of "one holy catholic church." Now, a Catholic hearing such an acknowledgment might legitimately be confused by this confession. When confronted with the alleged confession and resultant confusion the Protestant might respond by saying that catholic means universal, not the Holy Roman Church, because in his catechism class that is what he learned. The uttered belief in the holy catholic church is justified by the belief that catholic means universal without specifying the presence of an interconnectedness to the origin of that belief, i.e., a person who so taught one. Further, whether this conversation took place prior to or after an historic event, Vatican II, the meaning attached to "universal" would be quite different. The pre-Vatican II Protestant sees universal in terms of another belief, more of a control belief, and that is that all persons that share faith in Jesus of Nazareth are a part of his universal church, a post-Vatican II belief would manifest the non-theological conception of tolerance for all, universal meaning that everyone is included in the church. Inclusive tolerance is the key word in defining this perspective. This too is based on a pre-theoretical control belief that suggest that love—that quality all wish to claim but amorphously understand—is manifested in inclusive tolerance.

The research of Rokeach clarifies the structural interconnection of our belief system. To alter belief one would then need to attend to the structural interconnection of belief. But this perspective supports the contention that belief is a highly complex mental structure, which is not easily got at by the non-cognitivist models presented in chapter 1. The mere attempt to claim some overall logical scheme for a belief system does not account for the proper functioning of the interconnectedness mechanism and regioning in which our believings participate.

THE UTILIZATION OF THE MAP BY WHICH WE STEER!

I have argued for a different account of belief and how the concept of belief one holds will influence, necessarily, the manner in which one views belief revision. Some have posited belief to be a propositional representation of some object in the real world, whereas others have suggested a dispositional account. I have suggested, following Frank Ramsey, that belief be viewed as a state whereby one steers one's life. Some beliefs, which have been called control beliefs, are more centrally and firmly held than others. All beliefs, following Rokeach, are held in various regions of one's belief system and new beliefs are shaped by the interconnection of those regions. But, one might ask, how are those interconnections made and sustained? What does it mean for a control belief to function in directing one to certain information and not others? I have claimed that there are certain cognitive processes that carry the information from beliefs currently held to new information for evaluation and examination. What are these? In this section I will develop some of the illuminative suggestions made by Tversky and his colleagues in analyzing what they call judgmental heuristics. He comments,

> The heuristics to be explored are relatively primitive and simple judgmental strategies. They probably produce vastly more correct or partially correct inferences than erroneous ones, and they do so with great speed and little effort. Indeed, we suspect that the use of such simple tools may be an inevitable feature of the cognitive apparatus of any organism that must make judgments, inferences, and decisions as humans have to. Each heuristic or, more properly, the misapplication of each heuristic, does lead people astray in some inferential tasks.[14]

In this section I want to discuss three of the heuristics discussed by Tversky: the availability heuristic, the representative heuristic, and the anchoring heuristic.

---

14. Ross and Nisbett, *Human Interference*, 190.

PSYCHOLOGICAL INSIGHTS

Three Heuristics and a Fourth

The first of Tversky's heuristics is identified as the "availability heuristic."[15] The availability heuristic refers to the making of a judgment about new information based on the frequency or probability of other occurrences or instances of the information in one's belief system brought to bear on the present judgment. Once again, this is an automatic cognitive process, not an occurrent introspective analysis of a past event. The similarity of the class of associations in a current assessment with past events assists the individual cognizer to recall these. For instance, one may assess the range of heart attacks among middle age men by the number of men one has known who have had heart attacks. Tversky writes, "Availability is a useful clue for assessing frequency or probability, because instances of large classes are usually reached better and faster than instances of less frequent classes."[16] Further, Ross and Nisbett clarify this notion: "When people are required to judge the relative frequency of particular objects, they often may be influenced by the relative availability of the objects on events, that is, their accessibility in the process of perception, memory or construction from imagination."[17]

Three examples taken from Tversky's work illustrate this phenomenon. I will summarize these illustrations. Tversky contends that a person is more likely to believe the unemployment rate is higher or lower contingent on their employment status, i.e., whether they are unemployed or employed. A person who is unemployed has a greater chance of recalling unemployed persons he has met waiting in the unemployment line and makes larger estimations about unemployment on the basis of that experience. He remembers more vividly the size of the group he has contact with, consequently imposing his plight on others. The person who, in the eighties, made substantial amounts of money under Reaganomics is more likely to say that the general condition of the society was better than the current state of affairs. (If one worked in an industry like steel in the eighties, one would respond that things had gotten worse.)

A second illustration Tversky uses is that a person from Indiana is more apt to remember athletes who are Hoosier than ones from Utah. The frequency of an event includes what one hears via the media on sporting

---

15. Tversky and Kahneman, *Judgment*, 163–78.
16. Ibid., 11.
17. Ross and Nisbett, *Human Interference*, 190.

events. For instance, New York Jets football fans are apt to remember that Joe Namath hails from a small town in Western Pennsylvania named Beaver Falls because of the frequency of hearing and reading this fact. Alternatively, few people will know that Claire "Red" George is also from Beaver Falls, and maybe a few more will recall his Iran Contra indictment and pardon. (I undoubtedly recall Clair George not only because I grew up in Beaver Falls but because he played the drums in a Jazz band that my father played trumpet in.)

A third illustration of the availability heuristics is summed up as follows. Tversky asked a group of subjects whether there were more words that began with the letter R than had R as its third letter. Persons, when answering this question, tend to generate lists of examples of words beginning with R. These far outnumber instances of words which persons can freely recall with a third letter R. The fact is that there are actually far more words whose third letter is R than those which begin with R. This paragraph illustrates the fact.

Tversky et al. argue that the availability heuristic biases individuals to make certain judgments based on frequency of recall. Unlike Paul, who sees bias as misguided motivation, reflecting the epistemic dominance of ideal rational agency, Tversky suggests that bias is cognitively and descriptively built into humans and helps them navigate in the world of experience. Some judgments that individuals make may then be construed to rest upon the likelihood of the person's experience historically. When my son was five years old he suggested that because he wanted to be a basketball player his skin better turn black because all the best basketball players—Jordan, Scotty Pippen, Ewing, etc.—were black.

Even those who are more statistically proficient fall into this error. Persons tend, according to Tversky, to judge antecedents by consequences of which they have statistical knowledge. For instance, if someone dies in an automobile accident, an initial question raised is whether the person was or was not wearing a seat belt. Given that seat belt counters have been around for decades now, the lack of a seat belt is most often cited as the cause of death. The causal connection is sustained by the recollection of the statistics of the loss of life provided by the insurance industry or government. Counter evidence, such as the thousands who die because they are hit broadside, their seat belts restricting their bodily movement from the force of energy, is not included in descriptions of accidents involving death.

The Representative Heuristic

The second judgmental heuristic introduced by Tversky and Kahneman is termed the "representativeness heuristic." This heuristic operates according to the application of resemblance or fit when categorizing information or an event. People "assess the degree to which the salient features of an object are representative of, or similar to, the features presumed to be characteristic of the category."[18] How much a new piece of information resembles or appears like a belief held in the varying compartments of one's belief system will direct one's appraisal of that information. Tversky describes representativeness in the following manner:

> Many of the probabilistic questions with which people are concerned belong to one of the following types: what is the probability that object A belongs to class B? What is the probability that event A originates from process B? What is the probability that process B will generate event A? In answering such questions, people typically rely on the representativeness heuristic, in which probabilities are evaluated by the degree to which A is representative of B, that is, by the degree to which A resembles B.[19]

As with the availability heuristic, the representative heuristic is illustrated by a number of experimental scenarios conducted by Tversky and Kahneman. I summarize in what follows. An initial category of the representative heuristic they cite as the "Insensitivity to sample size." The likelihood of a group of people to respond in a particular way often depends on the similarity of those persons with the random sample. For instance, if a group of men are asked what the average height of males is, they will respond correspondingly to what appears to be the height of the men in the group. In a group of ten men, if seven happen to be six foot, the likelihood is that they will respond based on that sample of the population.

I refer to another experiment: "Imagine an urn filled with balls, of which 2/3 are of one color and 1/3 of another. One individual has drawn 5 balls from the urn, and found 4 were red and 1 was white. Another

---

18. Ibid., 196.
19. Tversky and Kahneman, *Judgment*, 4.

individual has drawn balls and found 12 were red and eight were white. Which of the two individuals should feel more confident that the urn contains 2/3 red balls and 1/3 white balls, rather than the opposite?"[20] Most persons responded to this problem by suggesting that the 4/1 sampling is stronger because the proportion of red over white is higher. Statistically, however, the sample 12/8 is higher and stronger.

Another type of the representative heuristic is identified as "Misconceptions of Chance." People expect that a sequence of events will reflect what one thinks of as *randomness*. For example, people regard the sequence of events H-T-H-T-T-H to be more likely than the sequence H-H-H-T-T-T because the latter does not appear random. The well-known gamblers fallacy is another example of this inferential strategy. If one is flipping quarters and heads comes up six or seven times in a row, the gambler will bet his money on tails because he thinks that chance corrects the apparent disrandomness.

A final example of representativeness occurs when particular descriptions were given of an individual and the subjects of the experiment were asked what was the occupation of the individual. This means that persons tend to ascribe certain characteristics to certain categories or classes of things. A subject group was given the following account: "The present authors have a friend who is a professor. He likes to write poetry, is rather shy, and is small in stature. Which of the following is his field: (a) Chinese Studies or (b) Psychology?"[21] Most persons responded Chinese studies because they appraised a relative fetidness between the professor's personality and what stereotypes they had of a sinologist or a psychologist. The representative heuristic guides one to find the fit of information to those categories one already holds to be true.

Ross and Nisbett sum up their account of the representative heuristic:

> Even more than the availability heuristic, the representativeness heuristic is a legitimate, indeed absolutely essential cognitive tool. Countless inferential tasks, especially those requiring induction or generalization, depend on deciding what class or category of event one is observing; such judgments inevitably hinge upon assessments of resemblance on representativeness.[22]

---

20. Ibid., 7.
21. Ross and Nisbett, *Human Interference*, 197.
22. Ibid., 25.

Although these examples led to inferential errors, this natural heuristic is also used daily to direct ones believings. Later, I will try to account for a broader perspective in utilizing these heuristics.

The Anchoring Heuristic

A final heuristic discussed by Tversky and Kahneman is identified as "anchoring." They suggest that people make adjustments in their evaluation and appraisal of data according to some judgment already made, an anchor in which the adjustment can be made. The anchor is a secure position from which one makes a judgment, even when there needs to be an adjustment or accommodation made to the information under inspection. This heuristic is related to the structural design I introduced from Rokeach. In the peripheral region of one's belief system change of belief occurs all the time, persons update and adjust their current perceptions based on data in flux. But what causes one to not challenge more deeply the control belief one has is one's ability to adjust in favor of the anchor. Data under inspection are modified to support the anchor thus preserving the control belief from challenge.

The heuristics I have identified from Tversky are joined by a fourth, vividness, discussed by Ross and Nisbett. I wish to briefly explore this heuristic in what follows.

Vividness

> Peoples' inferences and behavior are much more influenced by vivid, concrete information than by pallid and abstract propositions of substantially greater probative and evidential value. We argue that part of the reason for the greater inferential impact of vivid information is theoretically trivial but pragmatically very important. Vivid information is more likely to be stored and remembered than pallid information is. Information that is easily remembered is by definition more likely to be retrieved at some later date and therefore to affect later inferences.[23]

Vividness is especially important as a heuristic in the formation of belief because it addresses the idea that beliefs once formed remain in one's belief system memorially. The vividness of information as it contributes to

---

23. Ross and Nisbet, *Human Interference*, 45.

the formation of belief remains more firmly a part of one's belief system and is more readily utilized in the framing of other beliefs. The more vivid the information, data, and experience, the more likely for these to be inferentially influential.

Ross and Nisbett list three factors in vividness. They cite the emotional, concrete, and approximate vividness of new information and experience. When a situation includes an emotional element vividly expressed, it is more likely to be inferentially influential than mere statistics. Also, when information is concrete and produces an image, it has a greater likelihood of being remembered. For instance, the Rodney King beating in Los Angeles is more likely to be remembered than a similar scenario in Buffalo or Detroit that was not covered on video. People saw the beating and lived the aftermath that is the Los Angeles riots. When we hear even descriptive language in quantity, we are likely to remember it. And finally, when an information is temporarily near or gotten by the hard work of an individual, it is more likely to carry vividness. Educatively, children who are given answers to problems to memorize are, according to this research, less likely to retain them long term than one who stretches and finds an answer on one's own.

To follow up these considerations, memorial availability is enhanced when one can imagine a situation in one's mind. When one develops an image in one's mind by reflecting on and rehearsing beliefs, one is more likely to remember them. Interestingly, the Hebrew word for "to meditate" means to wrestle within one's mind, to gurgle, to rehearse in one's mind. Talmudic Judaism took up this image by suggesting that one should imagine oneself arguing with Moses, Hillel, even God when arriving at a decision regarding the law. The fostering of memory by visually acting out an event ensures its vividness. Religious liturgy communicates in imagery, for instance, events in its history that contribute beliefs by which the religionist's life is defined. The vividness employed in the initial encounter of some information remains with believers. Ross and Nisbett suggest that vividness works in concert with the other heuristic identified earlier, availability. In summary, they write:

> The most obvious mediation of the effects of vividness on inference is availability. More vivid information is more likely to be remembered and hence to be disproportionately available for influencing inferences at any time after the information is initially encountered.... The factors influencing such impact include (a) the likelihood that more vivid information provides a larger quantity of information and receives more attention and "time in

thought"; (b) the greater likelihood that more vivid information will recruit additional information of similar input from memory; and (c) the greater likelihood that more vivid information will be pondered and rehearsed.[24]

SOUR GRAPES: IRRATIONAL STRATEGIES FOR BELIEF OBSTINACY

Thus far in this chapter I have discussed the importance of a psychological contribution to the concept of belief, the structuring of belief systems, and heuristic strategies for understanding relationships between beliefs. Those have supported the contention of psychology's assistance to the goal of understanding belief perseverance and modification. I have focused on how we form and hold and modify our beliefs in a naturalistic, descriptive fashion. Thus far we have argued for the dismissal of the ideal cognizer which historic and analytic epistemology presume to be the case for their models. Another area of belief retention that ought to be addressed has already been raised by Richard Paul. Of our critical thinking theorists, Paul is the most inclined to blame misguided retention of beliefs on irrationality. His model, again, emphasizes the presence of bigotry and bias as the cause of irrational retention of belief and he argues that these will be improved by mastery of informal logic. Self-deception is conquered as one becomes more rationally disposed to apply logic.

There are several cognitive strategies, though, that help one make better sense of irrationality and the self-deceptive formation and retention of beliefs. I am thinking primarily of the strategies that resolve cognitive dissonance following the suggestion of Jon Elster in *Sour Grapes: Studies in the Subversion of Rationality* and *Solomonic Judgments: Studies in the Limitations of Rationality*. I have already suggested that the dispassionate model of cognition advanced by McPeck, Ennis, and Paul needs to be rejected. Following Peirce, the very act of believing requires a transition from some mental state of agitation to a state of tranquility. The state of agitation or seizure Peirce called doubt. Doubt is too narrow a depiction of agitation because it does not adequately describe what one does when one passes from a state of agitation to a state of settled belief. I include other negative states of disruption such as cognitive dissonance and positive ones such

---

24. Ibid., 62.

as wonder and amazement. They also stimulate or restrict inquiry and the passage into or out of the state of belief. Emergent for the argument up to this point is also the contention that beliefs already present within one's belief system function as information conduits in every activity of believing, and these activities include the presence of emotive disruptions. Cognitive dissonance (to be defined shortly) is one of the processes which demonstrate the presence of irrationality which is insufficiently addressed by the theorists in chapter 1. Merely learning the rules of fallacy identification does not engage these automatic processes. The limitations of our belief revising, then, stems as well from the ongoing presence of what occurs in the agitated cognitive state.

I want to suggest that the active presence of thought transpires constantly. The mechanism of one's mind is constantly and continuously framing, revising, reforming information. This is obviously not a passive behaviorally disposition account a la G. Ryle, but an acknowledgment that even when our cognitive system is functioning badly, it still is quite active. The work on the limitations of rationality cited above demonstrates this. I will synthesize Elster's perspective with some of the foregoing work that I have attempted to bring to the fore in this chapter.

Elster's work points to the presence of some cognitive manifestations that lead to irrationality and that support the contention that we are not as rational as our Enlightenment faith contends. He cites the work done first by Leon Festinger on cognitive dissonance in supporting this claim. Cognitive dissonance occurs when there is present in one's belief system two contradictory beliefs both of which one is disinclined to dismiss. Festinger describes two elements that occur in a cognitive dissonant state. He writes:

> The basic hypotheses I wish to state are as follows: 1. The existence of dissonance, being psychologically uncomfortable, will motivate the person to try to reduce the dissonance and achieve consonance. 2. When dissonance is present, in addition to reduce it, the person will actively avoid situations and information which would likely increase the dissonance.[25]

The argument here is that cognitive dissonance, once it occurs, is a state in which one is motivationally directed to seek consonance. He suggests that dissonance can be identified by the language of frustration or disequilibrium. Dissonance evokes the state of impassioned avoidance of the conflicting notions to which one is attending. Cognitive dissonance is a

25. Festinger, *Cognitive Dissonance*, 3.

Psychological Insights

state, like doubt, from which one desires deliverance. Cognitive dissonance requires the presence of the motivation to avoid for any period of time the eruption of dissonance.

Elster builds on the work done by Festinger and suggests three cognitive processes that placate the disrupted mental state. The first of these he calls "adaptive preference." Adaptive preference is the adjustment of wants to possibilities; it is "a causal process which takes place behind the back of the individual concerned."[26] When one is confronted with having wants that stand in opposition and that cannot both be satisfied, this cognitive process shapes that which guides one's choice.

A second means of resolution in cognitive processes is called "preference change by reframing." This process occurs when the relative attractiveness of options alter when the situation of choice is reframed in a way that rationally should have no effect on the preferences. L. J. Savage provides an example of this phenomenon; a customer who is willing to add $X to the cost of a new car to acquire a fancy radio, but realizes that he would be unwilling to add $X for the radio after purchasing the car at its regular price. Tversky and Kahneman describe this; "Many readers will recognize the temporary devaluation of money that makes new acquisitions unusually attractive in the context of buying a house."[27] People often will spend money on non-essential items because of the situation they are in: when one buys a new house, that is the time for other new items.

A final strategy used to resolve the presence of cognitive dissonance Elster identifies as "wishful thinking." Wishful thinking is the "shaping of beliefs by wants so as to produce a belief that a desire state actually obtains or will obtain."[28] A desire for promotion may cause one to dwell on certain evidence that the promotion is forthwith. The song, "I saw her diary underneath the tree and started reading about me" by Bread is a case in point. This ballad is about a person who reads diary comments about the man a particular woman is concerned about, the woman whom he happens to be in love with. So he construes that the words of her diary must be about him, the pain of her writing about someone else is too hard to bear; naturally he avoids the disrupted state of inferring that the words are not about him. The poor chap is crushed when he finds out this has merely been wishful think-

---

26. Elster, *Rationality and Relativism*, 126

27. Elster quotes this from Tversky and Kahneman on page 127 of "Belief, Bias and Ideology."

28. Ibid., 127.

ing on his part. These three strategies generate new beliefs that are illusory and assist old beliefs by not addressing their substance when dissonance creates the environment for it.

In this chapter I have argued for a much more complex notion of belief and belief holding. I have suggested that belief is a map by which we steer our life. I have also suggested that our beliefs are housed in three regions of our belief system which are interconnected by cognitive heuristics that sustain them and function in their perpetual existence. The way in which we hold our beliefs leads to the acknowledgment that belief revision might not be such an easy task. Certainly it is greater than the on-the-paper-thesis-of-epistemology theorists have maintained. We now see that cognitive diversity is present within the very way of structuring our beliefs, so that one possesses complementary and contradictory, inconsistent and yet coherent beliefs of which one might be orally unaware yet which are in use when new beliefs are being formed and old ones revised. Our look at cognitive dissonance pointed to another factor at play here: drives and motivations are used to obscure the presence of questionable beliefs.

But my chapter leaves us with a sense of tension. How are our beliefs accessible so that they are revisable? How is it that one can overcome the problem of our cognitive and doxastic diversity? How do we identify and attribute beliefs to ourselves when there is such complexity as this? Aren't we concerned with meliorating our beliefs? In what ways now might this improvement take place when we are not even so sure what it is that we believe? We query about the circumstances in human life that has given rise to illusory believing, or wishful thinking. I contend that insight into the nature of the noetic effects of sin provides a deeper analysis of the problems we bear as minimally rational agents. I will pursue these kinds of issues in the next chapter with a look at Augustine's understanding of the fractured mind which is in need of repair.

CHAPTER 4

Gnothi Seauton and *Quaestro Mihi Factus Sum*

The Problem of Noetic Sin in Augustine

GNOTHI SEAUTON (KNOW THYSELF) was the command given to Socrates by the Delphic oracle[1] and it was this imperative that framed the Socratic mission of inquiring after wisdom and understanding. Socrates believed answering the question of self-knowledge was essential for living the good life (happiness) and for offering a critique of socially embedded errors. As a consequence of Socrates' influence, the quest for self-knowledge is foundational for the philosophical enterprise; in fact, historically, other types of philosophical knowledge were viewed as dependent upon its realization. One might make the claim that all of philosophy is an historical footnote to the Delphic command given to Socrates. Furthermore, one might claim that modern epistemology and its foremost expression, internalist foundationalism, which I have discussed earlier, is a footnote to the Cartesian understanding of this Delphic command. Its frustration would inevitably lead to skepticism at best, futility at worst, for the philosophical endeavor. Consequently, engaging the problem of self-knowledge was not only the

---

1. Plato's *Protagoras* contains the command *gnothi seauton*. It is in the *Apology* that Socrates spells out the quest for self-knowledge as the basis of his philosophical endeavors citing the story of the Delphic oracle, the divine mission he felt he was on as a result, and ending the *Apology* with the phrase classically translated: The unexamined life is not worth living.

command given to Socrates, but has been the quagmire for philosophers ever since.

In the first couple of chapters of the treatise, I have advanced that self-deception and personal illusory believing muddles the ideal rational agents proposed by the Cartesian tradition. I have suggested that the concerns raised for both the normativity of our belief structure and its fractured state calls for a deeper assessment of the roots of this condition and problem. I promised an account of Augustine's notion of the noetic effects of sin to provide for this deeper assessment. In light of the place that self-deception has played thus far in Paul, the theorist whom I consider has the most promising model, and against the background of our cognitive failings cited by Elster and others, I will use the question of self-knowledge in Augustine as a portal through which I will discuss the noetic effects of sin developed by Augustine.

Augustine and John Calvin, the two strategic theologians/philosophers of the Reformed tradition, contended for the centrality of self-knowledge as well. In the *Soliloquies* 1.2.7, Augustine asserted that the reason for his inquiry into rationality was that "I desire to know God and the self."[2] The tenth book of *On the Trinity* is devoted to heeding the call of *gnothi seauton*, that is, know thyself. In fact, he claims that humans need "to act on the command to know thyself."[3] Book X is an attempt to figure out how one goes about acting on that claim. One also sees this same contention and focus in Calvin. In the *Institutes of the Christian Religion*, Book One, he writes, "Nearly all the wisdom we possess, that is to say, true and sound wisdom, consists of two parts: the knowledge of God and ourselves."[4] Further, Calvin claims that, "Accordingly, the knowledge of ourselves . . . arouses us to seek God, but also, as it were, leads us by the hand to find Him."[5] These two, knowledge of self and knowledge of God, are intertwined, mutually supporting the purpose and the quest of the *imago dei*. Clearly, without knowledge of self, the knowledge of God would be adversely affected, while the knowledge of self is impossible without the knowledge of God, in Calvin's terms, as Creator and Redeemer and, in Augustine's terms, as Trinity.

Although knowledge of self is central to Augustine and Calvin and the core of what it means to be human, this knowledge is obstructed and

2. Augustine, *Soliloquies*, in *Augustine's Earlier Writings*, 26.
3. Augustine, *Trinity*, 292.
4. John Calvin, *Institutes*, 35.
5. Ibid., 37.

distorted because of sin. Contemporary Reformed philosophers such as Alvin Plantinga and Nicholas Wolterstorff identify this distortion as the noetic[6] effects of sin. Augustine fittingly addresses the noetic effects of sin as it pertains to self-knowledge in the Latin phrase used in the title of this essay: *Quaestio Mihi Factus Sum*, I have become a riddle (quandary) to myself. (See *Confessions* X, chapter 33.) Calvin too sees man as a riddle to himself as a consequence of hypocrisy and pride, as he argues in the *Institutes*, Book I, chapter 1.

It is important to recognize that in Augustine and Calvin the noetic effects of sin do not utterly and completely destroy humankind's ability to know. God's grace preserves the *imago dei* so that man can know imperfectly and fallibly. Since the Spirit of God is the Spirit of truth, whenever truth is discovered, the Spirit has been involved in its discovery, even when not recognized by fallen humans. The possibility of finding truth in science, politics, or art is the consequence of the grace of God and the Spirit's activity.

Augustine praises God for the natural abilities of humankind that remain even after the fall and even in the presence of sin's noetic effects. Let me quote him at length:

> Man shows remarkable powers of mind and reason in the satisfaction of his aims, even though they may be unnecessary or even dangerous and harmful; and those powers are evidence of the blessings he enjoys in his natural powers which enable him to discover, to learn and to practice those arts. Think of the wonderful inventions of clothing and building, the astounding achievements of human industry! Think of man's progress in agriculture and navigation; of the variety in conception and accomplishment, man has shown in pottery, in sculpture, in painting . . . consider all the multitudinous variety of the means of information and persuasion among which the spoken and written word has the first place. . . . Consider man's knowledge of geometry and arithmetic, his intelligence shown in plotting the positions and courses of the stars. How abundant is man's stock of knowledge of natural phenomena![7]

---

6. The word "noetic" derives from the Greek word *nous*. This word is translated *mind* thus indicating that sin affects humans intellectually, to the core of the structure of their minds.

7. Augustine, *City of God*, 1072.

He claims, though, that if God in his grace did not preserve some measure of the natural reasoning abilities of humans, they would of necessity be destroyed. We see in this quote that the full scope of human intellectual activities are preserved enough to discover truth. But it is grace that permits this and grace that sustains the acquisition of truth in non-believers as well as believers.

Furthermore, Calvin believed that the mind, though fallen, was not totally incapable of discovering truth. He wrote in Book II of the *Institutes*:

> The power of human acuteness also appears in learning these because all of us have a certain aptitude. But although not all the arts are suitable for everyone to learn, yet it is a certain enough indication of the common energy that hardly anyone is to be found who does not manifest talent in some art. . . . Hence, with good reason we are compelled to confess that its beginning is inborn in human nature. . . . Where we come upon these matters in secular writers, let that admirable light of truth shining in them teach us that the mind of man, though fallen and perverted from its wholeness, is nevertheless clothed and ornamented with God's excellent gifts. If we regard the Spirit of God as the sole fountain of truth, we shall neither reject the truth itself, nor despise it wherever it shall appear, unless we wish to dishonor the Spirit of God.[8]

In this section of the *Institutes* Calvin celebrates the political, social, artistic, and scientific knowledge of humans, all the while reminding his readers that when and where a secular author discovers truth, it belongs to the Lord. He also lays claim to the notion that Christians ought to look to the work of the secularist as a vehicle for arriving at an understanding of God's creation. This does not mean that fallenness is not present, it simply qualifies it as such. It is God's kindness, providentially executed through His Spirit that breaks through the perversion of the human mind so that the truth and goodness and beauty of the creation might be known.

Holy Scripture contends for the noetic effects of sin and for the importance of self-knowledge as well. For example, one reads in Romans 1 that God's wrath is directed against those who "suppress the truth." To suppress suggests some measure or sort of self-awareness and understanding done with motivation. Further in the same passage, Paul writes that as a result of the prideful, idolatrous orientation of humans "they became futile in their thinking and darkened in their understanding." I take this to mean

---

8. Calvin, *Institutes*, 273.

that there is a disorder, disorientation, and aimlessness that accompanies humankind's fallen noetic structure. In Ephesians 4, Paul reiterates this theme by warning the church at Ephesus to forsake the *nous* (mind) of the Gentiles because "[they] live in the futility of their minds. They are darkened in their understanding, alienated from the life of God because of their ignorance and hardness of heart." Self-knowledge is the concern of Scripture as well. One reads of the call to "Examine yourselves," (2 Cor 13:5), and that the spirit of a man knows (see 1 Cor 2:11) the man himself even though it is a shadowy type of knowledge that requires the fullness of love (see 1 Cor 13:12–13). Although I might multiply these by a substantial number of other texts, the concerns of *gnothi seauton* and the fact of *quaestio mihi factus sum* are clearly evident and pervasive in God's kind disclosure of truth revelatorily.

THE *NOUS* AND ITS STRUCTURE

As I indicated above, I want to claim that Augustine does, in fact, have a conception of the noetic effects of sin. In this section, to enable the reader to understand what this conception entails, I will first provide a brief discussion of the composition of the *nous*, (mind or *mens*) so that one might comprehend what has fallen and then demonstrate, textually, support for a series of noetic canons necessary for self-knowledge inherent to the human cognitive apparatus. These points seem to me to be essential for understanding *gnothi seauton* and for the background in ascertaining Augustine on the riddle of noetic sin.

Charles Cochrane in his magisterial work, *Christianity and Classical Culture*, demonstrates the centrality of the doctrine of the Trinity in Augustine's work. He shows how the questions of metaphysics and epistemology, which were quagmires for ancient culture, were answered to Augustine's satisfaction through understanding the Trinity. I concur with Cochrane and would claim that Augustine's reflections applied to the topic of humanness demonstrates his trinitarian emphasis. Augustine articulated his position of the trinitarian construct of the human mind (*nous*) in his *On the Trinity*, *The City of God*, and the *Confessions*. He believed that, since humans were made in the image of God and God is a Trinity, that image itself must be trinitarian. It is important to note that the trinitarian image in man does not make man equal in substance to God. It only suggests that man in his being, in his existence, will mirror the Divine Being.

There is an extended discussion of the Trinity in the eleventh book of the *City of God*. In this book Augustine suggests that the Trinity be understood in terms of the triad of existence, knowledge, and love. The particular way one understands the Father is as Being (existence), the Son as Logos (knowledge), and the Holy Spirit as Love. These are peculiar designations for each member of the Godhead. But it is important to know that the Godhead is One: three persons, but one substance. It is important to note as well that the Godhead possesses what the Trinitarians from the east called *perichoresis*. This means that every act of the Father was mutually an act of the Son and every act or thought of the Spirit was equally the Father's and the Son's. The three are coterminous, inescapably cohering and mutually self-reflective and inter-related. The Trinity perfectly and flawlessly exists in perichoric activity and contemplation.

In creating humans in God's own image, man is made with existence, with knowledge of his existence and with a love for his own existence. Man is being, knowledge, and love. In chapter 26 of Book XI of the *City of God*, Augustine writes,

> We do indeed recognize in ourselves an image of God, that is of the Supreme Trinity. It is not an adequate image, but a very distinct parallel. It is not co-eternal and, in brief, it is not the same substance as God. For all that, there is nothing in the whole of God's creation so near to him in nature; but the image now needs to be refashioned and brought to perfection, so to become close to him in resemblance. We resemble the divine Trinity in that we exist; we know that we exist, and we are glad of this existence and this knowledge. In those three things there is no plausible deception to trouble us.[9]

Further, in chapter 28 he contends that, "Now we are human beings, created in our Creator's image, whose eternity is truth, whose truth is eternal, whose love is eternal and true, who is a Trinity of eternity, truth and love, without confusion or separation; and the constituents of the world which are inferior to us could not exist at all, could not have shape or form, could not aspire to any ordered pattern, or keep that pattern, had they not been created by him who supremely exists, and who is supremely wise and

---

9. Augustine, *City of God*, 459.

supremely Good."[10] In both of these quotes the reader will notice the trinitarian patterns: supremely exists, supremely wise, supremely good. But we also see the perichoretic focus as well. Look at the language from chapter 28; whose eternity is truth, whose truth is eternal, whose love is eternal and true. The aspects of the triune God coinhere; in like manner although without the same perfection, the three aspects of the *nous* coinhere as well. Humans possess all three aspects of their being yet are one.

Augustine clarifies the notion of three aspects co-inhering in Book XIII of the *Confessions* as well. Augustine writes,

> I should like men to consider three aspects of their own selves. These three are something very different from the Trinity; I only make the suggestion as a mental exercise which will allow people to find out and to feel how far distant they are from it. The three things I mean are existence, knowledge, and will. For I am, and I know, and I will. I am a being that knows and wills. I know that I am and I know that I will. I will to be and I will to know. Now he who is capable of doing so will see how there is in these three an inseparable life—one life, one mind, one essence—and, finally, how inseparable a distinction there is between them, yet nevertheless there is a distinction. Every man has this as a fact in front of him.[11]

Humans possess three distinct aspects of the self, yet these are inseparable.

Augustine provides a final formulation of the trinity of the mind in *On the Trinity*, Book X. He writes,

> So when one talks about these three things in a person, disposition, learning, and practice, one judges the first according to what he can do with his memory, his understanding, and his will; one estimates the second according to what he actually has in his memory and understanding, and where he has got to with his will to study; the third however is to be found in the use the will now makes of what the memory and understanding hold, whether it refer them to something else or whether it takes delight in them as ends in themselves.[12]

---

10. Ibid., 463.
11. Augustine, *Confessions*, 323.
12. Augustine, *Trinity*, 298.

Nous is memory, understanding, and will, and as we see in the above passage, each aspect is operative in the whole. He goes on to say in the same context,

> These three the memory, understanding, and will, are not three lives but one life, nor three minds but one mind. So it follow of course that they are not three substances but one substance.... After all, I remember that I have memory and understanding and will, and I understand that I understand and will and remember, and I will that I will and remember and understand, and I remember my whole memory and understanding and will all together.[13]

His final formulation is, then, that the self/mind is composed of memory, understanding, and will, that these make up one mind and not three, and that these are mutually and self-referentially involved in one another as aspects of mind. All other cognitive processes are fitted under one of these categories.

For Augustine, the will functions or operates as a cognitive mechanism. And, as Hannah Arendt reminds her readers, "the will is loving attention to the contents of memory and understanding."[14] Affective knowledge is every bit as much a part of the whole of cognition as what post-Cartesians have taken to be rationality. Will as an aspect of the mind portends its significance and its necessity for every act of true knowledge. This as an aspect is not readily appreciated in the history of epistemology, but certainly reflects the language of Scripture where "to know" is used to indicate intimacy between lovers or in the wisdom literature where love is used in the context of intimacy with wisdom. In the prophet Hosea knowledge is understood as loving covenant faithfulness to God from His people and so when he exhorts Israel to "press on to know the Lord," he is referring to affective knowledge that includes the memory of God's covenant dealing, the understanding of those dealings and of God's immutable nature and the love of direction and attention that these require when rightly functioning. As we move into a discussion of the specific noetic effects of sin, the triadic nature of the mind and its affective orientation must be kept in view.

---

13. Augustine, *Trinity*, 298.
14. Arendt, *Life of the Mind*, 102.

DOES AUGUSTINE HAVE A NOTION OF THE NOETIC EFFECTS OF SIN?

As intimated above, Augustine posits that humans have a basic knowledge of self. It is manifested in the conception, *Si Fallor, Sum*. One knows and appreciates one's own existence in a limited manner. But the kind of self-knowledge necessary for the Cartesian system to obtain is an impossibility for Augustine when divorced from divine illumination. Divine illumination is obscured and hidden because of the sinfulness of fallen creatures and can only be restored with understanding through the grace of redemption. In this section I wish to establish the parameters of Augustine's perspective by first discussing the nature of sin and to posit through an analysis of several passages which will serve to establish, exegetically, that Augustine asserts that one's noetic structure is tainted by sin.

Augustine understood sin to be the culpable distortion and disobedient rejection of the order of God's design in creation intellectually, socially, and morally. It is the consequence of a perverse will and a failure to conform to God's will. It results from the reluctance of a creature to give due acknowledgement to his Creator. Sin springs from the love of self inordinately sustained by lustful interests. Sin is sustained by the pursuit of those things that justice forbids.

I call attention to several features of Augustine's position that I believe will be helpful later on in uncovering the noetic effects of sin. Firstly, Augustine viewed sin as a perverse preference. In Book VII, chapter 16 of the *Confessions*, Augustine says of sin and wickedness that these are "a perversity of the will turning away from you, God, the supreme substance, toward lower things—casting away, as it were, its own insides and dwelling with desire for what is outside itself."[15] Sin confuses the order of value established by God and evidenced in the created order and preferentially seeks lower goods at the expense of higher goods. In *On the Free Choice of the Will*, Augustine contends that people have inordinate desires, that is, the longing and loving of something that one can lose against one's will.[16]

The perverseness of the will leads to a second feature of sinfulness, negligence. In Augustine, one erroneously pursues things "outside oneself" while neglecting the things of greater importance. Negligence is culpable behavior nonetheless. Much like a doctor who fails (neglects) to read the

---

15. Augustine, *Confessions*, 266.
16. Augustine, *Free Choice*, 10.

chart of a patient in a hospital and then prescribes medication that would be harmful, negligence is blameworthy, a perversity of will or a laziness obstructing one from rightly choosing to pursue more consequential issues. Negligence of the inner man for Augustine and the divine illumination of outward processes are due to the infatuation one has with other things perversely loved.

Ignorance of truth results from the perversity of the will and the negligence that stems from it. Ignorance of truth is often the result of a malfunctioning mind. Let me illustrate this from Augustine's work *On the Usefulness of Belief*. Augustine believed that human agents are created with a desire to discover and to know things that are true about themselves and the world about them. Sin distorts that natural longing for the truth and shows itself in what Augustine views as misguided pursuits. In *On the Usefulness of Belief* he thinks these misguided endeavors occur in three ways.[17] First of all, one confuses belief (thinking with assent) with credulity. Properly designed image bearing agents pursue true belief; fallen agents are satisfied with easy believisms and ready opinions, that is, with credulity. Credulity accepts too readily information provided without the thoughtfulness that goes into believing with awareness. Credulous believers accept and adopt, in ignorance, positions or perspectives advanced by others which seem to the credulous person as satisfying their wants and needs.

Additionally, Augustine argues that curiosity is not the same as the intentional desire found in truth seekers. In the *Confessions* Book X, Augustine discusses how it is that pagans are quite interested in finding out about things that have occurred in the lives of other people, but not quite as concerned to discover themselves. Ignorance manifests itself in vain curiosity and idle speculation and not the robust yearning and passion for truth that one has gotten through and by God. It is interesting that until the time he was nineteen, Augustine was quite satisfied with being a credulous believer. His curiosity about friendship and other things went untamed. Upon reading *Hortentius* by Cicero, Augustine placed himself on the path of pursuing with great rigor and abandon truth itself. It was not until ten or so years later that he found the truth in Christ. But vain curiosity that often looks for the limitations of others, is the result of a human agent's truth seeking design malfunctioning.

Finally, ignorance is a result of confusing cleverness with wisdom. Humans were created for happiness (i.e., the life of wisdom) but in their

---

17. The reader can find this discussion in *St. Augustine: Earlier Writings*, 309–15.

fallen state, they are satisfied with wittiness and cleverness. Cleverness is coy; it seems to provide an insight, but that insight stems from the ignorance of the propounder of a clever thought and those who naively receive it. Cleverness is often associated with deception, which is a suppression of the truth.(see Romans 1). Ignorance of the truth is perpetuated because of the sinful human tendency to accept the appearance of something for what it truly is. Its clearest example is found in Satan's conversation with Eve in the garden. Eve wrongly accepted a foreign cleverness in place of the wisdom of God, which had forbade eating of the forbidden tree.

Sin as ignorance, as perversity, and as negligence, is perpetuated through habituation, culminating in its necessity. In Book XVIII of the *Confessions* Augustine discusses this progression. Sin voluntarily engaged becomes habit and habit becomes necessity. Necessity in turn leads to a kind of deadness with respect to the glory, beauty, and truth of God known in self, creation, and in God. Let me quote two passages to illustrate this point. In chapter 5 Augustine claims that "From a perverse will came lust, and slavery to lust (inordinate desire discussed above) became habit, and the habit, being constantly yielded to, became necessity. These were links, hanging each to each and they held me fast in hard slavery."[18] And then a bit later in the same chapter, he writes, "For the law of sin is the strong force of habit, which drags the mind along and controls it even against its will though deservedly, (culpably), since the habit was voluntarily adopted."[19] One finds this same kind of analysis of the progression of sinful necessity in James 1. James writes, "One is tempted by one's desire, being lured and enticed by it; then, when that desire has conceived, it gives birth to sin, and that sin, when it is fully grown [habituated] gives birth to death. Do not be deceived, my beloved." Habit emerges from inordinate desire actualized which is then crystallized in one's behavior. Finally, habituated sin becomes a necessity, that is, much like when someone who is addicted to something cannot help but live out that addiction. Sin as habit, as necessity, is most difficult to undue and rehabilitate. Only through the ongoing grace of mortification after regeneration can this be realized in one's life.

Augustine applies the conception of sin discussed above to the notion of the mind to form an idea of the noetic effects of sin. Briefly before establishing the effects discussed by Augustine, it is important to demonstrate, textually, that, in fact, it is his position that some kind of radical damage

18. Augustine, *Confessions*, 168.
19. Ibid.

has been done to the mind. I will proceed to do so by offering some commentary on passages from several different works. I do so to establish not only that Augustine contended that there was some sort of effect of sin on the mind, but to show that it was a consistent, intertextual, position. Let me proceed to identify several of these passages, chronologically from earlier texts to later ones.

Consider claims from the earliest of Augustine's Christian works. Writing in the *Soliloquies* soon after his conversion, Augustine came to understand that, although the mind initially saw and understood truth because of its design, the mind is "vitiated and sick,"[20] and it is "impossible" to see clearly without faith.[21] The mind, as well as the moral life, must experience the intervention of grace to address its sickly condition. In a passage found in *On True Religion* (date 390), Augustine presents a realist conception of truth. He contends that falsehood is not found in the thing observed, but in the one who observes. In other words, the one who observes does so falsely because of sin. "Falsehood arises not because things deceive us, for they can show the beholder nothing but their form, and that they have received according to their position in the scale of beauty. Nor do the senses deceive us, for when they are in contact with natural objects they report to their presiding mind nothing but the impressions formed upon them. It is sin which deceives minds."[22] The mind damaged by sin cannot interpret rightly the data delivered to it because of its sinfulness. Furthermore, when Augustine became a presbyter in 391, he wrote the treatise entitled, *On the Usefulness of Belief*. This great work is pivotal in understanding his *credo ut intelligum*, the faith seeks understanding perspective. He discusses the results of the fall on the mind by contending that where truth seeking was the proper domain of the self made in the image of God, now vain curiosity or credulity governs the pursuits of fallen minds. He contends that this is a consequence of the damaged soul/mind. One is incapable of beholding the truth, "since the eye of my soul has been damaged by my sins and by my being habituated to the plagues of lethargic opinions. As eyes which are scarcely opened after a long period of darkness and blindness turn away and refuse the light which, nevertheless, they desire, especially if one try to

20. Augustine, *Soliloquies*, 30.

21. This passage goes on to describe the necessity of faith in coming to know God and the world. Later in his *Retractions*, Augustine criticizes his *Soliloquies* and what he considers to be its overconfidence in human reason. But the position that the mind has been affected is clear from the above passage.

22. Augustine, *On True Religion*, in *Earlier Writings*, 259.

point them to the sun, so in my case."²³ The mind has been darkened, the result of sin. These passages from early in Augustine's work demonstrate the beginning of his understanding of noetic sin; the mind has been adversely affected because of the fall.

The *Confessions* help in understanding the middle period of the development of this doctrine. Given that later in the chapter such of the discussion of one of the effects of sin, *akratic* believing, will get most of its attention from the *Confessions*, I will confine myself to two references. In Book VIII, Augustine, in a context in which he discusses the inner man and the law of God implanted on him, claims, "For the law of sin is the strong force of habit, which drags along the mind and controls it even against its will—though deservedly, since the habit was voluntarily adopted."²⁴ Later in Book X, Augustine writes that "truth does not reveal her light to them (minds)" because "this human mind of ours, so blind and sick, so foul and ill-favored, wants to be hidden itself," and people "hate the truth" when it is about themselves, but perversely enjoy it when it is about others.²⁵ In this stage of development, Augustine's confidence in reason (his early confidence was due to the neoplatonic views he had held earlier and which affected his early writings as a Christian) weakens and the reader gets the strong sense of the blindness and diseased state of the mind. Because of the effects of sin, the knowledge of oneself is derailed.

As one moves into the later Augustine, one identifies a clearer and more pervasive awareness of the noetic effects of sin and, as a consequence, the need for divine grace to intervene and correct the problems associated with a fallen mind. In a treatise published about 415, *On Nature and Grace*, Augustine avers in chapter 3,

> Man's nature was created at first faultless and without any sin; but that nature of man in which every one is born from Adam, now wants the physician, because it is not sound. All good qualities, no doubt, which it still possesses in its make, life, senses, intellect, it has of the Most High God, its Creator and Maker. But the flaw, which darkens and weakens all those natural goods, so that it is in need of illumination and healing, . . . it has gotten from original sin.²⁶

---

23. Augustine, *On the Usefulness of Belief*, in *Earlier Writings*, 294.
24. Augustine, *Confessions*, 169.
25. Ibid., 233–34
26. Augustine, *On Nature and Grace*, 523.

This quotation implies that some measure of the good qualities of mind and life persist even in fallen man, but he requires the healing grace of the God of creation to restore him to the pristine position of knowing God and the world aright. It is interesting to note that, in the very next section of the text, Augustine argues that it is God's free grace that makes the restoration possible, not any meritoriousness resulting from the abilities of a person, so that all might give God the praise He alone merits.

I wish to call your attention to one final passage to conclude the general discussion of the *nous* and sinfulness. This passage is taken from the *City of God*. The *City of God* was written over an extended period of time and reflects mature Augustinian thought on the notion of knowledge, the Trinity, and the image of God, man. Augustine writes that even though the mind was the seat of understanding and reason, "the mind of man is itself weakened by long-standing faults which darken it. It is too weak to cleave to that changeless light and to enjoy it; it is too weak even to endure that light."[27] Even though persons were created to enjoy felicity, man's mind must be first "renewed and healed day after day" and the "mind had to be trained and purified by faith; and in order to give man's mind greater confidence in its journey towards the truth along the way of faith." This passage is interesting on two accounts. Firstly, because of the clarity of the notion of noetic sin: the mind is weakened and blinded by its sinfulness. And secondly, Augustine provides a succinct overview of what I might call noetic sanctification. The mind, due to its weakened state, needs to be renewed daily to be enabled to do its task properly. A component of the mediatorial function of Christ affected through his Spirit is to provide the model and the grounds for the sanctification of the mind to occur. This passage from Augustine is reminiscent of Paul's exhortation to the Roman Christians to "be transformed by the renewing of your minds, so that you may discern what is the will of God" (Rom 12:2).

Augustine has provided a clear account of what he takes to be the human mind. It is important to understand that for Augustine the notion of humanness is thoroughly trinitarian, patterned after the aspects of existence, knowing, and loving. I have sought to explain what constitutes sin for Augustine and have concluded by giving ample illustrations, textually, supporting the claim that Augustine understood the mind to be pervasively affected by sin. I ended this section with the quote from the *City of God*

---

27. Augustine, *City of God*, 430.

which indicates that while sin is present, the work of renewing the mind might occur when one, in grace, comes to know the God who is over all.

Augustine was not an epistemic infallibilist in the Cartesian sense but a fallibilist in the sense that he understood the radical debilitating effect of noetic sin on reflexivity. Hence, one is not as radical as one may think! One might better contend that Augustine bequeathed to the Western tradition what came to be understood as Calvin's perspective on the noetic effects of sin and with Calvin, Anselm, Edwards, and others the necessity of meditation on the Trinity if one were to come to know oneself. As Bourke contends in *Augustine's Love of Wisdom*, "Augustinian philosophy is theocentric: all things and all events are to be explained by reference to the Divine Being."[28] Consequently, *gnothi seauton* is promise reduced to futility due to sin's aberration of the design of God which was to facilitate self-knowledge.

A RIDDLE TO ONESELF: THE PROBLEM OF SELF-DECEPTION AS NOETIC SIN

I have become a riddle to myself and that is my infirmity.

So it seems to me, though I may be deceiving myself. For here too there is a sad kind of darkness in which the abilities that are in me are hidden from me so that when my mind questions itself about its own powers, it cannot be certain that its replies are trustworthy.[29]

In this last section of the chapter I intend to explore the implications of being a riddle to oneself. It has been suggested that sin affects the *nous* thoroughly: memory, understanding, and will. Its weakness and frailty hinder the full realization and actualization of self-knowledge. And because the *nous* is weakened by sin, the call to know thyself is thwarted and remains fallow without the grace of God, both commonly and redemptively. As the quotations indicate above, deceiving oneself is the result of the darkness that has attended the fallenness of humankind. Self-deception is the quagmire of the *nous* and the riddle of existence. Self-deception, as the result of noetic sin, tends to be the standard of fallen humans, hindering the realization of the Delphic oracle.

Self-deceptive practices distort the self-knowledge canons listed above as a consequence of humankind's corruption, for Augustine. The command

28. Bourke, *Love of Wisdom*, 118.
29. Augustine, *Confessions*, 243.

is frustrated outside the intervention of God's grace and kindness. A possible way of defining self-deception in Augustine is to claim that it is the motivated evasion, misrepresentation, or suppression of the truth in completely acknowledging oneself through pride, *akrasia,* and fragmentation of thought. It is falsehood to oneself; self-deceivers lie to themselves about the truth regarding themselves due to the triad pride, *akrasia,* and fragmentation. Augustine's perspective is a robust conception of self-deception. In what follows I will explore this conception as humankind's riddle by exploring its three domains: pride, *akrasia,* and the fragmentation of thought.

Noetic Sin: Pride

Pride, for Augustine, is the root of all sin.[30] In pride "the soul has exalted itself and was excessively overconfident in its own powers."[31] It is the desire for "vain reputation and empty ostentation."[32] Pride is the turning away from God as the source of self-knowledge, which Augustine identifies as apostasy.[33] Adam and Eve followed the example of the devil in pride: the free rejection of God's design for one's own distorted advancement. The inner beauties that humans should recognize due to the charitic canon, are "claimed for itself" so that, in pride, the self-knower "turns away from Him [the Triune God] and slithers and slides down into less and less which is imagined to be more and more; it finds satisfaction neither in itself nor in anything else as it gets further away from him who alone can satisfy it."[34]

In Augustine pride is understood by considering its two manifestations, which, in effect, are violations of the commands to love the Lord with one's whole being and to love your neighbor as yourself. Firstly, pride is an overestimation of the self, producing a disoriented self-love that makes proper self-knowledge impossible. As Augustine indicates, it is living by the rule of the self not by God's rule.[35] This overestimation of the self is a rejection of the command to love God with all of one's being. Secondly, pride is a privatization of the self, a disregard for the insights one might gain as a social agent who interacts with others and God. Unfortunately, pride

---

30. Augustine, *Free Choice,* 147.
31. Augustine, *Literal Meaning of Genesis,* 432.
32. Augustine, *On the Usefulness of Belief,* in *Earlier Writings,* 291.
33. Augustine, *Free Choice,* 147.
34. Augustine, *Trinity,* 292.
35. Augustine, *City of God,* 252.

culminates in the quest for power over others. The quest for dominance, politically and socially, so magnanimously articulated in the *City of God* is the result of a privatized prideful mindset. As such, the privatization of the self and its pursuit of dominance is a repudiation of the command to love one's neighbor. Loving God aright and loving neighbor as self are essential in Augustine for a proper knowledge of self.

The overestimation of self is a dismissal of who God is, the significance of His illuminating presence, and God's prerogative in defining His own likeness, i.e., mankind. The opening book of the *Confessions* beautifully expresses the thought that humans have been made to live to the praise of God's glory and to revel in it, to take pleasure in the splendor of the Almighty. In Book X, Augustine cries out after his conversion, "Late have I loved thee, beauty so ancient and yet so new."[36] Humans, as fallen and noetically weak creatures, seek pleasures that "are beautiful to us, sweet to hear, to touch," but do so as a "mangled corpse."[37] Taking the place of the praise of God for His beauty is "the vanity of human praise" which leaves humans empty; it "does not satisfy the hungry spirit because it offers nothing to eat except what is hollow and full of air, the hunger itself forces it to appeal to something else as richer and more fruitful."[38] As such, humans turn away from the essence of beauty and instead concentrate on, worship, and adore things thought to be beautiful without divine reference. God is not only beautiful and majestic, but is the source of truth. Without God there is no discovery of truth. But, "pride does not lead to a perception of the truth. If there were no pride, there would be no heretics, schismatics, no worshippers of creatures or images."[39] It is pride that deceives one to "love the works of the artificer [God] more than the artificer" and to "scrutinize the creation contrary to the commandment of God and to enjoy it rather than God's truth."[40] The consequence of this overestimation of self and disordered view of creation is that "they have not known the author and maker of the universe. So they abandon themselves to idols, and, forsaking the works of God, they are immersed in the works of their own hands, all of them visible things."[41] Human "pride and impious madness, oppose his

---

36. Augustine, *Confessions*, 235.
37. Ibid., 246.
38. Augustine, "Epistle 118," 108.
39. Augustine, *On True Religion*, in *Earlier Writings*, 248.
40. Ibid., 258.
41. Ibid., 261.

name in the perversity of their hearts"[42] replaces what ought to have been an expression of gratitude. The self is governed by the inordinate desires that follow from pride: "the lust of the flesh, the lust of the eyes and the ambition of this world."[43] The turning in pride to these concupiscences ensures that "truth is far removed from the minds of vain men who have gone too far among worldly concerns."[44]

In addition to the overestimation of the self, Augustine suggests a kind of privatization occurs in pride that hinders one's love of neighbor. This privatization—that is a concern with the power the self exerts—is manifested in the quest for dominance and in utilizing knowledge for one's own hegemony. In the first book of the *City of God*, Augustine characterizes the city of the world, the city of pride, which "aims at dominion, which holds nations in enslavement, but is itself dominated by that very lust of domination." One might contend that the whole of the *City of God* is an exposition of this statement. Later in the first book Augustine outlines the progress of prideful power through the extravagant theatrical productions in Rome as a means of power and the civil and religious structures that supported it. Pride capitalizes on the self-interest of the bearer of power in which he utilizes the amusements of the stage and the alleged benevolence of the state to further his own ends. Even peace, Book XIX, must be understood in light of the privatization of prideful power. Augustine argues that the bearer of power engages in war against others to procure a peace, a peace of injustice,[45] that perpetuates his self-interest.

Pride as privatization is an anti-social, anti-community, anti-commonwealth mindset. In *The Literal Meaning of Genesis*, Augustine discusses the two loves introduced in the *City of God*: the love of God and the love of self. He says that "these two loves—one of which is holy, the other unclean, one social, the other private, one taking thought for the common good because of companionship in the upper regions, the other putting even what is common at its own personal disposal because of its lordly arrogance"[46] is "the tumor of pride."[47] Privatization run amok creates the

---

42. Augustine, *City of God*, 7.
43. Ibid., 261
44. Augustine, *On the Usefulness of Belief*, in *Earlier Writings*, 291.
45. Augustine, *City of God*, 869.
46. Augustine, *The Literal Meaning Of Genesis*, 439.
47. Ibid., 330.

condition for the destruction of society that Augustine warns against.[48] Augustine was the first great theorizer of power relationships and views these as the consequence of privatized pride. In the *City of God* Augustine contends that Rome itself was culpable and blameworthy for the invasion of the barbarians because of the perversion of prideful power that went unchecked in the society. The moral structure of the universe by God's design punishes those who violate God's normative framework. Rome fell because of its failure to love its neighbor and to follow the God of hosts. The hegemonous were self-deceived and infatuated with their power but failed to recognize that it doomed them to destruction.

Privatization of prideful power has an additional manifestation in the work of Augustine. I have in mind the misappropriation of knowledge due to pride. In *Epistle 118*, Augustine writes that "knowledge puffs up" and when it does, it hinders the quest for wisdom that humans were made to achieve. In this epistle, Augustine chastises a fellow cleric for his vain pursuit of knowledge. He points out that his fellow cleric only wanted to know so that others might praise him and recognize him. Much like the snobbery attached to some in modern education, this cleric desired status in the community and education was a means to the power attached to it. Knowledge divorced from the exercise of love toward one's neighbor is a perversion and degenerates knowledge according to Augustine; it is used to oppress others. As such "knowledge" can become the invention of the power broker to maintain his position, instead of utilizing knowledge as a tool for the liberation of humans.[49]

Pride as self-exaltation or as privatization strips humans of the glory of bearing God's image. God's image is realized in man's direction toward God in humility and in beneficent action taken in love for his neighbor. In pride, a man becomes "like a snake who does not walk with open strides but wriggles along the tiny movements of its scales, so the careless glide little by little along the slippery path of failure, and beginning from a distorted appetite for being like God they end up in becoming like beasts."[50] Pride deceives one so that he suppresses or evades the understanding of self as illuminated by God or causes him to fail in recalling that "man's true

---

48. Augustine, *City of God*, Book I.

49. It has been interesting to me that Augustine's perspective is similar to some of the postmodern theorists like Foucault; knowledge is power in the sense of a tool for domination. And those in positions of power identify what constitutes knowledge and do so as a means of perpetuating that power.

50. Augustine, *Trinity*, 331.

honor is God's image and likeness in him, but it can only be preserved when facing him from whom its impression is received." This self-deception ends in greediness "to experience his own power" and so he "tumbles down at a nod to himself into himself and then, while he wants to be like God under nobody, he is thrust down as a punishment for his own half-way level to the bottom to the things in which the beasts find their pleasure. And thus, since his honor consists in 'being like God,' man perverts this by existing in 'disgrace like an animal.'"[51]

Self-deception and Fragmentation

The second domain of self-deception as the consequence of noetic weakness is what I would like to identify as fragmentation. A number of philosophers have posited that persons suffer from a kind of division in the mental or believing structure that facilitates self-deception. Psychologists of various sorts contend for a division of the self as well using categories like ego and id or belief/disbelief system to identify the fault lines of the divisions. Prior to these suggestions Augustine provided an account of the divisions of the self or what I identify as fragmentation.

As noted above, Augustine attempted to diligently apply the notion of the Trinity to all aspects of human existence. This led him to posit a trinity of the "outer man" and a trinity of the "inner man." The outer man is governed by one's perceptual features and the knowledge derived from them is identified as sense knowledge. The inner man is characterized by reason, which develops rational knowledge. Divine illumination enlightens and clarifies sense knowledge and rational knowledge, culminating in self-understanding and wisdom about oneself.[52] In Augustine's model of self-knowledge a coordination of these elements is involved in the proper functioning of the human agent made in the image and likeness of the Triune God. Fragmentation is the disordering of that proper function such that coordination is hindered and radically obscured. This lack of coordination leaves one's belief structure fragmented, compartmentalized, and divided.

51. Ibid.

52. A complete examination of Augustine's epistemology is beyond the scope of this book. Helpful introductions can be found in Nash's *The Light of the Mind* and Gilson's *The Christian Philosophy of St. Augustine*.

Fragmented believers are inconsistent and incoherent in their belief systems and lack the cognitive power to affect coordination. In Book XI of *On the Trinity*, Augustine claims that "the rational soul lives a misshapen kind of life when it lives according to the trinity of the outer man; that is, when instead of bringing a praiseworthy will to bear on the things that form the senses from outside and referring them to some useful end (which requires divine illumination and rational knowledge) it fastens on them."[53] By this he means that the divided, fragmented mind malfunctions placing disproportionately more stress on the external than it intrinsically requires.

A second feature of the fragmented mind is that the lack of coordination identified in the previous paragraph suggests that the mind simply does not do a very good job of thinking; it does not think well. In *On the Free Choice of the Will* Book II, Augustine argues that in a properly functioning human agent the various senses, outer and inner, will share in the evaluation of data received. The inner sense makes sense of the information provided by perceptual states and, in turn, refers it to the understanding in which concepts, derived from the perceptual states, are developed. In a weakened mind, self-deceiving itself, the divisions among the elements of cognition are pronounced, thus inhibiting the flow of information and evaluation. The complete act of thought for Augustine requires there to be an ordered functioning of thought after the normative design of God in creation. Hence, the entire process of intellection is tainted and deformed leading to a poor intellectual life and a dwarfed understanding of the self. The intellectual life of man was ordered to be a "simply undivided mind" and the distribution of functions[54] needed to cohere in order to discover the truth. Fragmented man intellectually suffers the dislocation of the distribution of functions.

Fragmentation or the divided mind ensures that man "only sees in parts not the whole."[55] There is a lack of wholism in the mind weakened by sin. The *nous* "slides away from the whole which is common to all into parts."[56] One can view this slide into parts in the history of philosophy or in the development of modern scientific disciplines. In philosophy, schools of epistemology are divided by emphasizing one aspect of intellection over another. There generally has been a denigration of the factor of passion

---

53. Augustine, *Trinity*, 307.
54. Ibid., 324.
55. Augustine, *On Order*, 215.
56. Ibid., 330.

or love in the rationalist tradition along with the vilification of the body, which has its origin in Plato. There has been a lack of concern for how folks know socially or historically or through acquaintances. As such the vision of knowing has suffered greatly. Wholeness here again suggests a malfunctioning of the process of thought and a putting together data gathered and utilized in arriving at a position.

One other area of fragmentation deserves attention. Knowledge (*scientia*) is discovered in various realms of human experience. One gains knowledge of the liberal arts or of the sciences in the process of intellection and in the context of history. Knowledge fragmented and isolated from other domains of knowing encourages the presence of self-deception. In Augustine's *On Christian Doctrine* he argues that one of the values of liberal education is that it provides a broad view of the best that humans have thought and considered throughout the ages. He believed that this had a kind of purifying effect on humans and taught them well that authority was necessary for new discoveries of knowledge. The fragmented mind does not consider the contribution that various realms of knowledge provide in one's pursuit of wisdom. There is isolation, negligence, and ignorance that accompany a limited or narrow encounter of fields of knowledge. Knowledge has as its goal wisdom, but wisdom cannot be had without the full scope of fields of knowledge being paid the attention and devotion they deserve as part of the pursuit of wisdom.

For example, let's say that one is charged with discovering a way to interpret the revelation of God. The fragmented mind will pay attention to procedures, values, and interpretive schemes that have already been adopted by the interpreter. One might be given to source analysis or may have been shot through with post-Wittgensteinian family resemblances or language games. Following the procedures dominant in the *scientia* of his background, emphasis will possibly lead to a narrow view of the meaning of the text that is the goal of all interpretation. Wisdom and insight into the nature of the text demands a whole cartload of other considerations be taken into account. The modern infatuation with disciplines and domains dominating the hermeneutical considerations of modern philosophy, theology, rhetoric, or grammar will invariably, for Augustine, thwart the attempt to really understand the text in wisdom. Our saturation with discipline domain methodology should be given pause in light of the insight of Augustine at this point. Fragmentation in the domain of the *scientia* ensures that the trinitarian value of wisdom and truth is perverted, a sign of the disordering presence of sin.

Fragmentation, then, includes a lack of coordination of mental operations, an inhibited ability to think well and rightly, an absence of wholeness and completeness in intellection and a thwarting of the goal of thought itself toward wisdom and the discovery of the truth. Within the fragmented and fractured mind of humankind, the realization and presence of self-deceptive engagement prevails.

Akrasic Self-deception

Akrasia is the final noetic effect of sin examined in this chapter. *Akrasia* means weakness of the will and has been principally used to indicate a lack of strength or power to perform certain actions. Incontinence is another term commonly used for this absence of resolve and power. Augustine applies *akrasia* to the mind as well as action. A clear example of the latter is found in a work, a kind of sermon, entitled "Continence." "Continence" is a work that deals principally with the problem of lusting after the flesh sexually. Given that this kind of incontinence was primary and problematic in Augustine, especially as a youth, he was apt to warn about its influence. *Akrasia* of the mind is extensively discussed in the tenth book of the *Confessions* and also in *On the Free Choice of the Will*. In this section I will refer to these passages from the *Confessions* and *On the Free Choice of the Will* to frame my discussion of *akrasia* as an aspect of self-deception in Augustine.

"I have become a riddle to myself" captures the central problem in Augustine's inquiry in Book X of the *Confessions*. He begins Book X with the acknowledgment that only God knows him thoroughly and expresses the desire to know himself as God knows him. He discovers that memory is a chief source of knowledge about himself and the things he knows. He identifies a number of things that he holds in memory such as images from perceptual experience, judgments made whether true or false, feelings and things he had learned on the basis of authority like the liberal arts. He then notices a number of intellectual constructs that he already seemed to possess as a human, like mathematics, the rules of morals, and the sense that true happiness is a good thing, that which humans were designed to experience. Augustine believed that humans, made in the image of God, had both the capacity to actively engage in accumulating knowledge through sense perception and that humans were endowed with, or in contemporary speak hardwired with, certain bits of information. Unlike the Platonist tradition, which asserted that *a priori* knowledge was the result of previous existences brought to light through recollection, Augustine contended these were the result of God's grace enabling one to think rationally and well according to God's design.

Augustine ponders why, if we have been given the sense of true happiness, do humans not experience it? Why are there fabrications or imitations of happiness around which humans surround their lives and for which they live? How is it that humans do not wish to be deceived, but do so throughout their lives, while failing to grasp or to see what constitutes happiness. Happiness, which is experiencing "joy in truth," is thwarted in life. How should one account for such a thing?

Augustine's answer to the above dilemmas is to posit the debilitating influence of *akrasia* on fallen humans. He claims that humans receive "the encompassing brightness of your light. But love of the shadow causes the soul's eye to become too lazy and weak to endure the splendor of the sight of you."[57] This affection for the shadow produces the desire to be hidden from oneself. The self, created in the image and likeness of God, craves truth. Fallen selves pursue pseudo-truths that mask the splendor and glory of God's truth in and over all of creation.

Augustine asserts that humans, by nature, do not like to be deceived. Although they might engage in deceptive actions toward others as a result of an absence of brotherly love, they certainly do not wish to be deceived or to deceive themselves. He writes "they do not like to be deceived" and "I have met many people who wanted to deceive, but no one who wanted to be deceived."[58] Yet, due to perverted affections, humans do just that; they deceive themselves by failing to pay attention to the truth through *akrasia* and restraining their desires disordering the value of created objects. The weakness of the will hinders humans from attending to that which makes for true happiness.

The noetically impaired, even though they wish not to be deceived, want and desire to be hidden (evasion) from that which constitutes true happiness. He writes, "This human mind of ours, so blind and sick, so foul and ill-favored, wants to be hidden itself."[59] In chapter 32 of Book X, Augustine reaffirms the desire not to be deceived and even considers that

57. Augustine, *Free Choice*, 75.
58. Augustine, *Confessions*, 233.
59. Ibid., 234.

he may be doing just that. But he suffers a kind of blindness as to whether he is deceiving himself because of the desire for hiddenness, the result of self-deceptive *akrasia*. He writes, "I may be deceiving myself. For here too there is a sad kind of darkness, the darkness in which the abilities that are in me are hidden from me, so that when my mind questions itself about its own powers, it cannot be certain that its replies are trustworthy, because what is inside the mind is mostly hidden."[60] A person is a "riddle" to himself because of the quest for hiddenness and the failure to be attentive to the conditions of the self.

The hiddenness of self-deceptive *akrasia* becomes even more problematic as one passes through life. *Akratic* responses become the habituated and necessitated responses of noetic sin.[61] "Besides, the more willingly and more indulgently a man follows and accepts something very weak, the more he becomes covered with darkness, and gradually he becomes unable to see what is supreme. He begins to think that some evil is deceiving him . . . yet he is really suffering deservedly because he has turned from the light of wisdom."[62] Further, "the human soul is rational, though it is bound by the mortal chains of the punishment of sin."[63] The human who fails to act rightly on the knowledge that God has imparted suffers gravely the effects of weakened will. "Thus, the man who does not act rightly although he knows what he ought to do, loses the power to know that is right; and whoever is unwilling to do the right when he can, loses the power to do it when he wills to do it." The terrible, irreversible effect of hiddeness is the debilitation of the power of the will to know and to do in the way it was designed by the course established for it.

Now one might claim that if weakness of the will is an effect of fallenness, how might one be held accountable for its presence? Augustine contends that the presence of *akrasia* as a result of the fall is not sin; its execution is and even more so, a person's failure to prayerfully seek the mercy of God to overcome its adverse effects is sinfulness. God's provision of a moral regulatory system (conscience) and the sense of desiring happiness are instances of His grace in a human's life that function to direct the will to plead for mercy. Further, the whole of creation cries aloud and bears

60. Ibid., 241.

61. The reader may recall my earlier discussion of the progress of sin from habituated to necessity.

62. Augustine, *Free Choice*, 75.

63. Ibid., 112.

witness to the reality of God's common grace, inviting humans to hear its beckoning and to turn to the fountain of grace, the Triune God. He writes, "through His creation [the One] beckons to hostile servants, instructs believers, comforts those who hope, encourages those who work, aids those who try and hears those who pray."[64] Humans because of the bondage of their desire to be hidden, choose not to respond to the overtures of God's kindness and, hence, are culpable for their response.

The *akrasic* self-deceptive attitude results from the desire for hiding from the full implications of the truth, a suppression of the truth so to speak, a lack of restraining what one loves and a failure of attention, and of focusing on the truth as delivered by God. Sadly, although humans do not wish to be deceived, their proclivity is to hide the source of true happiness, the joy of living by the design and order of the most Holy Triune God.

I have been exploring the presence of *akrasia* in fallen humans, but now I wish to look at the implications of *akrasia*. I take from Augustine the idea that *akrasia* is a responsible, motivated, affective floundering of the will in restraining disordered desires and/or in exercising *kavanah*[65] in the pursuit of true happiness. *Akrasia* occurs in judgment about the nature of things and in control over the pursuits in which one would be engaged. With these features in mind, let us pursue their implications in Augustine's *Confessions*, Book X.

In failing to control one's affections and in not being attentive to the things that pertain to true happiness, humans, weakened intellectually by sin, judge poorly. *Akrasia* leads to an imbalance in evaluation situations that produces misjudgment. Affective disequilibrium creates the context in which a person considers some pleasures too loosely, wanting their immediate satisfaction and the gratification derived from them and at other times makes one judge too severely which gives way to a harshness of judgment about the pleasure one should uncover in things.[66] In cases like these a double-mindedness ensues in the person creating, as Scripture indicates,

---

64. Augustine, *Free Choice*, 129.

65. I have chosen to use the Hebrew word "*kavanah*" for several reasons to describe the proper state of mind toward happiness. The concept of *kavanah* captures several things. One is attention. *Akrasia* is a failure of attention as I said earlier in the text. But *kavanah* also implies appreciation and integration, according to Abraham Joshua Heschel in his work *God in Search of Man*, 314–17. So, *akrasia* is the floundering of the will by the absence of attention, appreciation of the value of things by God's design and the integration of these in one's total perspective on life.

66. See Augustine, *Confessions*, page 242 for a discussion of these fluctuations.

unstableness in life. Restraint fails and *kavanah* is thwarted; the floundering will judges the pleasure of the moment as acceptable, only to reverse the judgment on another occasion.

Augustine uses church music as an example of this problem. He notices that there are times when he finds excessive pleasure in the tones and melody of the music sung in church worship. He recognizes how this takes over his spirit and, because of *akrasia*, he desires the melodious sounds more and more. Later, he realizes that this lack of restraint, this lust for a pleasure, must be tempered. As such, Augustine becomes very severe in his judgment about the pleasures accompanying church singing and seeks to become deaf to the sounds in which he once took pleasure. In this example, there is a failure of restraint and a failure of *kavanah*. The latter failure results from not considering the joy of praising God as the motivating affection in song leading to a misjudgment about the value of music. Hence, all *akrasic* self-deception includes the component of motivation as indicated earlier.

Further, *akrasia* contributes to an overestimation of the value of sensate states. Pleasure is a good state, but is suspect to excessive or disproportionate value being attached to it. Because humans botch evaluating states, some are given a more significant place than they merit. For instance, many today believe that pleasure and happiness are synonymous. This certainly is not a new thing, but in a culture dominated by hedonism (pleasure is the highest good) the attentiveness and appreciation necessary to understand pleasure is lost. Pleasure is a momentary sensate state and needs to be understood as such. Happiness (the discovering of joy in truth and conformity to God's design in one's life to the praise of His glory) is an enduring state, a permanent one that does not require the immediate flashes of pleasure required by its overestimation. Overestimating the value of sensate states facilitates a lack of constraint in pursuing them. *Akrasia* in judgment leads to *akrasia* in action.

Augustine discusses another type of overestimation associated with *akrasia* in chapter 34 of Book X. This kind of overestimation concerns judgments about the beauty of human artistic productions.[67] He writes that the "love of beautiful shapes of all kinds, glowing and delightful colors . . . must not take hold of the soul; that is for God to do." He continues, "Certainly God made these things very good, but it is He Himself, not these things,

---

67. Augustine, *Free Choice*, 243.

who is good."⁶⁸ Light illuminates God's beautiful colors, but may become a snare when not understood for its extrinsic value and witness. An infatuation with the luminous colors of the universe gives rise to the overestimation of artistic endeavors by man. Oftentimes this leads to a misjudgment about what is of value aesthetically, culminating in the dogma of today's culture that beauty is in the eye of the beholder (subjectivism) and that its appreciation only says something about the beholder's sensate state.

Additionally, the lack of restraint in appreciating colors and artistic productions according to their derivative value leads to excessive manufacturing of goods that in the end are really not necessary for the welfare of humans or for their happiness. Augustine writes, "men themselves in their various arts and manufactures have made innumerable additions: clothes, shoes, vases, products of craftsmanship; pictures too and all sorts of statues—far beyond what is necessary for use, moderate or with any religious meaning."⁶⁹ The will is weakened by the "lust of the eyes" and the inordinate desire for possessions. The lust of the eyes leads to a coveting after things and a misapprehension of what one needs for the good life. Augustine is adept at showing the implications of *akrasia* spiraling out of control. He also makes for good commentary on the infatuations that contributes to a consumerist culture such as is found in the United States.

The progress of corruption associated with the overestimation of sensate states culminates in the inability to find the "right rule" for discovery or knowing beauty aright.⁷⁰ The right rule that Augustine has in mind assesses beauty and also determines its appropriate value and use. It is a rule that tells them "not to go too far, and to keep their strength in God."⁷¹ Without adherence to this rule or principle, humans mistake lassitude and license for happiness.

Weakness of the will fosters another kind of problem. Curiosity, when divorced from the pursuit of truth, skews proper design and knowledge. The beautiful, as discussed above, contributes to a distorted sense of pleasure when inappropriately judged. Curiosity is the lust to know and to find out things because of personal intrigue and not for the purpose of wisdom. In a very telling passage on page 246 Augustine writes, "From the same

---

68. Ibid. The confusion over beautiful things and their value contributes to the confusion over the things that men make themselves.

69. Ibid., 244.

70. Augustine, *Free Choice*, 245.

71. Ibid.

motive men proceed to investigate the working of nature which is beyond our ken—things which it does no good to know and which men only want to know for the sake of knowing. So too, and with this same end of perverted sciences people make inquiries by the means of magic." When reading this passage, one might be reminded of the Frankensteinian types of experiments undertaken today, ones in which the modern mind considers himself to be Prometheus.

Finally, *akrasia* fosters empty and vain thoughts, and an unbridled tongue in evaluation of things and rationalization.[72] Empty and vain thoughts take over one's life when one fails to harness them for the good. Rationalizations are attempts to justify the things and thoughts that one wishes to have suppressing counter evidence or by misrepresenting the truth. The desire for distinction or the pursuit of titles and acclaim dominate one's mindset such that one needs to find reasons, albeit fabricated, to pursue these. *Akrasia* "wants to possess the lie"[73] and employs the means of excluding oneself from proper disclosure from God while becoming unconscious of the truth.

CONCLUDING COMMENTS

I have argued in this chapter that Augustine provides a normative design for self-knowledge fostered through canons possessed by humans in God's gracious order and creation. But I have claimed that humans are thwarted in the pursuit of self-knowledge as a result of the principal noetic effect of sin, self-deception. Self-deception, the intentional misrepresentation, evasion, and suppression of the truth to oneself because of pride, fragmentation, and weakness of the will, masks the image made in the likeness of the Divine Trinity. Although given the command, *gnothi seauton*, and provided the resources (canons of self-knowledge), humans self-deceptively fail in this endeavor. Humans remain forever *Quaestio Mihi Factus Sum* without the intervention of God's renewing grace. Furthermore, the Cartesian distortion of the Augustinian insights discussed in earlier in this paper plagues modern epistemology. The history of philosophy is characterized by the quest of self-knowledge, but fails to account for the presence of noetic self-deception, the consequence of the fall, thus resulting in the state of futility acknowledged in much of the postmodern milieu.

72. Augustine, *Free Choice*, 248–50.
73. Ibid., 254.

The aberration of Descartes, his failure to recognize the important aspects of the Augustinian position, finally leads to philosophy's futility or frustration. Augustine's position should be viewed as one of both promise and frustration. The limiting effects of noetic sinfulness hinder the realization of wisdom, but grace facilitates the integrated reflection and understanding of self through the Trinity in the proper exercise of the canons of self-knowledge. Self-knowledge in the end is the illumination of the self by the Trinity in grace and mercy.

CHAPTER 5

Toward a Responsibilist Model of Believing

IN THE PREVIOUS CHAPTERS I have advocated a reorientation of the critical thinking enterprise. Like much of the traditional dominant critical thinking literature, I have been concerned with ways and procedures that will serve to enhance our understanding of how to go about improving believing. I have differed with many of them with regard to the internalist conception of justification and belief. This perspective claims that belief is a propositional representation of the state of affairs in the world which is available to a believer. In fact, a belief must be amiable if one is to be justified in one's believing. The basic premise of this work has been that one cannot provide the best advice or counsel about intellectual operations, critical thinking or belief melioration without also attending to the illuminating provocative studies of cognitive processes and with a look at the noetic effects of sin. The literature in this area by Tversky, Kahneman, Ross, Nisbett, and Rokeach, coupled with Augustine's analysis, point toward a fuller and more complete understanding of critical thinking.

I propose that an alliance of critical thinking concerns—predominantly identified as epistemological—with psychology in light of our intellectual fracture will yield a more realistic conception of how belief melioration occurs. In turn, this will enable and empower people to confront their propensity to tenaciously hold beliefs. This outlook takes into account the idea that the ideal thinker does not exist, and that we should focus our attention on minimally rational agents who are constrained by the information provided in chapter 3. This alliance contends that the traditional conception of critical thinking actually presents a far too limited model of our cognitive life. By focusing on belief exclusively as proposition, it fails to engage the complexity of our believing. To draw an analogy to Kant, the idealistic model proposed by the critical thinking theorist fails to follow the ethical principle that for one to be required (ought) to behave in a particular way necessitates that the person in fact *can* behave in the way required. In this context, a person must be able to fulfill his ethical demands, if that one is also to be considered ethically culpable for his action. In like manner the epistemic agent must be able to perform and fulfill his epistemic demands if that one is deemed epistemically condemnable. I have argued that the epistemic dominance of the critical thinking movement posits an ideal agent who simply *cannot* meet the demand of the model; "ought" presumes "can" if one is to be liable for his beliefs.

In this chapter I want to propose a model of a critical thinker that does not fall prey to the ideal demand discussed earlier. I want to focus my attention on what might be called a "responsibilist" model of critical thinking. In what follows I will attempt a definition of the kinds of features of the cognitive life one will possess if one is to be identified as a responsible critical thinker. This model will take into account the psychological insights of the previous chapter and the conception of belief developed earlier. Further, I will focus on processes of the cognitive life practices designed to improve these processes and passions which direct them. I want to also pull together some of the insightful perspectives from our early theorists and suggest ways in which they contribute to what Paul has called an "holistic" view of critical thinking.

A RESPONSIBLE CRITICAL THINKER

Important to the task of developing critical thinkers are the analogies that might be drawn between ethics and epistemology. Paul and McPeck acknowledged the connection between these areas; they did not, however, supply an adequate account of how these are related. We will explored this issue in light of chapter 3 with the goal of initially identifying a responsible critical thinker.

A critical thinker is blameworthy in W. K. Clifford's account if he violates the principle of believing on insufficient evidence. This presumes the critical thinker is able to collect and analyze all pertinent data in arriving at a belief, to lay out on the table for evaluation all beliefs that support or deny the proposition under inspection. I have already argued against this account. To argue against this account does not negate the idea that one can and ought to be held accountable for one's believing. Although deciding on a particular belief is not absolutely volitional, this does not indicate that the processes that go into our believing are beyond voluntary control to some extent. A responsibilist model of critical thinking will attempt to address just how this might be by taking into account the processes, passions, and practices that inform believers. A person is warranted in believing on the basis of how responsible an agent is in his cognitive life in arriving at a particular belief. By this I mean how reliable and how much integrity the individual demonstrates intellectually.

The analogy that I advance between ethics and epistemology is based on what ethicists call an ethic of character, not an ethics of duty. The models of critical thought that I focused on earlier in the book were examples of an ethic of duty. An ethic of duty identifies principles and norms that a person must fulfill if his action is deemed morally acceptable. An ethic of character, though, is far more concerned with the intellectual virtues, talents, and dispositions of individuals and argues that these are in fact improvable through practice. A theory of critical thinking reformed to consider character as a central intellectual concept will focus on constant and stable virtues and talents which go into our believing and which inform the structuring of one's belief. As a person's actions can be evaluated according to that person's reliability, so can cognitive activities and their products be judged by the reliability of the critical thinker. On this model a person's belief will be judged by the intellectual/cognitive processes and dispositions that go into determining a belief.

People acquire beliefs about certain states of affairs because their cognitive faculties are functioning particular ways. For instance, if I am called upon to remember the first name of someone I met yesterday, whether I am justified in recalling her name as Joan or Sally is largely a result of the reliability of my memory. The function of memory is to recall an event, name, date, or circumstance from a particular moment in the past. When someone fails to recall accurately that information, the person's cognitive faculty of memory is deemed unreliable, at least in the area at hand. When a cognitive process is functioning correctly by fulfilling its function, it is operating properly. A person will be warranted in holding or forming a belief to the extent that it is a product of the proper functioning of a particular intellectual process. This is, I think, at the heart of a responsibilist account of critical thinking. According to Aristotle in the *Nicomachean Ethics* 1139a 17–18, "But the virtue of a thing is relative to its proper function." When cognitive malfunction occurs, even if the belief is true, a person is not warranted in holding that belief. The position I will stake out is that a person's cognitive equipment in belief forming, holding, and modifying must be operating well when arriving at a particular belief in a specific context.

The conception of a faculty functioning appropriately clearly has analogies to the way that persons talk about a variety of mechanisms in life. Consider any number of engines or machines. The proper function of a machine is to perform in the way that it was constructed to function. For instance, several years ago I had a Nisson Sentra that had a fuel filter that sifted much from my gasoline before entering the carburetor. The mechanism did not fulfill the end of its design, which was to filter much from the gasoline so that the carburetor would run effectively. For a mechanism to malfunction in this way, calls into question its adequacy and even may suggest a poor quality in its design.

My analysis suggests, as do other character (virtue) conceptions, that critical thinking in a responsibility model is a teleological conception; its goal/purpose is to discover the truth. The end of a faculty is its proper function according to its particular design. The activity or process of a specific mechanism called upon to function in a particular area will be judged by the execution of its task. The quality of a mechanism is demonstrated by its adherence to the design that it possesses, be it a car engine or human cognitive agent. A mechanism is considered reliable when it so fulfills its design.

The proper execution of a faculty or mechanism seems to be incomplete in the above discussions. I refer again to a fuel filter to illustrate an additional feature of appropriate functioning. For the fuel filter to fulfill its design requires that it operate in an appropriate environment. There is little sense in talking about the proper function of a fuel filter divorced from a carburetor. Surely on an assembly line a fuel filter may spit gasoline without any problem or malfunctions but this does not constitute it being a reliable fuel filter. To be reliable it must function properly in an environment. This environment includes other mechanisms taken in its total design. The total design of a fuel filter is related to the engine with its pistons, carburetor, crank shaft, etc. This is the environment in which it is to function properly. But I think there is more. The environment of the engine and its proper function must be conducive to its operation. An engine might be running well, fulfilling the end of its design, and properly functioning, but when one drives into the local pond, the environment in which a mechanism is functioning contributes to its incorrect execution and operation.

I also think that there are degrees to which a mechanism functions properly which corresponds to its growth or evolution at a specific time. The notion of proper function does not have to contain an absolute state for it to be valuable. The growth of insight and understanding of a mechanism will increase the potential for melioration. Carburetors were, at least in gasoline-powered engines, thought to be a necessary component of an engine. A number of years ago the fuel filter was introduced as a way of cutting down the muck that entered a carburetor and hence protected the life of the carburetor. Fuel filters potentially had the mechanical malfunction potential to which I alluded earlier. Consequently, engine manufacturers developed the idea of the fuel injected engine to negate the necessity of carburetors and fuel filters. For anyone who drives a fuel injected engine, its benefits are clear.

The proper function of our cognitive faculties is analogous to the reliable functioning of other mechanisms. The substance of these faculties I will discuss in a later section. To be considered reliable, cognitive faculties must function properly according to their design in a congenial environment. The structuring of belief that I argued for in an earlier chapter can, on this account, be improved by making more reliable the processes of cognition through practice and experience. This account suggests that the operation of our cognition and the formation of particular beliefs depends on the belief's relationship to the cognitive processes that generate or sustain it (them). Human beings improve their cognitive lives by acquiring qualitative character traits of the mind, which have been identified historically in Aristotle and St. Thomas Aquinas as intellectual virtues. In the next section I will explore how a responsibilist conception of critical thinking relates to the concept of intellectual virtue.

AN EXPLORATION OF INTELLECTUAL VIRTUE

For the critical thinking enterprise, Richard Paul reintroduces the discussion of intellectual virtue to the forefront. He defines the intellectual virtues as "the traits of mind and character necessary for right action and thinking; the traits of mind and character essential for fair-minded rationality; the traits that distinguish the narrow-minded, self-serving critical thinker from the open-minded, truth-seeking critical thinker."[1] To this definition he adds the comment, "our basic ways of knowing are inseparable from our basic ways of being. How we think reflects who we are. Intellectual and moral virtues or disabilities are intimately interconnected."[2] Paul acknowledges the necessity of drawing a close relationship to the character of a person and his belief. The emphasis that I claim is slightly different: my focus is on the cognitive faculties and cognitive affections that go into reliable and responsible belief. In what follows, I will first examine Aristotle's conception of intellectual virtue because his approach focuses on the cognitive operation/faculty/power side of the divide. I will then attempt to build on Aristotle's conception by suggesting a taxonomy in which we might understand some of the virtues Aristotle and others have suggested. Following Paul, I will then talk about how our pedagogical practices need to develop these intellectual traits. And finally, I will discuss the affective side of the intellectual domain with an analysis of intellectual passions.

Aristotle's Account of Intellectual Virtue

> Is virtue something that can be taught? Or does it come by practice? Or is it neither teaching nor practice that gives it to man but natural aptitude or something else?
> (*Meno* 70a)

Much of what Aristotle proposes as a description of the nature of virtue, both intellectual and moral, is a response to this quotation from Plato. How does one go about acquiring virtue? Is it innate or is it learned? Does one possess virtue at the end of a period of practice? What is virtue? At the heart of the discussion of intellectual virtue in Aristotle's *Nicomachean Ethics* one will discover potential answers to these and other similar questions which pertain to virtue. I will reconstruct Aristotle's notion of intellectual virtue in this section and will only refer to moral virtue when it helps to enhance or illuminate our discussion of intellectual virtue. Much of the revival of interest in virtue currently centers on the evaluation and exploration of moral virtue. Aristotle suggests that moral virtue depends upon intellectual virtue of a particular kind (i.e., *phronesis*) for its existence. Hence, any discussion about virtue today as it pertains to Aristotle specifically warrants engagement in some sort of exegesis of the crucial notion of intellectual virtue.

1. Paul, *Critical Thinking*, 555.
2. Ibid., 194

Toward a Responsibilist Model of Believing

What then is virtue and, more specifically, intellectual virtue? To understand this question with a view to Aristotle's explication of it, one must consider virtue, *arete*, in light of the general argument of the *Nicomachean Ethics*.

In the *Nicomachean Ethics*, Aristotle argues that *eudaimonia*, or happiness, is the *summum bonum* of existence. In the structure of the *Ethics* the virtues, both intellectual and moral, are examined in terms of their relationship to *eudaimonia*. Aristotle suggests that happiness, as an activity of the human soul, is manifested in the exercise of the state of virtue. The excellence of a thing is demonstrated in the proper functioning of the thing itself. So that in terms of the human soul, the proper function of it is happiness, which results from the acquisition of the virtues in one's life. Aristotle wrote:

> If we take the proper function of man to be a certain kind of life, and if this kind of life is an activity of the soul and consists of actions performed in conjunction with the rational element, and if a man of high standards is he who performs these actions well and properly, and if a function is well performed when it is performed in accordance with the excellence appropriate to it; we reach the conclusion that the good of man is an activity of the soul in conformity with excellence or virtue, and if there are several virtues, in conformity with the best and most complete.[3]

This quotation from the *Ethics* provides the outline of how Aristotle will develop the concept of *eudaimonia*. To highlight several crucial components of *eudaimonia*, Aristotle says that it is an activity (*energia*) of the soul in conformity with virtue and realized most perfectly in the highest of the virtues.

Aristotle defines the soul in Book I, chapter 13 of the *Ethics*. He initiates a discussion of the virtues in Book II and concentrates on the notion of moral virtue from Book III to V. In chapter 6 he returns to the discussion of intellectual virtue from Book II concentrating on the idea of *phronesis*, practical wisdom, as the bridge between moral virtue and happiness. Aristotle culminates his discussion of virtues in Book X, where he suggests that contemplation (*theoriteke*) is the most complete virtue, the highest of the hierarchy of characteristics that leads to happiness. MacIntyre summarizes

---

3. Aristotle, *Nicomachean Ethics*, Book I, 1098a 17.

this thought by stating that "virtues are those qualities which enable a person to acquire *eudaimonia*."[4]

Aristotle posits that "Happiness, the result of both intellectual and moral virtue, is the activity of the soul."[5] But one may ask and rightly so, what is virtue (*arete*)? *Aretai* are praiseworthy characteristics and qualities of human soul that enable one to attain happiness. Aristotle wrote: "The good which we have been seeking is a human good.... By virtue we do not mean excellence of the body, but that of the soul, and we define happiness as an activity of the soul."[6]

The virtues are qualities and states of the soul that are praiseworthy and honorable and educatively acquired by practice or instruction. Intellectual virtues are manifested when they function in accordance with their *telos* (end). For example, the virtue of a shoemaker is that characteristic which enables him to produce good shoes, or that which causes an artist to create something useful and beautiful. Virtue is not possessed by the young or individuals who have limited cognitive experience. Educatively, the child must be guided through experiences that will prepare him or her to acquire the appropriate virtues.

In the statement above, Aristotle argues that happiness is an activity of the soul, and virtue is a state, which via activity, produces happiness. It is crucial for one to understand the notion of activity (*energia*) if one is to develop an appreciation for Aristotle's view as an answer to the *Meno* passage cited above. Aristotle is contending that virtue evolves through a set of experiences which serve to produce a disposition to behave in certain ways. The *Meno* passage asked, how is virtue acquired? Unlike Plato, who contended that virtue was knowledge and that it is knowledge of the ideal forms acquired through recollection and remembrance of previous existence, Aristotle posits that virtue is always manifested in experience. Now there are several problems with knowing what Aristotle meant by experience. Was it every and all experience? Was it experience implanted on the soul? How are experiences connected so that one might possess knowledge?

There is another aspect of the question of how virtue is acquired that requires consideration prior to answering some of the above questions. Socrates asked, is virtue natural? By this he meant is virtue an innate part of man. This was a common position held by the pre-Socratic philosophers

4. MacIntyre, *After Virtue*, 148.
5. Aristotle, *Nicomachean Ethics*, Book I, 1102a 15–20.
6. Ibid., 1102a 10–15.

such as Heraclitus. Aristotle believed that it was not an *innate* component of man's existence, but that man had the *potential*, if stimulated properly, to possess virtue.

There are two passages from Aristotle's works that illuminate this discussion. The first is found in the *Posterior Analytics* Book XIX, 99b 30:

> So it emerges that neither can we possess them from our birth nor can they come to be in us if we are without knowledge of them to the extent of having in such developed state at all. Therefore, we must have a capacity (*dynumis*) of some sort, but not such as to rank higher in accuracy than these developed states.

Aristotle refers here to states of knowledge and to premises from which scientific knowledge (*episteme*) is acquired. He is arguing that as a person, one has the "potential" to develop higher order cognitive skills. The capacity or potentiality to develop such skills remains latent until the proper kind of experience is present, stimulating the potentiality into an actualized state. A capacity, of course, never needs to be fully developed or actualized. It can continue in an underdeveloped condition sempiternally. A person might possess the ability to become a great singer but without the proper education in vocalizing, this capacity is stifled. In fact, without early training in many instances, the capacity experiences atrophy. This is why in the *Politics* Aristotle suggests that the "Fate of the empires rests on the education of Youth." In the field of scientific knowledge (*episteme*) the capacity is cultivated via training and instruction. More will be said about his later in the book. Suffice it to say that Aristotle suggests than humans possess a potential for the virtues and that they are more fully developed in one's life through experience.

A second passage that discusses the notion of a capacity being developed via activity into a virtue is found in the *Ethics*, Book II, 1103a 25–30. Aristotle wrote: "The virtues are implanted in us neither by nature nor contrary to nature: we are by nature equipped with the ability to receive them, and habit brings this ability to completion and fulfillment."

Furthermore, of all the qualities with which we are endowed by nature, we are provided with the capacity first, and display the activity afterward.[7] One has the potential for such and such characteristics but they necessarily have to be developed through activity. Aristotle is arguing that it is foolish to talk about something like a good house builder outside of the

---

7. One can look further into this subject by reading Aristotle's *Metaphysics*, 1019 15–35.

house builder building houses. Latent qualities make no one virtuous. It is only *operative* qualities that are virtues. Capacities, according to Aristotle, reside in the rational dimension of the soul, which will be the focus of the discussion in the next section.

The division of the soul

Thus far we have established that Aristotle answers the *Meno* question regarding the origin of virtue by claiming that the potential for virtue is latent in the soul. The interpreter of Aristotle must discover how the soul cultivates and develops potentials through an examination of the soul itself. In fact, the virtues, moral and intellectual, are differentiated by the divisions of the soul. But what are these divisions of the soul and how do they function? Aristotle suggests that "the soul consists of two elements, one irrational and one rational."[8] The virtues correspond to these two elements, with moral virtue being related to the irrational part of the soul whereas intellectual virtue resides in the rational element.

Aristotle identified two sections of the irrational element of the soul. He wrote: "The irrational element of the soul has two parts: the one is vegetative and has no share of reason at all, the other is the seat of the appetites and of desire in general and partakes of reason insofar as it complies with reason and accepts its leadership."[9] Moral virtue is a disposition of the desiderative part of this bipartite irrational element of the soul. It must be noted that moral virtue in this schema is coextensive with *pathos* and desire.

Having identified the location of moral virtue in the desiderative portion of the soul, we must now explore moral virtue in relation to intellectual virtue and how moral virtue is distinguished from it. An initial distinction has already been mentioned, the idea that moral virtue is located in the irrational section of the soul whereas intellectual virtue is in the rational section. A second difference pertains to the relationship each has to reason. In the quotation from 1102a 25–30, one reads that the desiderative part of the soul submits to the leadership of reason, specifically right reason, *orthos logos*. This kind of reason is present as a result of moral deliberation that utilizes one of the intellectual virtues to identify the appropriate moral virtue to be exercised in a given situation. Not only does moral virtue submit to the leadership of reason, but it cannot actually be said to be present in a

---

8. Aristotle, *Nicomachean Ethics*, Book I, 1103a 5–10.
9. Ibid., 1102b 25–30

moral situation without the intellectual virtue *phronesis* identifying which moral virtue needs to be put into action.

The relationship of moral virtue to intellectual virtue needs to be unpacked a bit more to ensure an understanding of the concept. Aristotle calls moral virtue a *meson*, that is, a mean. The mean is the median between excess and deficiency in human behavior. Aristotle uses courage as an example of a mean. He suggests that "a man who exceeds in fear and is deficient in confidence is cowardly."[10] Courage is the mean between these two. We find intellectual virtue guiding in each specific instance the necessary manifestation of the appropriate mean. Hence, Aristotle posits "that virtue or excellence is a characteristic involving choice, and that it consists in observing the mean relative to us, a mean which is defined by a rational principle, such as a man of practical wisdom would use to determine it."[11]

A third distinction between intellectual and moral virtue concerns how each is acquired. Moral virtue is formed by habit. By this Aristotle means that as a person performs virtuous acts in the process of growing up and does so on a regular basis, resulting in the acts becoming habits. One might behave courageously and in so doing this moral virtue becomes a component of one's life. It is through the exercise of the moral virtues that pleasure and pain are shaped so that one feels a sense of pleasure at the right time in accordance with the correct action.

Further, the moral virtues are not inherent to man. By this Aristotle meant that moral virtues are not natural to mankind. The virtues must be acquired. The method of acquisition for moral virtues is habituation.[12] This is not to say that one does not possess the ability to acquire the moral virtues, this has already been established. But it needs to be cultivated to be actualized. It is via the process of engaging in virtuous activity that the moral virtues become habit, that is, by practicing a virtuous activity.

A person is not, according to Aristotle, naturally self-controlled, for example. Mankind has the capacity to be self-controlled, but self-control is only cultivated by habit. Aristotle suggests: "We are by nature equipped with the ability to receive them, the habit brings this ability to completion and fulfillment."[13] Also, given that the virtues are acquired by desiring in the irrational part of the soul that is not governed by reason, perversion

10. Ibid., 1102b 30–35.
11. Ibid., Book II, 1107b 1–5.
12. Ibid., 1103a 25.
13. Ibid., 1103a 20.

may take place. The perversion of virtue can manifest itself in either excess or want, both of which are identified as vice. Cowardice and irresponsible action are vices that manifest themselves in opposition to courage, a moral virtue. Consequently, moral virtue is a mean between the extremes of want and excess. It is through the cultivation of a disposition through habituation that a moral virtue is established.

To support this claim, Aristotle posited that action is of utmost importance in the development of moral virtue. When one performs an action, it solidifies the disposition to act in that way again. Contemporary social psychological studies support this claim as well. Through the process of engaging in an action, a belief/disposition is acquired.

Imagine a person who is interested in bettering his personal work schedule. He wants to make the best use of the time possible so he is told that if he acquires the habit of evaluating the next day's work prior to going home, he will have a jump on the day. So he makes himself check the following day's calendar prior to leaving the office. An action has been taken that, if performed on a regular basis, becomes a habit.

Aristotle suggests that the desiring part of the soul taking action can lead to bad habits. He says: "By reacting in one way or in another to given circumstances some people become self-controlled and gentle and others self-indulgent and short-tempered. In a word, characteristics develop from corresponding activities."[14] He further warns that because habits are inculcated in us from early childhood, it is imperative to cultivate the proper passions corresponding to virtues.

I have already mentioned that the moral virtues are discoverable in the mean between two extremes. But how can one find the mean? It is *kata ton orthon logon*, according to right reason. The according to right reason principle is established via rational judgment. MacIntyre wrote: "The genuinely virtuous agent acts on the basis of a true and rational judgment."[15] The ability to make true and rational judgments occurs due to the intellectual virtues.

Intellectual virtue, on the other hand, is acquired by teaching and consequently takes "time and experience." Aristotle elaborates how this is the case in each of the virtues. *Tekne* or art is an example. Through doing or making, a person becomes an artist. The artist must project mentally prior to the act of creation of the art work just what it is he will make. The object

---

14. Ibid., 1103b 20–25.
15. MacIntyre, *After Virtue*, 150.

must be beautiful and useful for these two criteria are the distinguishing marks of *tekne*. Each intellectual virtue must correspond to truth (*alethia*) in a different manner of *tekne*, its function is to produce beautiful and useful objects, and as it does so *tekne* will correspond to truth. The process of education developing intellectual virtue ought to commence early in the life of the child so that the potentials for such virtue can be stimulated and maturity arise. "Let it be assumed that there are two rational elements: with one of these we apprehend the realities whose fundamental principles do not admit of being other than they are, and with the other we apprehend things which do admit of being other. . . . Let us call the one the scientific and the other the calculative element."[16] Aristotle is propounding that the intellectual virtues will function in proper relationship to the part of the rational soul that is appropriate for each. The first division is concerned with things that are invariant, immutable, and eternal. The other portion of the soul is concerned with variant and temporal situations.

For the interpreter of Aristotle it is essential to understand the function of a virtue as it corresponds to the appropriate portion of the soul. Each intellectual excellence, when it is operative, will be commensurate with the object of inquiry. For example, the intellectual virtue *nous* or intelligence is concerned with first principles. First principles are immutable. The operation of *nous* must correspond to the first principles in each case of operation to the extent that it insures that true first principles are identified. Aristotle posits that, "truth is the function of both intellectual parts of the soul. Therefore, those characteristics which permit each part to be as truthful as possible will be the virtues of the two parts."

A component of the truth function in an intellectual virtue is that the part of the soul governing the activity of the virtue must be similar in form to the object of inquiry. In *Deanima* Book III, 420a 13 Aristotle wrote: "The thinking part of the soul must be capable of receiving the form of an object, that is, must be potentially identical in character with its object without being its object."

As a condition for truth to function in an intellectual virtue, there must also be a correspondence between the object of inquiry and the appropriate virtue. For example, intelligence (*nous*) will identify forms from experience and inductively generalize universals from them. The claim made at this point is that *nous* will have the feature necessary for it to identify its intended function.

16. Aristotle, *Nicomachean Ethics*, Book VI 1139a 10–13.

Thus far I have claimed that intellectual virtue is of two kinds, scientific and calculative. I have also suggested that a condition of the existence of an intellectual virtue is that it will produce truth, that is, it will identify the genuine state of affairs. An intellectual virtue will accurately describe the object of inquiry. Another condition is that an intellectual virtue will have some kind of structural similarity to the object of inquiry without which there would not be the possibility of describing what is true.

I want now to propose a framework for understanding Aristotle's intellectual virtues. As has been pointed out, the rational element of the soul is divisible into two parts: the scientific, which deals with invariant truth, and the calculative, which focuses on the variant. Aristotle lists five virtues each of which falls under one of these two categories. They are: *sophia* (theoretical wisdom), *episteme* (scientific knowledge), *nous* (intelligence), *phronesis* (practical wisdom), and *tekne* (art). Each of these virtues will function in accordance with the two conditions mentioned above. Each virtue will leave some correspondence to truth or the real state of affairs and each will concentrate upon a particular object of inquiry. Aristotle writes that the "soul will express truth by way of affirmation or denial," and that in a specific realm of inquiry. It must be emphasized that there are two states of true beliefs about certain kinds of things. Other doxastic states are not included in the intellectual virtues, for they yet can be shown to be false.

Doxastic states are often held because of an initial perception by an inquirer. Earlier, I stated that Aristotle believed that knowledge, particularly intelligence, resulted from experience. Doxastic positions result from experience as well. The difference between the two is that intelligence is acquired via a series of experiences and immediate knowledge whereas "doxa" results from a perception without the accompanying justification for the claim. The process involved in intelligence, or for that matter *episteme*, is that which ensures warrant for a particular belief.

Let me offer an illustration from religious knowledge to illuminate the discussion of doxastic states. Many people claim that they have had an encounter with God, that they have perceived Him and formed an opinion based on that experience. Soon the opinion is generalized so that others are instructed to conform to the substance of the perception. Someone requests warrant for believing that the initial perception of God is the true state of affairs. To believe an assertion or command, even from one who claims to have experienced God, is not believing in a responsible fashion. It cannot be justified until the appropriate virtue examines the truth claim

Toward a Responsibilist Model of Believing

in accordance with the process utilized by the virtue for justification. An opinion may be true or false; the intellectual virtue that pertains to the field of inquiry from which the *doxa* emerges is that which affirms or denies that it is true.

Intellectual virtue is both a state of one's life and includes a cognitive process by which the virtue is manifested. *Nous*, for example, is called a cognitive disposition, in the *Posterior Analytics* Book XIX, 100b 5–17. In this section, Aristotle claims that *nous* provides even more certain knowledge than *episteme*. The reason for this is that *nous* deals with first principles, those universals that permit and allow for *episteme* to occur. Aristotle posits that *nous* supplies *episteme* with the appropriate information fit to conduct its inquiry.

Intelligence discovers the first principles by either immediate recognition of the principle via intuition or more likely through induction. Induction occurs as a result of sense perception, experience, and memory. Actually, memory stores up a series of like occurrences, which form an initial experience. As a number of these experiences emerge inductively an individual develops knowledge of the universe from the particulars. Aristotle expressed this concept in the *Analytics* as well. He wrote: "out of sense perception comes to be what we call memory, and out of recently repeated memories of the same thing develops experience; for a number of memories constitute a single experience."[17]

The method employed to secure knowledge of the universal is inductive reasoning by the person who possesses the virtue of *nous*. *Nous* is identified as the *hexis* or disposition for inductive reasoning.[18]

Episteme is the *hexis* of demonstration and syllogism. It is concerned with necessary, invariable, and eternal truth and is the "quality whereby we demonstrate these truths." *Episteme* utilizes both demonstration and definition to arrive at necessary truths.

Sophia is the intellectual virtue that encompasses both *nous* and *episteme*. In the *Ethics* Aristotle claims that "*sophia* must comprise both *nous* and *episteme*. It is science in its consummation, the science of things most highly valued. In fact, happiness is said to exist as an activity in conformity to *sophia*."[19] It is the life of theoretical contemplation (*theoriteke*) that is the process of the highest intellectual virtue and is most like God.

17. Aristotle, *Posterior Analytics*, Book XIX, 100a 5–10.
18. Modrak, "Aristotle on Knowing First Principles," 74.
19. Aristotle, *Nicomachean Ethics*, Book X, 1177a 10–15.

The productive intellectual virtue is called *tekne*. This intellectual virtue is the most quickly dispensed with in the *Nicomachean Ethics*. Aristotle distinguishes *tekne* from *phronesis* and the theoretical virtues. *Tekne* is concerned with things coming to be as a result of the producer.[20] Both technological virtue and *phronesis* correspond to things that actually are. Aristotle suggests the latter is more significant than productive intellectual virtue. Art, a productive virtue, is not concerned with things that exist or come into being by necessity. The significance of a virtue is evaluated in terms of what other things are affected by it.[21] *Tekne* finds its value in its beauty or usefulness but does not cause action to occur. *Phronesis* stimulates action in moral situations. *Nous* creates the movement of knowledge for *episteme* to be established. But *tekne* does not have that kind of effect on other things.

Aristotle discusses the third of the intellectual virtues, *phronesis*, for the vast majority of chapter 6. *Phronesis* or practical reason is that which establishes what the right principle or rule is which governs action. Whereas, theoretical virtue resulted from it suitability to demonstrate truth, *phronesis* is characterized by its ability to deliberate over particulars and to arrive at a true principle of what one ought to do to arrive at the right action.

The man who possesses practical wisdom will be characterized by the following elements. Practical wisdom makes one aware of the means to accomplish an end. Aristotle wrote: "the capacity of deliberating well about what is good and advantageous for oneself is regarded as typical of a man of practical wisdom."[22] Practical wisdom is also viewed as the capacity to see what is beneficial for oneself and others.

Aristotle believed that practical wisdom was concerned with the investigation of a particular kind of object. This activity he calls deliberation. Deliberation is different from the demonstration found in scientific knowledge. Scientific knowledge is said to be known in certainty. In deliberation one is calculating and investigating the truth of an action and the "truth" of an action is "what one ought to do." There is an openness to deliberation which is constantly tested to determine its accuracy. Aristotle calls practical wisdom in deliberation, reasoning. To acquire excellence in deliberation demands that the particular end being sought is attained. Aristotle wrote:

---

20. Ibid., Book IV, 1140a 10–15.
21. Ibid., 1104a 15.
22. Aristotle, *Nicomachean Ethics*, Book IV 1140a25

"excellence in deliberation will be correctness in assessing what is conducive to the end, concerning which practical wisdom gives conviction."[23]

Earlier in this section I suggested that without the intellectual virtue of *phronesis* virtue is impossible. *Phronesis* identifies the right rule or reason that one should adopt to insure the manifestation of a moral virtue and to acquire the end desired by the agent. Without *phronesis* the moral life is impossible. In *phronesis* one finds "intellectual activity concerned with the good state in harmony with correct desire."[24] Truth is the goal. *Phronesis* is the surest means to attain that goal.

This section began with a question from Plato's *Meno* about the origin of virtue. I have suggested that Aristotle answers this question by identifying the role of an *energia,* capacity, in one's life. I have also argued in this chapter that Aristotle posits two kinds of virtue. Moral virtue resides in the irrational portion of the soul and is a disposition which is acquired through repetition and practice in the behaviors of virtue.

Intellectual virtue is also a disposition, but is a disposition of the cognitive faculties. These virtues are concerned functionally with truth and the truth sought by the particular virtues will correspond to like-minded things which are the focus of the inquiry. As cognitive faculties, each intellectual virtue has a certain process of activity related to it. Each virtue will automatically and routinely be operative once the educative processes of experience and instruction enable the virtue to become a virtue. I have also suggested how each of these excellences correspond to a particular portion of the rational soul.

Intellectual Virtue

The tradition associated with Aristotle that I analyzed in the previous section provides a context to discuss a responsibilist account of intellectual virtue. Aristotle's account emphasizes the idea of proper function as central to an understanding of the intellectual virtues. The proper functioning of a cognitive mechanism occurs when it functions according to its design. Intellectual virtue advances this notion by suggesting a kind of consistency and reliability of function in friendly environments to the function. If one has been drugged with an hallucinogen, one's environment at that moment will be hostile to cognitive operations. If one is limited by experience,

23 Ibid., 1142b 25–30.
24. Ibid., 1139a 25.

perspective, or information, one's environment is not conducive to particular judgments. For instance, memory is a source of beliefs, both new and old. If one's experience of history is limited to particular notion about who fought in World War II, one's understanding and insight into what occurred will be dwarfed. The fuller and richer one's experience, the greater potential for intellectual virtue to emerge or characterize one's life. Sosa defines intellectual virtue as "a quality bound to help maximize one's surplus of truth over error.... [W]e assume a teleological conception of intellectual virtue, the relevant end being a proper relation to the truth.... The virtue of a virtue derives not simply from leading us to it, perhaps accidentally, but from leading us to it reliably."[25] A virtue is a cognitive excellence that operates in a consistent and reliable fashion. Its end or telos is truth. A virtue is functioning properly when securing that goal in specific situations. In light of my discussion of Aristotle and this definition we might ask what cognitive mechanisms might be identified as intellectual virtues?

There are three kinds of cognitive processes, specifically dealing with belief formation, revision, and maintenance, that are possible candidates for these virtues. The first category I will call "generative virtues"; the second, "transmissive virtues"; and the final category, "metamorphic virtues." Unlike Aristotle who argues for wisdom as the chief of the virtues, this account contends for an equality of the virtues. The operation of the virtues will depend on the situation which calls for their reliable execution, so that there will be circumstances that require particular cognitive processes to function properly while excluding the necessity of others. I will now discuss these categories and suggest some operations in what follows.

Generative intellectual virtues are those cognitive processes that generate new beliefs but not from prior existing beliefs. These faculties lead to beliefs but not from, inferentially, other beliefs that one holds. There seem to be two faculties that fit this description. The first is perception. I hear the noise of birds singing outside early in the morning. From this perceptual experience, I develop a belief that birds are singing outside. The proper function of a perceptual state is to interpret phenomena as it appears to a perceiver. One's worldview prepares one, of course, to see things. The belief that birds are singing does not necessarily depend referentially on a set of other beliefs. A second generative faculty is intuitive reason. Intuitive reason is the faculty of grasping simple necessary truths. This would include simple mathematical problems. Historically, intuitive reason was identified

---

25. Sosa, "Knowledge and Intellectual Virtue," 225.

Toward a Responsibilist Model of Believing

as the source of the immediate knowledge of a certain state of affairs and has also been identified as an apprehension of self-evident truths.

Transmissive virtues are those that utilize pre-existing beliefs in the operation of arriving at some new beliefs. The process of transmission is inferential from one's belief or set of beliefs to a new belief. I would suggest three transmissive virtues that cover much of what some of our earlier critical thinking theorists advance in their perspectives. Inferential processes figure prominently in those positions. Inductive reasoning, the ability or power to engage in induction and the habit of doing so is a transmissive virtue. The representational heuristic that I analyzed in an earlier chapter is an example of the mind working inductively. The representational heuristic functions quite often in a proper manner. It identifies new data as an instance of categories previous held. It has the potential for reasoning well or improperly. The transmissive virtue of induction will serve to direct one's process of representing data toward the truth. The two other transmission virtues are deduction and memory.

Ennis' work provides much by the way of the operation of deduction. Deduction is advocated across the board by all epistemically minded critical thinking theorists because, as Aristotle said, it leads invariably to the truth. Memory does not fare quite as well with the critical thinking theorists discussed earlier. In this account memory is a transmissive virtue. Memory serves to provide induction in many cases with other beliefs that bear on a particular subject. It also connects with another one of the heuristics in chapter 3. This heuristic capitalizes on how *vivid* a particular belief is implanted in the memory. I also showed how this heuristic functioned inappropriately in remembering details of automobile accidents. Memorial beliefs, either present or not present to one's consciousness, serve to shape new beliefs. Hence the importance of memory to function properly in the formation of new doxastic conditions.

The last category of intellectual virtue I have called metamorphic. What distinguishes metamorphic virtues is that they function to transform or reform one's believings. These virtues are of particular interest to me because they address the question of belief revision on a larger scale. There are changes in belief, as I indicated before, that occur because of a change in circumstance of which one becomes aware. The example of Timothy and perceptual change illustrates belief revision in the peripheral area of one's believing. The deeper, more engraved, belief of the central region and intermediate region are addressed by the metamorphic virtues. Metamorphosis creates a chain reaction because of the structural connections of beliefs mentioned previously. The metamorphic virtues I would contend for are wisdom, reflection, and creativity. Each of these leads to greater overall consistency and comprehensiveness in one's believings and in metamorphosing one's worldview.

A Spring Gathering Force

Pirqe Avot, the *Ethics of the Fathers*, is one of the most widely read and best loved of the tractates in the Jewish Talmud. This wonderful book of lore, insight, and maxim brings together many of ethical precepts of the greatest Rabbis of the Mishnaic period, i.e., prior to 200 CE. According to *Pirqe Avot*, Rabbi Yohanan Ben Zakkai, who is credited with preserving Judaism after the Roman destruction of the temple in 70 CE, had five preeminent disciples. In *Pirqe Avot* he sums up their abilities. The greatest of his disciples is a Rabbi named Elazar Ben Arakh. Yohanan Ben Zakkai describes Elazar as *kemayan hammithgaber*, a spring that gathers force. He was referring to the creative mind that Elazar possessed. A few comments about this verse introduces for us the topic of creativity.

Yohanan Ben Zakkai's comments about Elazar illustrates the importance of creativity among the sages of Israel. The verse I referred to above describes several other great Rabbis in the language of the fine virtues that they possessed. One is characterized as a deep cemented cistern who does not lose a drop. This means that the Rabbi had the well-developed transmissive virtue of memory. Another Rabbi is cited for his piety. The comment about Elazar is inclusive of the other virtues; he is commended for his creativity because it includes memory and piety. Creativity indicates both a mastery of the tradition and its practices, and, because one who is pious is one who is a disciple, the creative one has been disciplined by the teaching of the tradition and now is able to teach as well.

The phrase "a spring that gathers force," illustrates that in the mind of these Rabbis, creativity is a dynamic activity occurring in the creative individual and not the product. In Plato, justification was centered on the proposition as a static representation of the world. Here the comment is on the mental power attributed to Elazar, not on a static state of affairs. The verb in Hebrew is identified as a "Hithpael," which means that it is reflexive; the subject of the verb is acting on himself. Elazar is a spring that gathers force reflexively on himself, his system of beliefs, his contributions to the tradition, piety, and growth in understanding.

The notion of creativity as a force has been advanced by such nineteenth- and twentieth-century thinkers as Emerson, Bergson, and Whitehead. Emerson in "The American Scholar" wrote: "The scholar is that man who must take up into himself all the ability of the time, all the contributions of the past, all the hopes of the future. He must be a university of knowledges."[26] The creative mind is the one that does not remain captive to past thoughts but swings forward transforming the past into the present.

David Perkins argues for the importance of the idea of creativity as well. He suggests that creativity seems to include what he calls potencies, plans, and values. Potencies are the "computational powers of the mind at or near the neurological level. Perhaps creativity depends on the person's performing certain mental operations very efficiently or effectively." Plans he identifies as the "patterns by which a person's development of his or her potencies is organized. . . . A plan is the same thing as a schema or frame." Finally, values refer to the larger values that direct and control a person's endeavors. To this list Laird-Johnson adds expertise and the ability to engage in analogical reasoning.

Michael Polanyi argues for the centrality of imagination in the creative endeavor. He writes: "But we can explain also what it is that qualifies the arts for this enterprise. Our lives are formless, submerged in a hundred cross currents. The arts are imaginative representation, hewn into artificial patterns."[27] Polanyi contends that scientific advance results from acts of the imagination on the part of the scientist—a well-prepared mind but one not necessarily bound to the procedures of the past. Originality and imagination are essential to creativity.

Creativity requires one to recognize an element of ineffability in one's experience. For some, especially those writing out of a religious context, the potential for creativity is that which most approximates what it means for humans to be made in the image of God. Dorothy Sayers in her *Mind of the Maker* writes: "if we conclude that creative mind is in fact the very grain of the spiritual universe, we cannot arbitrarily stop our investigations with the man who happens to work in stone, or paint, or music, or letters."[28] Even

---

26. Emerson, "The American Scholar," 62.
27. Polanyi, *Meaning*, 101.
28. Sayers, *Maker*, 172.

Responsible Belief

common man has the potential, she contends for expressions of creativity. It remains the ineffable part of human existence to exercise this virtue.

A Taoist work, *The Way of Chuang Tzu*, captures the ineffable aspect of creativity in a poem entitled "The Wood Carver":

> Khing, the master carver, made a bell stand of precious wood. When it was finished, all who saw it were astounded. They said it must be the work of spirits. The Prince of Lu said to the master carver, "What is your secret?" Khing replied: "I am only a workman: I have no secret. There is only this: When I began to think about the work you commanded I guarded my spirit, did not expend it on trifles, that were not to the point. I fasted in order to set my heart at rest. After three days fasting, I had forgotten gain and success. After five days I had forgotten praise or criticism. After seven days I had forgotten my body with all its limbs. By this time al thought of your Highness and of the court had faded away. All that might distract me from the work had vanished. I was collected in a single thought of the bell stand.
>
> Then I went to the forest to see the trees in their natural state. When the right tree appeared before my eyes, the bell stand appeared in it, clearly, beyond doubt. All I had to do was put forth my hand and begin. If I had not met this particular tree there would have been no bell stand at all.
>
> What happened? My own collected thought encountered the hidden potential of the wood; from this live encounter came the work which you ascribe to the spirits.

Hokmah

> For wisdom, the fashioner of all things, taught me. There is in her a spirit that is intelligent, holy, unique, manifold, subtle, mobile, clear, unpolluted, distinct, vulnerable, loving the good, keen . . . . For wisdom is more mobile than any motion; because of her pureness she pervades and penetrates all things. For she is a breath of the power of God, and a pure emanation of the glory of the Almighty; therefore nothing defiled gains entrance into her. For she is a reflection of eternal light, a spotless mirror of the working of God, . . . more beautiful than the sun, and excels every constellation of the stars, . . . for she is an initiate in the knowledge of God. (Wisdom of Solomon 7:22, 24–26, 27; 8:4)

We saw earlier in Aristotle the idea that wisdom was the highest of the virtues. For Aristotle, wisdom was the knowledge of first principles, of invariant truth. Wisdom was only discoverable by the one who had leisure and could spend his time in the contemplation of eternal things. In the tradition from Wisdom of Solomon, we receive a glimpse of how beautiful and inviting wisdom really is. The passage above invites persons to pursue and desire her beauty.

Wisdom, as a metamorphic virtue, is an organizing principle of one's entire belief system. By wisdom one knows what ends and goals in life are worth pursuing. Wisdom directs an individual towards the most efficient ways of substantiating beliefs or altering them. Wisdom, as a virtue, includes intellectual humility, the courage and insight to acknowledge the limitations of one's thought. Wisdom takes that which is of value in our lives—beauty, truth, love, and justice—and applies herself to exposing which lines of thought, inquires, or problems should be pursued, not for the sake of domination, but for the sake of liberation.

Nicholas Maxwell advances the following definition of wisdom:

> Wisdom is the desire, the active endeavor, and the capacity to discover and achieve what is desirable and of value in life, both for oneself and for others. Wisdom includes knowledge and understanding but goes beyond them in also including: The desire and active striving for what is of value, the ability to experience value, the capacity to help solve those problems that arise in connection with attempts to realize what is of value; the capacity to use and develop knowledge, technology and understanding as needed for the realization of value.[29]

Wisdom utilizes what is of value in her interpretation of life. Wisdom cuts across the domains of our structured believings, uses the virtues I mentioned earlier, and brings to bear all that one knows, imagines, and understands in making a determination about a problematic situation. Wisdom understands the emotions and passions that go into having a perspective. Possessing this insight permits the one with wisdom to make decisions, not infallibly, but faithfully and insightfully. Wisdom does not see situations as pre-defined and inflexible, but as fluid and filled with potential. Wisdom is not limited to one dimension of thought but, more so, cuts through the multi-dimensionality of problems as they arise.

---

29. Maxwell, *Knowledge to Wisdom*, 66.

Patricia Kennedy Arlin sums up six features of wisdom. She suggests the following aspects:

1. The search for complementarity.
2. The detection of asymmetry in the face of what appears symmetrical and in equilibrium.
3. Openness to change: its possibility and its reality.
4. A pushing of the limits, which sometimes leads to a redefinition of those limits.
5. A taste for problems that are of fundamental importance.
6. A preference for certain conceptual moves.[30]

These six features, according to Arlin, are manifest in the finding of problems embedded in difficult situations. They might also be applied to our own discovery of problems within our belief system.

Finally, wisdom allows one to search out the limits of one's own worldview. A worldview is not as neatly constructed as Paul contended, but he was quite right in emphasizing its influence on our believing. The view expressed earlier was that our worldviews are so complex and diverse because of the way in which we hold beliefs, the mere application of logic to them will not secure the desired coherence of epistemology. Wisdom pushes one to recognize the interfacing and diversity of one's believings and engages one in a fuller exegesis of one's belief. Wisdom perceives the ways in which one goes about one's believings.

Reflection

All three theorists in chapter 1 advocated reflection as a primary feature of critical thought. Unfortunately, they failed to develop the concept in an adequate fashion. The view proposed here includes two aspects of reflection. The first is clearly spelled out for us in Dewey's notion of reflection. The second fails to make its way into the critical thinking literature because of its religious connotation. This is the art of contemplation. The Deweyan perspective describes the process of reflection when a felt problem exists. Contemplation does not need a problem to exist to be operative.

Dewey defines the talent of reflective thought as "the active, persistent, and careful consideration of any belief or supposed form of knowledge

30. Arlin, "Wisdom," 231.

in the light of the grounds that support it, and the further conclusions to which it tends."[31] Reflective thinking tends to follow a particular pattern which he sees as characteristic of the scientific method. This pattern includes the following features: (1) a felt difficulty, the presence of a problem that needs some sort of solution, (2) the problem is clarified and defined by what one knows, by past experiences, and by analyzing the features of the problem, (3) one conjectures an hypothesis, (4) the consequences and implications of the hypothesis are deduced, and (5) the hypothesis is acted upon to determine if it is confirmed by experience.[32] Without further discussion, I will assume Dewey's discussion is correct.

Contemplation, on the other hand, is the search for self-knowledge in the midst of the illusions of life. It is the consideration of the implications of our positions, the penetration of the falsehoods we establish to sustain us. Contemplation is the studious consideration of our beliefings in the face of reality. As Heidegger indicated, the objects that present themselves to us for thought move away from us because we constrain them into categories and schemas that feel comfortable to us. Contemplation breaks through these by allowing reality to speak to us across the void of our illusions.

Kavanah is an essential feature of contemplation. This Hebrew word connotes attentiveness to the desire of the mind to understand itself. *Kavanah* is paying close attention to the text that one may be studying. As one pays attention to the text or an object or a belief, *Kavanah* respects and appreciates the struggles associated with an honest development of a position. *Kavanah* is the art of listening for the hidden voices crying out in one's soul for appreciation.

The direction of contemplation is to remain open to mystery. For one to conclude and appreciate that one does not have the capacity to grasp all there is. With Socrates the contemplative accepts the limitations of one's own thought and yet seeks to understand more completely from those able to teach them about wisdom. Contemplation is the virtue of looking back at oneself, one's position in the world, and one's attitudes. Contemplation supposes that solitude and silence are necessary features in developing a sense of self-knowledge.

---

31. Dewey, *How We Think*, 6.
32. For an explanation of this pattern, consult *How We Think*, chapter 6.

THE IMPORTANCE OF PRACTICE

The responsibilist account I am advancing contends that the intellectual virtues discussed above are ones that emerge *in the context of practice*. Humans possess the potential for such virtues to function, but practice provides the context for them to grow.

Historically, the academic disciplines, along with one's experience in life, set the stage for the development of the virtues. Discipline derives from the Greek word *mathētēs*, for disciple. The disciple is one who forms talents, attitudes, and behaviors in conformity with the tradition of a master. A disciple is one who has been disciplined such that the master's teaching is inculcated in his life and character. This included both theoretical and practical knowledge. The practice of the master provided the setting for the realization of the formation of the disciple.

MacIntyre in his influential *After Virtue* emphasizes the importance of practices in the formation of virtue. He writes:

> By practices I am going to mean any coherent and complex form of socially established cooperative human activity through which goods internal to that form of activity are realized in the course of trying to achieve those standards of excellence which are appropriate to, and partially definitive of that form of activity, with the result that human powers, to achieve excellence and the human conceptions of the ends and goods involved, are systematically extended.[33]

He claims that the virtues are developed as the socially established practices are learned and experienced by individuals. Further practices that aligned themselves with intellectual virtues are doxastic practices, i.e., belief forming practices. A feature of doxastic practices would include that they ought to express a plurality of approaches to a subject matter. Following several theorists in philosophy of science, Lakatos and Lauden among them, a plurality of practices, what they call research programs, should be learned. Secondly, these practices are learned long before one is critically aware of them. Thirdly, there are practices that aid one in the generation of belief, others that assist the transmissive virtues and still others that facilitate the metamorphic virtues. Finally, as MacIntyre expressed, these are socially established practices that grant legitimacy. The context of our practices creates the plausibility structure embedded in our belief system.

---

33. MacIntyre, *After Virtue*, 187.

Toward a Responsibilist Model of Believing

Practices and Structuring Belief

There are several implications that I would like to draw from these considerations about practices as they relate to my description of belief systems in chapter 3. These provide us with several caveats to consider in our doxastic forming practices.

The first caveat emerges from the last feature of the practices above. In analyzing doxastic practices, one should give due consideration to the univocal tendency of socially constructed practices. To learn and inculcate dominant social practices, critical thinkers must be aware that these represent embedded power structures as well. Practices, consciously or unconsciously, take the form of supporting the form of power advocated by the framers of the practice. The practices are inculcated in what I contend to be an idolatrous fashion. That is, one pays homage to the practice and its source. Practices embody perspectives or worldviews. When the practices advocated are univocal, this cuts off the potential for challenging the power sources of one's beliefs because belief systems are gotten by authorities and early experience. If the practices that sustain these are univocal—as has so often occurred in the past, whatever perspective one holds—it limits the potential to challenge the dominant views of one's culture or control beliefs of one's personal belief system. A plurality of practices should be learned so that one dominant perspective does not remain unchallenged, socially or individually.

Also, one needs to learn to recognize the diversity of one's belief system by being exposed to a plurality of practices. In describing the structure of a belief system, I argued for a structure that isolates contradictory beliefs from one another. At times this provides a safety net for individuals, but more so it hinders persons from seeing the contradictions embedded in a belief system. Practices are potential ways to train the mind to recognize its diversity. Wisdom serves to push the limits of one's understanding and recognition of that diversity and divergent practices assists wisdom in discovering the deeply embedded contradictions of our believings.

Paul and Ennis advanced the importance of learning transmissive practice such as informal or formal logic. McPeck stresses the importance of knowing the depth of a discipline so that one can raise issues and question pertinent to that discipline. (As I argued earlier, he is too univocal in his approach to engage the diversity I mentioned.) At this point, I would like to mention an approach to critical thought and practice that encourages all three types of virtues mentioned above—generative, transmissive, and metaphoric. This practice is ancient in origin, supports the demand for plurality for which I have been arguing, and is social in development. The cognitive practice approach I have in mind is unfamiliar to most. It is what is known as Talmudic study.

The word Talmud derives from the Hebrew *lamar*, which means "to study." The Talmud contains lore, law, marital instruction, economic advice, institutional counsel, story, narrative, and myth. The Talmud includes discussions of every aspect of life, touching not only religious concerns but also the most practical concerns. The knowledge of the Talmud—its law, regulations, narratives, and practices—is required by the Rabbis (teachers) if one is to be a faithful (responsible) adherent of Judaism

The issues mentioned earlier of diversity, plurality, memory, and logical acumen are all emphasized within the Talmud. Abraham Joshua Heschel captures the essence of the Talmud in the following statement:

> The essential value of the intellectual experience is the experience itself; its value is not to be looked for in external gain that may and should ensue, but in the intrinsic insight that will endure. The study of Torah is a challenge to the mind as well as an act of being involved in the dialogue of God and man, an act of sanctification of time. True learning is a way of relating oneself to something which is both holy and universal.[34]

Talmudic learning, in essence and practice, is the cultivation of human character in the wide reaches of human experience.

The Talmud is dialogical. Several main perspectives, each with a different position on a subject, converse with one another about a point of the law. The law, which is understood as given by God, is subject to a variety and multiplicity of understandings and interpretations. The various positions reflect Rabbis arguing, debating, dialoguing, and deliberating over interpretations handed down from previous authorities. The text of the Talmud contains authorities conversing over the meaning of a law. Their authoritative pronouncements are included in the Mishnah. The mishnaic interpretations of the law date in the period prior to 200 CE. The Mishnah is the central component of the Talmud around which the rest of the dialoguing partners refer.

A second major component of the Talmud is called the Gemara. The Gemara is a running commentary on the mishnaic discussions of the pre-200 CE age by Rabbis who lived in between 200–600 CE. The discussions of

34. Heschel, *Insecurity*, 57.

the Gemara arrive at no conclusions. These Rabbis engage in deliberations about the points of interpretation that the mishnaic Rabbis made regarding the law. The interpretation of the earlier Rabbis by the later sages illustrates the ongoing nature of conversation with a tradition. The later Rabbis attempt to pose questions of application of the law, questions about the questions which the Rabbis saw and maybe did not see.

Surrounding these two on a page of Talmud are other sources which join the conversation. The commentary by Rashi who lived from 1040–1105 is included. Also, the commentary by the Tosaphot, the disciples of Rashi. There is also a section for cross references in other places of the Talmud, with additional cross references to other medieval law codes such as Maimonides or Rabbi Jacob Ben Asher, d. 1340. All of these are on one page providing the conversation of the ages and inviting response. The sources ask probing questions of other sources, apply what we now call informal logic to the debates, and it invites others, the reader, to become involved in its debate. The Talmud approaches issues from a logical/epistemological perspective, practical perspective, creative perspective, and liturgical perspective with the goal of making the student a learner and cultivating his intellectual powers.

The diversity and plurality, in determining the meaning of the text is summed up in the following Talmudic story as retold by Michael Walzer. This is taken from the tractate Baba Metzi 59b and is the Gemara which elaborates the Mishnah on Deuteronomy 30:11–14. The story involves a dispute among a group of sages; the subject does not matter. Rabbi Eliezer stood alone, a minority of one, having brought forward every imaginable argument and failed to convince his colleagues. Exasperated, he called for divine help: "If the law is as I say, let this carob tree prove it." And the stream immediately began to flow backward. But Rabbi Joshua said, "No proof can be brought from a stream of water." Again Rabbi Eliezer said: "If the law is as I say, let the walls of this schoolhouse prove it." And the walls began to fall. But Rabbi Joshua rebuked the walls, saying that they had no business interfering in a dispute among scholars over the moral law; and they stopped falling and to this day still stand, though at a sharp angle. And then Rabbi Eliezer called on God himself: "If the law is as I say, let it be proved from heaven." Whereupon a voice cried out, "Why do you dispute with Rabbi Eliezer? In all matters the law is as he says." But Rabbi Joshua stood up and exclaimed, "It is not in heaven!"[35]

35. Walzer, *Interpretation and Social Criticism*, 31.

IN PRAISE OF COGNITIVE EMOTIONS

The responsibilist account of critical thinking I have offered in this chapter stresses the cultivation of our intellectual powers such that they become virtues through practices. Powers/practices and finally cognitive passions fill out the responsibilist account of a critical thinker. As was argued earlier, certain passionate, states such as wishful thinking or rationalization, lead one to irrational beliefs. The cognitive passions I will discuss in this last section cooperate with the virtues and practices mentioned above to form humankind into responsible epistemic agents. Responsible agents are those who are well equipped to tackle and confront the problems of truth and value in our world.

Persons are moved to enquire or cease from searching because of the intellectual passions they possess. Paul mentions the importance of some intellectual passions but he fails to recognize how deeply embedded in human life cognitive emotions are. He claims that humans are not truth-seekers by nature. I think more the point is that people do manifest the traits of intellectual passion directing them toward understanding and truth from an early age. This does not suggest that other passionate states like self-deception, wishful thinking, or rationalization cannot distort the thinking process. I have already contended that they do. When I observe children, I cannot help but be amazed at the intense desire that most of them possess for understanding. Now it may not be that the child completely covers all of the areas of logic and insight belonging to the virtues, but children do manifest cognitive *passion* toward understanding. Aristotle was right by this account when he wrote in his *Metaphysics* that "by nature man desires to understand." In other words, the design humans bear from God is oriented toward truth. Given the right context and environment and experience, cognitive virtues will emerge from one's desire and passion.

When I was a child, early on I developed an intense love for baseball. I played for hours, without exhaustion, without worry about whether I was better than other kids; I played for the sheer excitement and joy of the game. I read every sports magazine or baseball story I could get my hands on. I experienced great joy in memorizing long lists of baseball facts and trivia about leading home run hitters and averages and pennants and World Series winners. When I was eight, my father would have his friends ask me questions about baseball facts to amuse them I'm sure, not because they were interested in baseball trivia. The passion I had for baseball served to cultivate a passion for information, which served to shape the cognitive mechanism of memory more than my school work at that time. Surely, later in life when I turned my attention to the study of Semitic languages and history, this early experience of cultivating an intellectual virtue assisted me.

The cultivation and utilization of cognitive passion in the virtues creates and sustains the environment of their fulfillment. Kieran Egan in his *Educational Development* suggests that at certain ages different cognitive functions are more ready to be expressed. At ages eight to nine, a child's capacity to memorize facts is at a premium. To have the desire to go after facts in some educative endeavor prepares the child for the exercise of a virtuous memory later on. The caveat from Gardner though is that potentials not utilized can become "crystalized." The potential becomes hardened so that one cannot use it later on. Intellectual passions drive the use of cognitive mechanisms so that through practice, they become virtues.

Israel Scheffler made an outstanding contribution to this discussion in an article entitled, "In Praise of Cognitive Emotions." He mentions two passions that figure largely in this topic. The first he calls the joy of verification and the second he identifies as the significance of surprise.

In addition to Scheffler's two and Dewey's one, the feeling of doubt, I would add two: the presence of wonder and intellectual love.

Wonder is the beginning of the love of wisdom, according to Aristotle. To want to know, one must wonder at and about the nature of one's life, the universe, and God. Heschel claims that:

> Wonder rather than doubt is the root of knowledge. Doubt comes in the value of knowledge as a state of vacillation between two contrary or contradictory views, as a state in which a belief we had embraced begins to totter. Doubt is an act in which the mind confronts its own ideas: wonder is an act in which the mind confronts the universe.[36]

Wonder is curiosity about a state of affairs. The great discoveries of science occur because wonder is their midwife. Wonder is larger than humankind even when they make the universe surround them. The response of God to Job from the whirlwind illustrates this: "Who is this that darkens counsel by words without knowledge? Where were you when I laid the foundation of the earth [universe]?" (Job 38: 2,4). The universe, its essence, structure, and significance, is deemed the abode of the wise God. Job learns his limitation from this encounter. The intellectual virtues are cultivated

36. Heschel, *Man is Not Alone*, 11.

when wonder excites us to search, and consider, and contemplate a universe greater than oneself.

Rabbi Abraham Joshua Heschel was keenly aware that wonder had been compromised in the modern world and needed to be restored and renewed. In his view, the presumption of the Enlightenment, that everything advances and progresses, has fostered the decline of wonder among humankind. He writes, "as civilization advances the sense of wonder declines. Such decline is an alarming symptom of our state of mind. Mankind will not perish for want of information; but only for want of appreciation."[37] He contends that although all humankind is naturally endowed with a sense of wonder, it is "our system of education that fails to develop it and the anti-intellectual climate of our civilization does much to suppress it." Further, "our system of training tends to smother man's sense of wonder, to stifle rather than to cultivate his sense of the unutterable." And we might say, with Heschel, that we have forgotten that "study, learning is a form of worship" and that we live *coram deo* even in the classroom. I think a significant reason for this loss and why wonder's recovery is necessary is that we have forgotten that the goal of education is wisdom, she is our garland, and that a college exists for the purpose of inducting learners, who have come to take the yoke of wisdom on themselves, into a collegium of scholars who make wisdom their abode. The collegium of scholars which seeks wisdom is one which is driven by intellectual passions that are native to the life of wisdom and its possession.

Wonder Established as the *Arche* of Inquiry

For something to be recovered—as wonder needs to be, in light of Heschel's comments—implies that it once was the case, but is no longer so in a full sense. One might say that as wisdom has been replaced by other ends and presumptions in education and culture, the intellectual passion of wonder has been derailed and, in the language of cognitive scientists, intellectually crystallized, hardened such that as a fluid capacity it no longer obtains. A quick survey of ancient literature will suggest that this was not always the case. In Hesiod's *Theogony*, Thaumas (wonder) and Electra (shining beauty) bear a daughter named Iris, the goddess of the rainbow, who functions to interpret the wonder and beauty of the activities of the gods among mankind. In philosophical literature, Plato, in his epistemological work,

37. Heschel, *God in Search of Man*, 46.

Theatetus, writes, with Socrates as his mouthpiece, "the sense of wonder is perfectly proper to a philosopher; philosophy has no other foundation." Throughout Aristotle's work, he returns to the theme of wonder and wisdom time and again, claiming in the *Metaphysics*, for instance, "human beings originally began philosophy because of wonder," and later while exploring the dimensions of theology, he writes, "the god is always in a good state and that deserves wonder, and if he is in a better state, that deserves still more wonder." So too Aquinas claims that "man's first experience of wonder sets his feet on the ladder that leads to wisdom." Suffice it to say, these ancients celebrated and practiced the intellectual passion of wonder.

In biblical literature, the significance of wonder and its connection to wisdom is even more apparent. Let me cite a few examples to illustrate this. It is quite interesting that in the early narratives found in Luke's Gospel, the theme of wonder is prominent. Think about it; people respond to the birth announcement with wonder and amazement. What does Mary do when she hears about the prophecies regarding her son? She marvels, wonders, and ponders these things in her heart. What happens when the people at Nazareth hear Jesus preach for the first time prior to their rejection of him? They are amazed and wonder at his words. In Matthew's Gospel, Jesus' wisdom is vindicated by her children dancing in the public square, who are then invited, in a passage perplexingly wondrous, to take his yoke of wisdom on them, the wisdom that brings peace and the proper ordering of life.

In the Old Testament, we find scores of examples of the connection between wonder and wisdom. Take for example Psalm 111 or 139, where God's works in creation, history, politics, and humanness are celebrated as wonders that stimulate reverence and awe as the foundation of wisdom. In Job 26, in his response to the failed wisdom of his interlocutors, Job claims that the things mysteriously visible to us are only the "outer fringe" of God's works, which are wonderful; there is a greater ontological depth in them that escapes human inquiry and knowledge and this invites wonder. In Job 28, the hiddenness of the significance of things causes one to wonder and confess that God is the only one who fully and truly knows wisdom, although he bids his followers to cherish her. In Isaiah 28, the farmer, in tilling his land, is filled with wonder when considering that God has made it to grow food in season and the like. And so I could continue to multiply the examples, but I take it from these, that at one point our partners in the covenant, understood that wonder was central to wisdom.

The Recovering Wonder

Wonder is the proper function of the intellectually passionate life directed in response to the marvel of something (persons, events, selves, God, creation). God has constituted us as wonder-manifesting creatures in response to the excellence and goodness and intrinsic value of the things that he has made. Remember Adam's response when he saw Eve for the first time. Wonder makes one desire to know the glory that is hidden and not apparent in those things that one encounters in life. And confesses that there is more to things than initially meets the eye. In the words of Josef Pieper, "wonder signifies that the world is profounder, more all-embracing and mysterious than the logic of everyday reason had taught us to believe. The innermost meaning of wonder is fulfilled in a deepened sense of mystery. It does not end in doubt, but is the awakening of the knowledge that being, qua being, is mysterious and inconceivable."[38] This means that the commonplace is not commonplace in a pejorative sense at all; it is filled, defined, by engagement with and possession of the marvelous. There is a kind of splendor in the ordinary. There *is* Narnia behind the thistles, and thorns and brush and rubbish and decay. It is not that it was once here; it *is* here. There is grandeur to this place and it behooves us to know something about it locally and memorially so that we might have eyes to wonder at its wonder.

With Heidegger, I view wonder as attunement.[39] When something is attuned, it is in harmony with the order of some reality and mirrors what it is. The passion of wonder reflects, is attuned to, the thing wondered about. C. S. Lewis captures this sense of attunement in his work, *The Abolition of Man*. In the section, "Men without Chests," he contends that when one calls something sublime, one is not talking about a personal feeling that one has; rather one is talking about the quality of the thing that is sublime and this merits the response of awe or wonder. Only those who are dulled to the sense of the wonderful do not wonder, do not respond to the merit that the wonderful intrinsically bears. Our discordant epistemological schemes do much to create this dullness. This absence leads, thinks Lewis, to the inability to connect our hearts, the proper seat of passion, to our minds.

I want to claim that when one intellectually, passionately wonders in the presence of the wonderful as the proper function of life leading to wisdom, one does so because those things are deserving conduits through

---

38. Pieper, *Leisure*, 115.
39. Heidegger, *What is Philosophy?* 83.

which a greater wonder and perfection is conveyed. Let me illustrate this through a poem written by Wendell Berry in a collection called *A Timbered Choir*. This poem is entitled a Sabbath poem.

> To sit and look at light-filled leaves
> May let us see, or seem to see,
> Far backward as through clearer eyes
> To what unsighted hope believes:
> The blessed conviviality
> That sang Creation's seventh sunrise,
> Time when the Maker's radiant sight
> Made radiant everything He saw,
> And every thing He saw was filled
> With perfect joy and life and light.
> His perfect pleasure was sole law;
> For all His creatures were His pleasures
> And their whole pleasure was to be
> What he had made them.

The timber and leaves are parts of a choir that sings the praises of the glory and radiance of God who made these things excellently, and effulgently for His pleasure and their welfare. The things created are worthy of the *pathos* of wonder in response to them. Their radiance was the radiance of God reflected in them. His glory made them glorious. His excellence made them excellent. God saw them as excellent, and they were in fact deeply and abidingly wonderful and excellent. In the words of St. Bonaventure, they are vestiges of God's glory.

The proper response of wonder to the wonderful is astonishment, amazement, and a delighted surprising insight and understanding that invites one to ponder, to contemplate, the significance of the magnificence encountered. These train us to be wonderers. The amazement that the child feels at the novel becomes the wonder that one experiences later in being apprehended by the marvelous and submitting to its reality. Wonder is present on every step of the ladder of contemplation that leads to wisdom and the knowledge of the Holy One.

The rightly ordered life will be oriented toward wonder. Intellectual sin dices and fragments, balkanizes and isolates, parts of the experience of life and its wonder from the completeness that leads to wisdom. It fractures wonder in its wake and, consequently, our capacity to wonder rightly at all is compromised. We violate the covenant of humanness by not manifesting the God designed response to the glory that confronts us.

Finally, recovering wonder and all its magnificence necessitates that one appreciate that the wonderful, and our radical astonishment and amazement at it, is rooted in what Jonathan Edwards identifies as the beauty of God pervading all that is. What amazement! Heschel contends that wonder is radical amazement. When humankind stops and remains silent before the vastness and greatness of the universe, the seed of wonder is born. He continues that "The beginning of our happiness lies in the understanding that life without wonder, is not worth living." What shall we do? The natural thing: let us open the eyes of our hearts to gaze, to ponder, to marvel, and appreciate the theatre of God's wonders that merit the response of wonder by our design. This recovering will encourage the wisdom required to worship God aright and to love him supremely.

Intellectual love, the desire for wisdom to be our partner in life, is most clearly expressed in the Hebrew wisdom tradition. Wisdom is the lover who calls out for humankind to engage her: "Love her and she will guard you" (Prov 4:6); "She will honor you if you embrace her" (Prov 4:8). In the Wisdom of Ben Sira (Ecclesiastitcus), love of wisdom is erotic: "Whoever pays heed to me will lie down in my innermost rooms" (Sir 4:15). The Wisdom of Solomon captures this erotic side of intellectual love as well:

> I loved her and sought her from my youth; I desired to take her for my bride, and became enamored of her beauty. . . . When I enter my house, I shall find rest with her; for companionship with her has no bitterness, and life with her has no pain, but gladness and joy. (Wis 8:2, 16)

Intellectual love for wisdom and knowledge pushes on to understand and desire more of her. Intellectual love casts out fear, is courageous and bold, pursuing its goal. Intellectual love recognizes the beauty of wisdom and knowledge.

Plato too saw that love, *eros*, directed one's pursuit of eternal things. In his *Timaeus* there is a clear expression of this passion that drives one's pursuit of knowledge.

> 28c. The creation and the father of this universe is found only by toil. . . . If this world is beautiful, if the artist is good, obviously he looked towards the eternal. For the one is the most beautiful of works and the other the most beautiful of causes.

Toward a Responsibilist Model of Believing

Intellectual love causes one to see the beauty of the universe and its causes and to seek these out. For Plato, the presence of *eros* directs us to inquire deeply and to discover the good.

I have suggested an account of a responsible critical thinker by focusing on three essential ingredients. These are: (i) intellectual virtue, which is the proper functioning of our cognitive processes, (ii) practices in which the intellectual virtues are cultivated, and (iii) cognitive emotions, which push one, through passion and desire, to know more. Surely, I have not exhausted what might be said or written. I have attended in these remarks especially to the area of providing a conception of critical thought that appreciates the psychological limitations and structures of thought, the noetic effects of sin, and focuses on how an agent might become apt (virtuous) to modify beliefs. But this analysis needs a more thorough account of the last subject raised and that is the place of beauty inviting humankind to explore her wondrous excellences in light of an ethics of belief, or what might be called an ethics of inquiry. I will pick this up in the next chapter looking to the ancient Hellenistic Jewish philosopher Philo of Alexandria as my guide and partner.

CHAPTER 6

Cosmic Beauty and the Ethics of Inquiry
Appropriating Philo of Alexandria

> *Even if the Maker made all things simultaneously,*
> *order was none the less an attribute of all that came into*
> *existence in fair beauty.*
> —Philo of Alexandria, *On the Creation*, 23.

> *Late it was that I loved you,*
> *Beauty so ancient and so new,*
> *Late I have loved you!*
> —St. Augustine, *Confessions, Book X, Chapter 27*

EARLY ON IN THIS book, I contended that there were two over-arching features of the post-Cartesian epistemological tradition that had hegemony in the critical thinking approaches I discussed. The second of these I identified with what I called methodism and briefly argued for its inadequacy in light of the failure of internalism, the main focus of much of my critique. The responsibilist model of the epistemic agent I offered in the last chapter in response to the limited epistemic agents that humans are provides a plausible account of going about belief melioration. It capitalizes on the design humans have been granted and yet takes into view the debilitating effects of noetic sin in the epistemological life. But one might query, what of method? Is there a retrieval of some form of method, which I identify with inquiry, responsive to the epistemic agents that humans are that might guide one toward belief melioration and improvement? Does beauty, discussed at the end of the last chapter, hold some promise to invite the kind of response needed for the human dilemma to improve believing? In light of these kinds of questions, in this last chapter I will explore the hope that a retrieval of an ethics of inquiry (*elenchos*) offers through a further engagement with the topic of beauty under the guidance of Philo of Alexandria, the Hellenistic Jewish philosopher of the first century.

In Alexander Solzhenitsyn's Nobel Prize in Literature lecture, he invoked Dostoyevsky's claim that "Beauty will save the world."[1] As he attempts to explore what he calls this "enigmatic remark" Solzhenitsyn avers that maybe "the old trinity of Truth, Goodness, and Beauty is not simply the decorous and antiquated formula it seemed to us at the time of our self-confident materialistic youth." More so, the "convergence" of these will soar again by the "ever surprising shoots of Beauty." Consideration of beauty and its capacity to empower might have a renewing effect on a culture that has "buried without a coffin" truth and virtue. I imagine through working my way through countless passages in Philo's works in which he engages the topic of beauty and inquiry that he would concur with this claim by Solzhenitsyn. Maybe this comment from Solzhenitsyn will be prophetic in the twenty-first century as he viewed Dostoevsky's from the nineteenth.

Philo's period, the middle-Platonist era as Dillon claims,[2] is one in which both Judaism and early Christianity engaged seriously the wisdom of the Greeks and how it might foster a deeper understanding of the Scriptures and God. A tradition of cosmological concern for Beauty emerged for both Jews and Christians during this era that influenced the fathers of the church, including St. Augustine and St. Gregory. And much of the background shaping of this tradition is the wisdom concern of Philo.

In particular, Philo's idea of the relationship of cosmology and beauty is robust and insightful and invites wonder and intellectual love and humility. According to Hart,[3] St. Gregory replicated Philo's position while recasting it in Christological terms. Given that Philo's cosmology is an example

1. Solzhenitsyn, *Reader*, 514.
2. Dillon, *Middle Platonists*.
3. Hart, *Beauty of the Infinite*, 408

of Jewish Wisdom cosmology, one can imagine the association it drew for Gregory as he sought to develop an understanding of the Wisdom/Word, Christ. For Philo the beauty that the cosmos bears is an intimation of the beauty that God supremely is. God, ever generous and kind, made all being to reflect God's own perfect beauty. This idea of intimative beauty is born out not only in Gregory and Augustine, but finds its expression in Jonathan Edwards, the Puritan Augustinian, as well. In *The Nature of True Virtue*, Edwards writes in words reminiscent of Philo's conception of intimative Beauty that "God is infinitely the greatest Being: and all the beauty to be found throughout the whole creation is but the reflection of the diffused beams of that being who hath an infinite fullness of brightness and glory. God is the fountain and foundation of all being and all beauty. From whom all is perfectly derived, and on whom all is most absolutely dependent . . . whose beauty are the sum and comprehension of all existence and excellence."[4]

One might query how this beauty is discerned. Philo contends that humankind was endowed with the design and order of being and intellect by the all beautiful God capable of perceiving the structure of God's magnificence radiating majestically the cosmos by giving him certain capacities for "science and art, for knowledge and for the noble lore of the virtues." Indeed, humans are characterized "by a love and longing for wisdom." But a fracturing occurred in humankind because of the fall and its effect of disassociating pleasure from rightful enjoyment in beauty and this requires a therapist and healer. This therapist has a priestly function to restore humankind and its capacities so that humankind might perceive anew the intimative beauty of the cosmos as it points to God. This priestly therapeutic activity is rooted in Philo's development of the Socratic notion of *elenchos*, inquiry.

In this chapter I briefly explore this intimative beauty by discussing how Philo understands beauty. I wish to suggest that for Philo when the beauty of the cosmos is perceived rightly, its power is unleashed so that the purpose of human existence to virtuously know the God of beauty and wisdom is realized. When this occurs, Philo contends that social and political structures become just and the creational mandate for humans to tend and guard the universe is executed rightly. The last paragraph of *On the Account of the World's Creation* bears this out as the summary of his argument about beauty and cosmology. He writes,

4. Edwards, *Nature of True Virtue*, 15.

> He that has begun by learning these things with his understanding rather than with his hearing, and has stamped on his soul impressions of truths so marvelous (beautiful) and priceless, both that God is and is from eternity, and that He that really is is One, and that He has made the world and has made it one world, unique as He is unique, and that He ever exercises forethought for His creation, will lead a life of bliss and blessedness, because he has a character moulded by the truths that piety and holiness enforce.[5]

Elenchos enables and molds the understanding of which Philo speaks.

CONTOURS OF BEAUTY

The intimative beauty that the cosmos is has a number of characteristics that Philo unfolds in his works. In particular, because of the copious references to beauty throughout his writing, I will primarily explore citations from only three of his works: *On the Account of the World's Creation*; *On the Cherubim*; and *The Worse Attacks the Better*. These three are examinations of parts of the first four chapters of Genesis and explore the order of the cosmos, the wonder of philosophy, and the difference of lower education and wisdom, culminating in being able to meet Cain on the plain. In the main *On the Account of the World's Creation* will supply most of my reflections and the development of intimative Beauty.

According to Philo, Moses supplies an exordium, Philo's term, in Genesis, the first chapters of which demonstrate his superiority as a philosopher. In Jewish Alexandrian thought, whether Aristobulus or Philo, it was believed that the Greeks learned philosophy from Moses and so Philo turns his readers' attention to the most lovely and beautiful description of cosmogony that is found in the first two chapters of Genesis. The beauty of the cosmos is located in its "harmony with the Law of God . . . which enables humans to be loyal citizens of the cosmos" (*Creation*, 13).

Philo waxes rhapsodically as he considers the wonder of the cosmos, the creation of God. He claims that its beauty is beyond the scope of ideas and language that humans might employ in describing it. He identifies the philosophers who do not know Moses as incapable of suggesting anything

---

5. Philo, *On the Account of the World's Creation*, 137. All references to Philo's work will be taken from the Loeb Classical Library. Volume I is where *On the Account of the World's Creation* is found along with *Allegorical Interpretation*, from which I cite later in this chapter. I will place in the body of the text the page number and/or the paragraph location of the various passages in Philo.

beyond words of "irrelevance" (*Creation*, 7). So magnificent is the beauty of the cosmos that while philosophers might be "painstaking" in analysis, yet the best they can do is provide a few myths while acquiescing to the ideas of others. Philo claims that "it is true that no writer in verse or prose could possibly do justice to the beauty of the ideas embodied in this (Moses') account of the creation of the cosmos. For they transcend our capacity of speech and of hearing, being too great and august to be adjusted to the tongue or ear of mortals" (*Creation*, 9). Only a few of the beauties of the cosmos are within the reach "of the human mind when possessed by the love and longing for wisdom." It is the Torah, the Law that Moses provides, that unlocks the mystery of the universe. As Philo contends, "perchance shall the beauties of the world's creation recorded in the Laws, transcendent as they are dazzling as they do by their bright gleams the souls of readers, be indicated by delineations minute and slight" (*Creation*, 9). You'll notice that the "dazzling" beauty of the cosmos revealed by the Law illuminates the souls of humans, it is intimative of its Cause and Principle, the all-encompassing Beauty, God. The cosmos is "God's beautiful masterpiece" (*Creation*, 11).

In Philo's view, humans engage in a kind of spirituality when engaged in philosophy as they meditate on the cosmos and its beginning through the illumination of the Law/Logos/Wisdom. On page 43 of *On the Account of the World's Creation*, he claims that "it was out of the investigation of these problems that philosophy grew, than which no more perfect good has come into the life of mankind." In a similar vein, the writer of the Wisdom of Solomon, written in the same era and probably in Alexandria, with similar language claims that "Wisdom is radiant and unfading." She invites her followers to know "the structure of the universe and the activity of the elements; the beginning and end and middle of times, the variety of plants, and the changes of the seasons." Philosophy is, when faithful to Moses, an "initiate into the knowledge of God." The quest for understanding the beauty of the cosmos is the form of life intended for those made in God's likeness. About his own life, Philo tells his readers that when he was young "he began to feel the sting of philosophy." Philosophy for Philo requires leisure and in an autobiographical passage states that he engaged in the "contemplation of the cosmos and its contents, when I made its spirit my own in all its beauty and loveliness and true blessedness" (*On the Special Laws*, III, Loeb Vol. VII, 475). His account of the creation of the cosmos is his engagement with the wonders disclosed by Moses.

Cosmic Beauty and the Ethics of Inquiry

As claimed above, beauty has its origin in the beauty God possesses. Philo asserts that the "Word of God surpasses beauty itself as it exists in Nature" (*Creation*, 110). He continues this thought with, "God is not only adorned with beauty, but is Himself in very truth beauty's fairest adornment" (Ibid.). The relationship of the beauty that God is and the cosmos, including the creation of humankind, stems from God's decision in how to go about forming in intellectual and physical form this beauty. In a wonderful passage found in *On the Cherubim*, Philo presents his case: "God is full of happiness unmixed. He partakes of nothing outside himself to increase his excellence. Nay He Himself has imparted his own to all particular beings from that fountain of beauty—Himself" (*Cherubim*, Loeb Vol. II, 61). He continues that the souls of humans must "mirror the beauty" that is in the invisible sphere which points to directly to God, so that humans might become a "house fit to receive God."

Philo believed that for physical objects to intimate the beauty that God is requires that God make a blueprint first from which these objects are derived, much like a contractor would do in building a house. This house of creation is a kind of cosmic sanctuary that is fit for God to inhabit due to its beauty. Again from *On the Account of the World's Creation*, Philo writes: "For God being God assumed that a beautiful copy would never be produced apart from a beautiful pattern, and that no object of perception would be faultless which was not made in the likeness of an original discerned only by the intellect. So when God willed to create this visible world, He first fully formed the intelligible world, in order that He might have the use of a pattern wholly God-like" (*Creation*, 15). This, of course, leaves all parts of the cosmos accountable to the Beauty that is.

Philo cites various attributes of beauty throughout his works that attest to its reflection of God. He contends that beauty is harmonious and that it is orderly. There is nothing beautiful without order. Philo suggests, as one can discern from the passages cited above, that beauty is correlative; physical beauty correlates the pattern of the intelligible world, the intelligible world to the being of God. In *On the Account of the World's Creation*, one can see the influence of the place that Pythagorean ideas of math had in his analysis of numbers like one and four and exhaustively seven. Of course Pythagoreanism had a central place in the development of middle-Platonism. And so the very order of the creation is symmetrical. Beauty is light enabling one to understand the order of creation. In a passage found later in *On the Account of the World's Creation*, beauty is shalomic.

Philo attests to the implication of beauty beginning on page 87 and following. Four reasons are given for why he has gone about writing *On the Account of the World's Creation*. In summary, Philo claims to show humankind's kinship with God (made in beauty, the pinnacle of creation) to enable humans to perceive beauty and long for its origin, that is God. A second reason is to create a kind of *Paideia* that fosters virtuous persons and is passes down to posterity. Further, these morally and intellectually virtuous beings are enabled to be dazzled by the beauty of the cosmos, stimulating them in science, art, and knowledge to discern its beauty. And finally, Philo suggests this is to equip humans to rule the cosmos for shalom under God.

Philo warns that without taking account of the beauty of the cosmos that intimates its Creator and forms the virtuous, lust, the quest for power, and greed wreak havoc and destruction (*Creation*, 51–53). In *On the Cherubim*, in times of moral decadence, music, philosophy, all culture, those truly divine images set in the divinely given soul, are mute. Only the technical practices that "pander and administer pleasure to the belly (lust, greed, and power) are vocal and loud-voiced" (*Cherubim*, 65). This compromise of the beautiful and its association with God is the effect of the fall and requires a reproving, healing agent, which we identify as *elenchos*.

SOCRATIC *ELENCHOS*

Again my concern is to examine Philo's *elenchos*, but to do so I now must establish its roots in Socrates. Another first-century-BCE philosopher, Cicero, contented that in the New Academy the Socratic method of inquiry was prominent. Eudorus initiated the concerns of Middle Platonism to Alexandria as an alternative to Antiochus and along with it some of the central commitments of Middle Platonism. Both Eudorus and Antiochus are descendants of the New Academy and were central to its revival. My argument is that Philo, following in the vein of Eudorus, is probably the clearest expositor of the elenchic tradition.

In establishing the roots of Socratic *elenchos* in Philo, I need not explore exhaustively Socrates' employment of it. I will suggest two aspects of the *elenchos* that resurface in Philo that shed light on the main focus of *elenchos*. The first example is from Plato's *Meno*.[6] Socrates encounters Meno, a Sophist and follower of Gorgias, and in typical Platonic fashion engages

---

6. Plato, *Protagoras and Meno*, 70a–80b.

him in a discussion this time about virtue. This discussion becomes an elenchic encounter in which Socrates draws out the implications of some of the beliefs that Meno holds, showing the inconsistency of these beliefs with others held in his belief system. Because of Meno's intellectual arrogance, the inquiry does not proceed very far before, in frustration, Meno lashes out at Socrates. In turn, Socrates enlists a young slave boy and by employing the elenchic method extracts from the boy certain positions that are in fact consistent with one another. The boy possesses intellectual humility, the mother of all sound inquiry, and because of this, the exploration continues. When the boy is stymied, instead of getting angry and lashing out like Meno, in his puzzled state Socrates leads the boy, pedagogically, to new conclusions and beliefs based on the *elenchos*. We see in the *Meno* that the *elenchos* of Socrates is pedagogical, but it requires the right frame of mind for its fulfillment. When the right frame of mind is not present, the *elenchos* becomes an examination that is more forensic and judicial and yet even though he ought to feel guilt, Meno does not feel shame, but attacks Socrates instead. The *elenchos* has a positive focus; one might say its proper function in this case is to foster the teaching moment so that even the one most unlikely to learn, increases in understanding. Philo uses *elenchos* in this light as well.

A second illustration from Socrates is his account of his own call to the philosophical life found in the *Apology*.[7] Socrates receives a divine mission to examine (*elenchos*) the best and brightest of his day so that he can understand why the oracle at Delphi would call him the wisest of persons. He then caries on an examination of Meletus and others frustrating them along the way because they too do not possess the virtue of intellectual humility. He claims that "God has appointed him to the duty of leading a philosophic life, examining myself and others." To fail to do so would be disobedience to God. He believed that this divine mission was for the welfare of the polis such that he was like a "stinging fly" to rouse them from its slumber by "persuading and elenchicing them." After his conviction, Socrates asserts in words memorial to all subsequent generations that "the unexamined (*a-elenchic*) life, is not worth living." Virtue and goodness, without which the polis cannot stand, require *elenchos*. *Gnothi Seauton* (know thyself) is the Socratic cry in the Protagoras, but without the *elenchos*, self-knowledge is an impossibility. The *elenchos* is concerned with enabling a person to fulfill his proper function of self-understanding, a positive endeavor that

---

7. Plato, *Last Days*, "The Apology," 63.

includes the more negative rebuttal that must occur to cut through the layers of self-illusion. It is the proper function of human life in deference to the divine mission.

In brief, we have explored the *tolodotic* (ancesterial) roots of the Jewish Hellenistic philosophic tradition by briefly demonstrating Plato use of the Socratic notion of the *elenchos* and by establishing a positive conception of the *elenchos* in Socrates claim simply by taking account of two passages from Plato's works in which the *elenchos* is at work pedagogically and therapeutically. It is through the employment of *elenchos* that Socrates confounds his interlocutors, but for those with intellectual love and humility an elenchic inquiry avails one to the beauty that the cosmos is. That Philo picks up this central notion from Plato's Socratic dialogues supports Dillon's contention of Philo standing in the venerable tradition of Middle Platonism.

TAKING ACCOUNT OF PHILO'S IDEA OF THE *ELENCHOS*

Wisdom is the context in which Philo's idea of *elenchos* must be cast and understood. If one fails to see it in that light, one will miss the specific applications of it when one considers the negative or forensic functions of the *elenchos*. Given the place that wisdom and cosmology play in Philo's thought, our casting of *elenchos* needs to begin with these notions in mind. To do so, I plan first to look at a couple of cosmological/wisdom passages that become central to Philo's use of the *elenchos* and how these order the fuller development of his *elenchos*. Wisdom is the province of the sage who executes *elenchos* rightly in discovering the beauty that is and the beauty that God possesses by God's nature.

In *On the Account of the World's Creation*, we see the importance of framing *elenchos* in light of wisdom and cosmology. He claims that Moses, superior to the philosophers, provides an account in the creation story of the "harmony" of the world and the wise person is the one whose life is regulated by God's law. Understanding the design of this world (*Creation*, 9) is within the grasp of the "human mind when possessed by love and longing for wisdom." The various faculties of the human mind, such as reason, memory, and our senses, are designed with the goal of perceiving the beauty of the cosmos, the knowledge of which is located in the mind of the Architect, God. The mind is so ordered that it discerns the order of the universe which is "fair beauty" for when "beauty is absent there is disorder" (*Creation*, 23).

After describing the order of creation, Philo hones his attention on humankind. He writes that "man is the end of creation." To discern the order of God's beauty in the creation of the world, "man bears within himself, like holy images, endowments of nature that corresponds to the constellations. He has capacities for science and art, for knowledge, and for the noble lore of the virtues." Humans have incredible capacities and capabilities to understand the cosmos in which they are placed. But capacities need to be actualized for them to discern the order of the cosmos and its beauty as these radiate the beauty that God is. The one who is the sage is the one who has the love and longing spoken of above and faculties activated and functioning in their design to understand the beauty of the universe that references God. The beauty of the mind is manifest in that "lover of virtue Moses" and the capacities of the mind including the conscience are activated by the exercise of *elenchos*. The realization of the good is the work of philosophy's engagement, which is *elenchos*. So to understand the beauty of the cosmos which it possesses from God is the result of the faculties functioning rightly by their design with *elenchos*.

In *Allegorical Interpretation III*, after Adam has disobeyed Wisdom, God calls out to reclaim him and does so that through the question posed, where are you? The mind receives "reproof" (*elenchos*) to check its own defection from God. He then writes that it is not only the mind that is called, but all "its faculties as well for without its faculties the mind is naked" (*Alleg. Int. 3*, Loeb Vol. I, 333). He continues that one of those faculties is sense perception, which needs *elenchos* so that it might do its job of "distinguishing between material forms" (*Alleg. Int. 3*, 335). Sense perception has both a passive and an active component; the passive is to receive empirically information about the world while the active, "*elenchos*," discerns the distinctiveness of empirical deliverances. When sense perception fails to utilize *elenchos*, it rejects its purification like the "Ammonities and Moabites." This neglect is their sin (*Alleg. Int. 3*, 355).

As a result, *elenchos* proves that Noah was a righteous and wise man and as such models rest, the end of Sabbath, the ordering of creation with understanding. Philo writes that what adjudicates, *elenchos*, is that Noah explores "the nature of existences" and makes a surprising find in his "discovery" that all things are a "grace of God" and creation unable to gift humans on its own receives grace as God's own possession (*Alleg. Int. 3*,

353). Noah is "noble (virtuous) and lives in fellowship with justice" and as such, finds "favor with God." Noah's inquiry, *elenchos*, culminates in the realization of the grace of God commonly radiating all the cosmos, the act of God's kindness and elicits from him intellectual humility.

Union with God in God's Sabbath rest is the goal of the wise life. The cosmological speculations of the philosophers fail to grasp this principle, and because of this, fail to understand the festive nature of wisdom's discovery of the cosmos as it bears the beauty of God. In *On the Cherubim*, Philo avers that "joy and gladness" and "peace" are God's. God's "nature is most perfect, He Himself is the summit, end, and limit of happiness." He "imparted of his own to all particular beings from that fountain of beauty—Himself, for all the good and beautiful things in the world could never have been what they are, save that they were made in the image of the archetype, which is truly good and beautiful." Recognizing this beauty in all things makes one study the heavens and all that there is demonstrating (*elenchos*) that the changes in the cosmos are ordered by the one who is unchanging. *Elenchos* is the operation of the properly functioning human mind with all its faculties and passions inquiring, discerning, examining, adjudicating, and proving the beauty of the universe, which bears the radiance of God's glory and beauty such that one might become a sage, a wise person, one in whom wisdom dwells.

The condition of proper functioning minds in elenchic activity is impaired because of the folly of human life in their post-lapsarian state. *Elenchos*, in light of this folly, bears a second function in Philo; the function of exposing falsehood and deception. *Elenchos* in this aspect is an inquiry that uncovers the inconsistency and illusions in one's belief system due to the problem of sin. God sends the power of exposing, *elenchos*, to humans because he is their parent. In *On Drunkenness*, Philo claims,

> Is not the Maker and Father of the universe He who presided at the beginning? So if you say that you now know, not even now have you true knowledge, since it does not date from the beginning of your own existence. And you stand no less convicted of mere feigning, when you compare two incomparables, and say that you know that the greatness of the existent is beyond all the Gods. For if you had true knowledge of that which is, you would not have supposed that any other god had power of his own. For when the knowledge of the Existent shines, it wraps everything in light, and thus renders invisible everything which seemed brightest in

themselves. But your ignorance of the One produced your opinion of the existence of many. (*Drunkenness*, Loeb Vol. III, 341)

Deception includes the distortion of reality purposefully and haughtily as we see in this passage. Further, it entails an inability to see what reality is, (the two incomparables), and misrepresents it as a result. There is folly in claiming that one knows who and what God is while failing to be illumined by the "light of the Existent." The paragraph itself is an illustration of the *elenchos* claiming that one has been convicted i.e. exposed in his inconsistency. Later (*Drunkenness*, 385) he prays that humans would be able to voluntarily submit to the direction of the *elenchos* to avoid "indiscipline and folly." Deception is a purposeful evasion of reality so one must pray that conscience do its elenchic work of conviction. In this case it makes one aware of the delusion so that one might gain "steadfastness of mind."

The theme of *elenchos*, its exposure and examination of the soul that deceives, is evident in the treatise entitled *On the Confusion of Tongues*. (*Confusion*, Loeb Vol. IV). *Confusion of Tongues* is, of course, about the story of Babel and the dispersion of languages in response to the arrogance of humankind. After engaging a variety of positions that were against the facticity of the story, Philo makes a striking observation about Babel. He states that he will, with the help of God and Moses, "demolish the plausible arguments of the sophists," who with cunning lips deceive others about the story. Philo embarks on an inquiry to achieve that demolition of deceit. Although all humans have the "treasures" of peace embedded on their minds, friendships of "falsehood" (i.e., deceivers) and enemies "of the truth" (i.e., liars) mask the truth (*Confusion*, 39, 49). These enemies of truth "surely are by nature men of contradiction, [and] all who have ever been zealous for knowledge and virtue, who contend (*elenchos*) with these neighbors of the soul; who test (*elenchos*) the pleasures which share our home." In both cases, the philosopher uses *elenchos* examining the false claims of the enemies of truth. He says this testing goes further claiming that the men of knowledge and virtue "test every sense, the eyes on what they see, the ears on what they hear, the sense of smell on its perfumes the taste on its flavours, the touch on the characteristics which mark the qualities of substances as they come in contact with it." Given the pervasiveness of erroneous claims by the sophistical thinkers above every area of life must be explored from the epistemological to the metaphysical because distortions will infiltrate those realms of human perspective. He says that even the "utterances of sentences" will be elencheinized.

The enemies of truth are called "impious ones" in paragraphs 125–27 on page 79 of *Confusion*. Philo writes:

> The impious man thinks the opposite, that the mind has sovereign power over what it plans, and sense over what it perceives. He holds that the latter judges material things and the former all things, and that both are free from fault or error. And yet what could be more blameworthy or more clearly exposed of falsehood by the truth than these beliefs? Is not the mind constantly convicted of delusion on numberless points, and all the senses guilty of false witness, not before unreasoning judges who may easily be deceived, but at the bar of nature herself whom it is fundamentally impossible to corrupt. And surely if the means of judgment within us, supplied by mind and sense, are capable of error, we must admit the logical consequence, that it is God who showers conceptions on the mind and perceptions on sense, and that what comes into being is not gift of any part of ourselves, but all are bestowed by God. (*Confusion*, 79)

The fractured intellect includes the mind and the senses, all that goes into knowing, fails to perceive things as they are, and just like Meno, or Meletus, or Gorgias, characterized by intellectual arrogance, the chance of repentance dims because, even though their error is exposed, they reject the intellectual humility necessary to acknowledge it and to continue the inquiry. The logical consequence is that the *elenchos* has brought the inquirer to the place of needing divine assistance and help. An advocate who is a healer must intervene. The second aspect that we have pursued I have identified as the work of exposing deception and illusory believing; the revelation of falsehood and lies as they affect the individual, but also as they affect institutional and corporate life. The malfunctioning of the mind, although it was designed to discern with wisdom the beauty of the cosmos through its design, now needs the corrective and revelatory power of the *elenchos* to unveil its contradictions and the complexities of beliefs.

I have suggested that *elenchos* for Philo is rooted in his Wisdom cosmology in which the human mind with its powers are structured to discern the beauty that radiates all things as they reflect the beauty of God. These powers to interpret the cosmos are activated by *elenchos*, a kind of *elenchos* that corresponds to each power in its uniqueness like perception, the power to distinguish distinguishes rightly, correspondingly one might say, due to its elenchic activity. The second claim I made was that because of the fall and the introduction of an alternative wisdom dominating the mind of humans, elenchic functions to expose and examine the deeply entrenched deceptions and falsehoods that characterizes one's belief system in this state. Exposing deception includes refutation of these false beliefs and the presence of inconsistency among these. I now proceed to what I see as the third function: the therapeutic, healing function of *elenchos*.

Because all knowledge of beauty is based on the grace of God, the exposure that occurs in function two is designed to lead to changes in one's belief system and in the believer if that one is to join the ranks of the wise. *Elenchos* has its focus on the restoration of the mind to discern beauty; its concern is for the healing of the believer, a redirecting of one's loves. In the *Unchangeableness of God*, Philo writes,

> But when the true priest *elenchos* enters us, like a pure ray of light, we see in their real value the unholy thoughts that were stored with our soul, and the guilty and blameworthy actions to which we laid our hands in ignorance of our true interests. *Elenchos*, discharging his priest-like task, defiles all these and bids them be cleared out and carried away, that he may see the soul's house in its natural bare condition, and heal whatever sicknesses have arisen in it. (*Unchangeable*, Loeb Vol. III p.79)

In this passage not only is *elenchos* called a true priest, but carries on the priestly duties of purifying people of their unholy thoughts by making them aware that they are unholy. Toward the end of the quote the priestly activity of *elenchos* is to bring one back to the natural condition of the mind. I take it to mean that *elenchos* restores one's faculties to function properly again, a kind of quickening of the mind similar to what Paul claims in Romans 12:1–2, the renewing of the mind to prove the will of God and to discern the beauty of the cosmos as it is intimative of God. *Elenchos* is a beam of pure light exposing the state of the one who has violated God's law with the view of renewing one's proper state. There are parallel passages regarding this priestly activity in the work *On Special Laws*, where the *elenchos* is called a priest to heal and to bring about purification (*Spec. Laws 2*, Loeb Vol. VII, 407; *Spec. Laws 3*, 509).

Not only does the *elenchos* have a priestly function that heals and restores, it has a prophetic function enabling one to perceive "this world as a cathedral" (*Who is Heir?*, Loeb Vol. IV, 319). In other words, humans live in a cosmic sanctuary. Living in this sanctuary requires the prophetic work of the *elenchos* so that one understands the "perfect joys of God even in the rain and other parts of the elements of the cosmos." Philo cries out, "look up and convict the errors of the multitude of common men, the blind race, which has lost the sight which it thinks it possesses." The old prophets, he reminds his readers, were called "seers" so that they might examine and instruct the "idleness and ignorance" of the makers of luxury. These seers bear "the holy text" so that through it one might be "reproved" (*elenchos*) and regain sight. Education in the holy text, the province of the prophets (prophets spoke as they were moved by the Holy Spirit), is what the *elenchos* does, reeducating and, consequently, healing those who have been foolish.

The prophetic aspect of the therapeutic function necessitates taking aim at cosmologies that wrongheadedly mask the beauty of the cosmos and the mind's design to discern it. In particular in the work called *The Eternity of the World* (*Eternity*, Loeb Vol. IX), the Stoics are the system he sets out to refute, that is to dismantle elenchically. Their cosmology claims that fire (*puros*) is the one unifying principle of the cosmos. He catches them in what would appear to be an obvious contradiction, that is, how can they claim an ongoing existence for the universe when fire by its nature consumes things and burns out. He identifies his engagement with the Stoics *elenchon* and calls this their "cardinal doctrine," which is a lie that leads to "death" (*Eternity*, 249). He calls them "ingenious quibblers" who conflate an apparent power with the real power of the universe. The stakes are significant because of the dominance of the Stoic worldview and its influence on the mind of the first century. To expose is to purify this from the minds of society at large and offers only a qualified place for it.

One function remains in Philo's use of the *elenchos*; its forensic function rooted in conscience. I also wish to contend against a view, closely related to the former, taken by a number of scholars, which concerns the connection between *elenchos* and the *sunoida* (conscience) word group found in Philo. Philo uses *sunoida* on at least thirty occasions and in some instances uses it interchangeably with or in parallel to *elenchos*. Two passages will illustrate this from the half dozen in which one finds *elenchos* and *sunoida* interchanged and illustrate the forensic function of the conscience ascribed to *elenchos*. The first of these is found in *The Worse Attacks the Better*. This work is a consideration of the attack leveled by Cain against Abel found in the book of Genesis, a book of the Bible primed for examination by Philo. In sections 23-24 (*Worse*, Loeb Vol. II, 218-19), Philo claims, "Sometimes he [the real man] assumes the part of witness or accuser and convicts (*elenchos*) from within, not allowing us so much as to open our mouth, but, holding in and curbing the tongue with the reins of conscience

Cosmic Beauty and the Ethics of Inquiry

(*suneidotos*). This challenger (*elenchos*) inquired of the soul when he saw it wandering" (*Worse*, 219). Notice that the nouns "real man," conscience, and challenger are used interchangeably and synonymously in a forensic, judicial sense.

A second passage, perhaps even stronger than the first, is found in *On the Decalogue* (*Decalogue*, Loeb Vol. VII). Philo writes, "For innate and living in every soul is the *elenchos*, whose way it is not to admit anything that calls for censure, by nature always hating evil and loving virtue, itself being both prosecutor and judge. When activated as prosecutor, it lays charges, accurses and makes ashamed; as judge it instructs, rebukes and exhorts to change . . . the conscience witnesses to falsehood" (*Decalogue*, 51). Philo explores the contours of the conscience that serves forensically as judge, accuser, and prosecutor. The job of punishment, the job of the court one might say, is to rebuke so that a rational agent, an agent with a conscience, feels a sense of shame as a result of demonstrated guilt, that is, the judge *elenchos* working with *sunoida*. These two passages lend support to idea of the *elenchos* as the tool of conscience and that the forensic aspect of *elenchos* is at the core of its meaning in this realm.

The job of the *elenchos* is to discern through the natural powers that humans possess the beauty of the cosmos wisely, and when that fails because of falsehood and self-deception it exposes and examines these, and it exposes and examines these with the priestly intent to restore and heal and the prophetic view of calling to task those perspectives that hinder that healing so that healing might occur, if healing and a turn toward restoration does not occur, what might *elenchos* do but to convict forensically by activating the conscience to distinguish between right and wrong, the just and the unjust, and the good and the evil. The conscience is a power of the human mind which has the function of discerning the moral law and when it goes right and when it goes wrong. The conscience "proves" that violations and sins have occurred (*On Virtues*, Loeb Vol. VIII, 206). Conscience employs *elenchos* to demonstrate errors of the good design of God, and in the *Worse Attacks the Better* (*Worse*, 299) it renders the right punishment for the infractions that have occurred. The justice of God demands a faculty like conscience to reprove and forensically convict those who neglect or pervert the beauty of God's cosmos and renders the judgment that is due those who have been so convicted in the court of God's righteous law. *Elenchos* is the proper function of *sunioda* in these passages similarly to how it functioned in sense perception or therapy. My earlier references suffice to demonstrate that *sunoida* and *elenchos* are used interchangeable.

In this chapter I have argued that the cosmos intimates the Beauty that God is, bearing beauty itself as a result of God's gracious creation. I have suggested ways that Philo understands beauty and have suggested that when beauty is discerned, its power is actualized, molding virtuous humans who mirror the Beauty that God is. Understanding the beauty of the cosmos as it reflects God's excellence affects the political, social, and familial realms of creaturely existence, thus contributing redemptively culture. Fractured though humans are, God utilizes a therapeutic agent to transform humans by wisdom. That agent is *elenchos*. Finally, I have explored a robust conception of *elenchos* embedded in the Wisdom cosmology of Philo and the proper functioning of human powers engined by the use of *elenchos* to discover the beauty of the cosmos. My sense is that through the exercise of *elenchos* in practice impassioned by wonder and intellectual love, humans might become responsible believers discovering the beauty of a cosmos as it intimate the beauty of the Triune God.

Conclusion
Recapitulation and Prospects

"The fate of empires rests on the education of its youth." This dictum by Aristotle receives support by the critical thinking movements currently exercising influence over the educational landscape. They contend that education of a particular variety, one steeped and baptized in the sanctifying streams of critical thinking, is needed if our democratic society is to persist. The extent of concern expressed by this movement is astonishing and impressive. College courses have been developed to provide remediation due to the absence of critical thought manifested by students; businesses have spent millions of dollars trying to educate or re-educate their employees, and reform documents have in one voice called upon educators at all levels to invest the time, energy, and finances at their disposal to address the crucial question of the absence of critical thought.

I have set out in this book to offer a proposal on fixing the fixation of belief that troubles my soul, which leads to belief melioration by doing three things. The first is to expose and refute aspects of the dominant epistemological framework for engaging belief tenacity and improvement. This framework advances several features of its dominant concern, justification. I identify these as internalism, the on-the paper-thesis-of-belief, and sacerdotal methodism with its cathartic effect. I do so in what I call in the last chapter an exercise in *elenchos*, an ethics of inquiry. After a few chapters of exploring this issue and in suggesting the design that humans possess, I offer an account of the fractured intellects that humans manifest in their post-lapsarian state of existence. This seems to me to be a highly plausible suggestion, but, I am sure to some it will be thought of as a smuggling in of theological concerns into the discussion. Given that I take Plantinga to be right about properly basic beliefs and how religious beliefs can serve in this way, I am not shaken by possible disdain. I also find Wolterstorff's view of faithful Christian scholarship to be convincing, and so in my analysis I hope for fidelity. The public square's refusal to permit religious beliefs to enter the fray illustrate the disembeddedness of life, culture, and education discussed so persuasively in Charles Taylor's book *Modern Social Imaginaries*. I adopt the language of the noetic effects of sin to describe this state of affairs.

I also set out in this treatise to provide a model of the believer based less on the traditional ethics of duty perspective, but on an ethics of character model. The place of virtue ethics and now virtue epistemology has a venerable tradition going back to Aristotle and shaped much of the thinking of the medieval philosophical tradition. Given its focus on cognitive traits and affective conditions, this seems to me to account better for the broken design humans bear which was discussed in the earlier chapters.

The third thing I set out to do to finish this task of fixing belief fixation is to discuss the importance of beauty as a framework for understanding the cognitive and affective life and how these respond to the intimations of God's Beauty in all that there is. I confess ancestors in this tradition including Philo of Alexandria, St. Bonaventure, and others. I further suggest that the cognitive design humans bear—which is an act of God's grace and is realized in the intellectual virtues discussed earlier—requires an ethics, in particular, an ethics of inquiry. I retrieve the work of Philo of Alexandria on *elenchos*, in my view a better alternative to the Cartesian method of doubt, to assist in this task. These three framing intentions provide a way to the improvement of our believing. In what follows I offer a recapitulation of how I go about this.

One problem that stands in need of being addressed is what I have identified, following C. S. Peirce, as the fixation of belief. People hold to their beliefs tenaciously. Once beliefs are formed and become a part of one's system of belief, their revocation is quite the formidable task. Beliefs tend to be locked away in compartments or segments of one's belief system and, as such, are difficult to amend. In this book I have asked whether the persons currently setting the trends have, in their models of critical thinking, the potential to handle adequately this problem of belief fixation. In chapter 1 I focused my discussion on three critical thinking theorists: Robert Ennis, John McPeck, and Richard Paul. Although I find much that is insightful, useful, and helpful to the project of belief melioration, I conclude that their perspectives rely far too much on analytic epistemology's

Conclusion

separation of psychological/historical contributions from epistemic considerations. Analytic epistemology has presumed that psychology and history, because they describe how one believes, are irrelevant to the critical thinking theorists task of establishing the norms for believing. This preoccupation with normativity limits these theorists in probing belief fixation. I identified the position advocated by Ennis, McPeck, and Paul as the on-the-paper-thesis-of-epistemology.

The on-the-paper-thesis-epistemology dominates the way in which critical thinking theorists approach the issue of belief fixation. Basically this position suggests that one is capable of placing on the table for inspection a belief and those things that pertain to its rejection or acceptance. The on-the-paper-thesis-of-epistemology advances the notion that one has the capacity for autonomy in believing and is able to separate oneself from one's history and other beliefs when applying norms or principles of acceptance or rejection to a belief. In chapter 2 I spell out the history and content of the on-the-paper-thesis-of-epistemology.

C. S. Peirce associates the dominance of the on-the-paper-thesis-of-epistemology with the direction philosophy took with Descartes. Descartes initiated the epistemological tradition that suggests that the most efficient way of remedying belief fixation is to get belief right when one initially accepts a belief. This means that a believer will only accept a belief if that belief survives an epistemological examination. A believer allegedly has the wherewithal to lay his or her one's beliefs for this examination to protect against the problem of needing to change belief. One is morally condemnable or commendable on the basis of one's epistemological examination.

I suggest this model of epistemology contains a preoccupation with justification (finding the norms of justification), with internalism (one's beliefs are internally present in one's mind, accessible, and one has cognizance of one's beliefs), and a particular notion of belief (that belief is exclusively a propositional representation of the real world). In chapter 2, I discuss each of these and reject them as possible ingredients that go into making critical believers who engage belief fixation. I suggest that the dominant epistemology's interest in answering the question of how one *ought* to believe can be illuminated by considerations of how one *does actually* believe. I conclude the chapter by discussing the psychological limitations to one's believing and by demonstrating that the impartial internalist model simply does not occur in life. Everyone is influenced by previously established beliefs and pre-theoretical assumptions that guide them in believing.

In chapter 3, I argue that understanding how one holds beliefs and what constitutes a belief are essential when addressing belief melioration/fixation. I advanced a psychology of belief that suggests that beliefs are maps by which one steers (Frank Ramsey) in life, they are propositional attitudes given the cognitive and affective condition they bear, and that beliefs are either memorial or occurrent. Memorial beliefs need not be accessible to guide and still direct one in acquiring new beliefs or solidify beliefs already held within one's belief system. Occurrent beliefs are few, but even these are related in complex ways with a multitude of other beliefs that are not necessarily accessible but nevertheless influence one's believing. In either case one need not be fully aware of adopting beliefs, of the inferential strategies used in developing beliefs, or in maintaining beliefs within one's belief system.

Some beliefs are more basic than others and comprise what Rokeach has called the central region of one's belief system. These beliefs I have called control beliefs following Wolterstorff or terminal beliefs adopting Kornblith's phrase. The complexity of believing is enhanced by one's tendency to isolate and fragment beliefs into compartments. Rokeach suggests two other regions of one's belief system. These are the intermediate and peripheral regions. The intermediate region is characterized by beliefs gotten by authority and the peripheral contains data beliefs subject to frequent change.

My discussion of the structure of belief was followed by an examination of judgmental strategies for arriving at beliefs. These strategies (the representational, availability, anchoring, and vivid heuristics) shed light on how people utilize their beliefs and their structure. The heuristics advanced by Tversky, Kaheman, Nisbett, and Ross illustrate how limited or minimal humans actually are.

A final psychological contribution to understanding how one holds, forms, and modifies beliefs is the work done by Jon Elster. His focus is primarily on the passionate states like wishful thinking or adaptive preference that one utilizes when confronted with cognitive dissonance. Cognitive dissonance occurs when two contradictory beliefs are present in a believer when arriving at a decision. Elster's work demonstrates how persons when caught in a situation of cognitive dissonance employ strategies of evasion so that the beliefs (vying to be the map by which one steers) might not be faced with the contradiction. The work done by Elster, Rokeach, Tversky et al. point this writer to conclude that the holding/modifying of beliefs is far more complex than the on-the-paper-thesis-of-epistemology portends. If the on-the-paper-thesis-of-epistemology that influences the critical thinking theorists in chapter 1 is found wanting, and beliefs are more complex than has been traditionally expressed, then the question of training critical thinkers to engage in belief melioration and change remains perplexing. How can we think about critical thinking so that the minimally rational agent (not the autonomous ideal) and the complexity of beliefs (not belief as conscious, propositional representation) are taken into account?

For some the kind of argument advanced through the first three chapters lends credence to the thesis that the post-Cartesian philosophical concentration on epistemology has become a thing of the past. Charles Taylor writes how philosophy is now "after epistemology." Richard Rorty writes that the epistemological orientation is a "tradition well lost." Cornel West argues for an "American evasion" of epistemological concerns. There are others, though, like Alvin Plantinga, Ernest Sosa, and Alvin Goldman, who wish to argue for a more naturalistic account for epistemology. This orientation seeks a union of epistemic concerns with naturalistic explanations that might be found in psychology, cognitive studies of all sorts, religious insights, and history. It is in the spirit of the design account, a good design given by a gracious God to enable humankind to detect the intimations of God's beauty in the cosmos, that I argue for a different model of the responsible believer.

In chapter 4 I explore a tradition of explaining the limitations of humankind though the work of St. Augustine. Augustine was concerned about fixation and melioration as evidenced by his claim that a renewal of mind needs to occur for humans because of sin's debilitating effects. Understanding God's beautiful, *shalomic* design has been vitiated by these effects manifesting in *akrasia*, fragmentation, and self-deception leaving humans as riddles to themselves and the cosmos as radically masked. I suggest that these considerations support the notion of the complexity of our believing and provide an explanation of the isolation, contradictions, and illusory believing discussed earlier.

My account of the critical believer concentrates on the proper functioning of one's intellectual faculties in a conducive environment (social, political, institutional) which through practice leads to intellectual virtue. So that I can avoid the critique I offered in chapter 2 of the ahistorical character of the on-the-paper-thesis-of-epistemology, I readily acknowledge my debt to Aristotle in an extended examination of his account of intellectual virtue. Aristotle focuses our attention on proper functioning and how, in a conducive atmosphere, humans have the potential for developing these virtues. I build on Aristotle's account (which I believe informs the best of an American epistemological tradition from Reidian common sense realism through Peirce and Dewey) by adopting Sosa's definition of intellectual virtue: "a quality bound to help maximize one's surplus of truth over error . . . we assume a teleological conception of intellectual virtue, the relevant end being a proper relation to the truth . . . the virtue of a virtue derives simply from leading us to it, perhaps accidentally, but from leading us to it reliably." Intellectual virtues are cognitive excellences that direct one's believing not in an absolute, but in a responsible fashion. "Responsible" is my preferred word to reliable because it allows for some human determination in bettering our cognitive life while avoiding the voluntarist assumption of the on-the-paper-thesis-of-epistemology.

I suggest three kinds of intellectual virtues: generative, transmissive, and metamorphic. Generative virtues are those that lead to belief without dependence upon prior beliefs, such as, simple perception or intuitive reason. Transmissive virtues use pre-existing beliefs in the formation of new beliefs such as memory or induction. Induction is a good example of where the critical thinking theorists of chapter 1 have much to offer. Their focus is on inductive concerns. Induction and memory working together also address the judgmental strategies discussed earlier. The virtues that deal with belief revision and renewal I have identified as metamorphic. Although I might feel more like Franz Kafka's Gregor, I have in mind cognitive excellences which serve to alter beliefs. These include creativity, reflection, and wisdom.

Intellectual virtues must have an environment and a context in which to be cultivated. Practices are the second ingredient in the model proposed. These are socially and historically defined ways of engaging a particular subject matter in one's experience, which, in turn, serve the maturation and responsible execution of one's cognitive processes. Too often these practices are univocal representing one point of view where other practices are equally representative of engaging a subject matter. One remembers that the babbling of Babel will always be the characteristic of humankind, both in one's own belief system and the practices evident in a subject area as a result of the noetic effects of sin. Practices leads to discipline and reliable execution of the cognitive and effectual life. Talmudic practice is an example of multifocal practice described in chapter 5.

Conclusion

Finally, intellectual passions (what Scheffler calls cognitive emotions) are cited as the third ingredient of a critical thinker. I include doubt, intellectual love, and wonder as passions that need an environment to be cultivated as well. I accept Aristotle's comment that humankind by nature desires to understand and it is through the cultivation of experiences which allow for doubt, intellectual love and wonder that these direct and participate in one's inquiries.

I have attempted to provide a model that recognizes humankind's potential weaknesses psychologically and that does not pretend to escape its historicity. The intellectual practices that provide the context for virtues and passions to mature are evolutionary in the sense that they give way to new practices that further help to improve one's believing. An historical consciousness (as Dewey contended) is necessary as one utilizes the plurality of practices available in learning how to arrive at belief. The exercise, though, of the cognitive processes that become virtues are naturally a part of the design of humankind and these exist as potentials until cultivated through practice, passions, and what I identify as *elenchos*.

There are good and bad days for humans in all their activities in life. Lebron James has several games a year in which he scores under 20 points and Andrew McCutcheon goes an entire season hitting under 300. The greatest of thinkers, the ones most characterized by intellectual virtues, are subject to errors as well. Humans are fallible epistemic agents. Educationally, teachers need to be aware of the possible miscues of themselves and their students. When correcting homework, for instance, I wonder how often a teacher attempts to walk through the mistakes children make. I wonder if allowing children to verbalize the procedures and their understanding of them utilized in solving a math or science problem would do more to cultivate intellectual virtues and responsible activities than mere red ink. I am curious whether a Jeopardy approach to homework or class activities may be beneficial as an approach in which an answer is provided for children and then they must discover the problem, practices, and passions to which the answer corresponds.

I mentioned in the penultimate chapter that Talmudic study is a good model of multifocal practice. An essential part of Talmudic study is "*pilpul.*" The Talmud is studied with another person of comparable ability with whom one argues, dialogues, and debates about the meaning of a text. This is called *pilpul*. Social inquiry is important to the task of creating intellectually virtuous thinkers. I have not included in my analysis how social inquiry or a social epistemics might influence intellectual virtue. I have only referred to social practices as possessing some authority in one's believing.

My sense is that the journey is not complete without providing a way to engage the beauty that things possess and the intimative value of these. Virtuous believers discussed need the empowering presence of a therapeutic agent, a kind of power, that enables one to function rightly and to discover the deep structure of belief in a believer. I offer what Philo of Alexandria suggests as a spirituality of inquiry rooted in the Socratic notion of *elenchos*. Philo understood the exercise of *elenchos* as the priestly presence of the Spirit in a way that is similar to the Paraclete passages from John's Gospel, although I do not discuss these. Calvin claimed that the Holy Spirit guides believers and, in common grace, non-believers to discover what is true in fulfillment of human design, even though bearing the noetic effects of sin. Philo gives a reasoned account through the notion of *elenchos* of how this inquiry occurs. Wonder, intellectual humility, and intellectual love serve with *elenchos* in renewing minds daily. Heschel is quite right when he declared that we need more text people and less text books, and that believers ought to see their study as an object of worship. And so, with Lewis, we need responsible, passionate believers who transform the "desert" of arid lives into "springs that gather force."

Finally, this model of responsible believers does not supply the final condition or state of humans. But it is a hopeful proposal for belief melioration in the midst of our intellectual failings. St. Augustine tells of the *telos* of this hope in the *City of God*. He writes:

> And a time will come when we shall enjoy one another's beauty for itself alone without lust. And this above all is a motive for the praise of the Creator, to whom the Psalm says, "You have clothed yourself in praise and beauty." The manifold diversity of beauty in the sky and earth and sea; the abundance of light, and its miraculous loveliness, in sun and moon and stars; the dark shades of woods, the color and fragrance of flowers; the many variety of birds, with their songs and their bright plumage; the countless different species of living creatures of all shapes and sizes, for we wonder and are astonished at these.[1]

---

1. Augustine, *City of God*, 1074–75.

Bibliography

Alston, William. "Concepts of Epistemic Justification." *The Monist* 68.1 (1985) 57–89.
———. "Thomas Reid on Epistemic Principles." *History of Philosophy Quarterly* 2.4 (1985) 435–52.
Anderson, Craig, Mark Lepper, and Lee Ross. "Perseverance of Social Theories: The Role of Explanation in the Persistence of Discredited Information." *Journal of Personality and Social Psychology* 39 (1980) 1037–49.
Aristotle. *Nicomachean Ethics*. Indianapolis: The Liberal Arts, 1975.
Arendt, Hannah. *The Life of the Mind*. New York: Harcourt Brace Jovanovich, 1971.
Arlin, Patricia Kennedy. "Wisdom: The Art of Problem Finding." In *Wisdom: Its Nature, Origins, and Development*, 230–43. Cambridge: Cambridge University Press, 1992.
Audi, Robert. *Belief, Justification, and Knowledge*. Belmont, TN: Wadsworth, 1988.
Augustine. *City of God*. Translated by Henry Bettenson. New York: Penguin Classics, 2003.
———. *Confessions*. Translated by Rex Warner. New York: Penguin Mentor, 1963.
———. *Earlier Writings*. Edited by. J. H. S. Burleigh. Philadelphia: Westminster, 1963.
———. "Epistle 118." In *Letters 100–155*, The Works of St. Augustine: A Translation for the 21st Century, edited by Boniface Ramsey. Translated by Roland Teske. Brooklyn, NY: New City, 1990.
———. *Literal Meaning of Genesis*. In *On Genesis*. The Works of St. Augustine: A Translation for the 21st Century, edited by John E. Rotelle. Translated by Edmund Hill. Brooklyn, NY: New City, 2002.
———. *On Nature and Grace*. In *Basic Writings of Augustine*, edited by Whitney J. Oates, 521–79. New York: Random House, 1948.
———. *On the Free Choice of the Will*. Translated by Anna S. Benjamin. Indianapolis, IN: Bobbs Merrill, 1964.
———. *On The Trinity*. Translated by Edmund Hill. Brooklyn, NY: New City, 1991.
Ayer, A. J. *The Problem of Knowledge*. London: MacMillan, 1956.
Bernstein, Richard. *Beyond Objectivism and Relativism: Science, Hermeneutics, and Praxis*. Philadelphia: University of Pennsylvania Press, 1985.
Berry, Wendell. *A Timbered Choir: The Sabbath Poems 1979–1997*. Berkeley, CA: Counterpoint, 1998.
Bogdan, Radu J., ed. *Belief: Form, Content, and Function*. Oxford: Clarendon, 1986.
Bonjour, Lawrence. *The Structure of Empirical Knowledge*. Cambridge: Harvard University Press, 1985.
Bourke, Vernon J. *Augustine's Love of Wisdom: An Introspective Philosophy*. West Lafayette, IN: Purdue University Press, 1992.

Bibliography

Bruner, Jerome. *Actual Minds, Possible Worlds*. Cambridge: Harvard University Press, 1986.

———. *Beyond the Information Given: Studies in the Psychology of Knowing*. Edited by Jeremy M. Anglin. New York: Norton, 1973.

Cherniak, Christopher. *Minimal Rationality*. Cambridg: MIT Press, 1986.

Chisholm, Roderick. *Theory of Knowledge*. Englewood Cliffs, NJ: Prentice-Hall, 1977.

Clifford, William K. "The Ethics of Belief." In *Ethics of Belief Debate*, edited by Gerald McCarthy, 19–36. Atlanta: Scholars, 1986.

Cochrane, Charles Norris. *Christianity and Classical Culture*. Oxford: Oxford University Press, 1940.

Code, Lorraine. *Epistemic Responsibility*. Hanover, NH: University of New England Press, 1987.

Feldman, Richard, and Earl Conee. "Evidentialism." *Philosophical Studies* 48.1 (1985) 15–34.

Copleston, Frederick. *A History of Philosophy*. Vol. IV. Garden City, NY: Doubleday, 1963.

Descartes, Rene. *Meditations on First Philosophy*. Indianapolis: Hackett, 1979.

———. *Philosophical Writing*. Edited by Elizabeth Anscombe and Peter Geach. Indianapolis, IN: The Library of Liberal Arts, 1954.

Dewey, John. *How We Think*. Buffalo, NY: Prometheus, 1991.

———. *Logic: The Theory of Inquiry*. New York: Holt, 1938.

Dillon, John. *The Middle Platonists: 80 BC to 220 AD*. Ithaca, NY: Cornell University Press, 1996.

Dooyeweerd, Herman. *In the Twilight of Western Thought*. Nutley, NJ: The Craig, 1972.

Edwards, Jonathan. *The Nature of True Virtue*. Ann Arbor, MI: University of Michigan Press, 1969

Elster, Jon. "Belief, Bias and Ideology." In *Rationality and Relativism*, edited by Martin Hollis and Steven Lukes, 123–48. Cambridge: MIT Press, 1986.

———. *Solomonic Judgements: Studies in the Limitations of Rationality*. Cambridge: Cambridge University Press, 1989.

———. *Sour Grapes: Studies in the Subversion of Rationality*. Cambridge: Cambridge University Press, 1987.

Ennis, Robert. "A Concept of Critical Thinking." *Harvard Educational Review* 32.1 (1962) 81–111.

———. "A Conception of Rational Thinking." In *Philosophy of Education 1979: Proceedings of the Thirty-Fifth Annual Meeting of the Philosophy of Education Society*, 9–26. Bloomington, IN: Philosophy of Education Society, 1980.

———. "A Taxonomy of Critical Thinking Dispositions and Abilities." In *Teaching for Thinking*, edited by Jonathan Baron and Robert Sternberg, 9–26. New York: Freeman, 1987.

Emerson, Ralph. "The American Scholar." In *The Complete Essays of Ralph Waldo Emerson*, 62. New York: The Modern Library, 1940.

Festinger, Leon. *A Theory of Cognitive Dissonance*. Stanford: Stanford University Press, 1957.

Feyerabend, Peter. *Against Method*. New York: Free, 1975.

Firth, Roderick. "Are Epistemic Concepts Reducible to Ethical Concepts?" In *Values and Morals*, edited by A. Goldman and J. Kim, 215–29. Dordrechts, NLD: Reidel, 1978.

Gadamer, Hans-Georg. *Truth and Method*. New York: Crossroad, 1975.

Gardner, Howard. *Frames of Mind*. New York: Basic, 1985.

———. *The Mind's New Science: A History of the Cognitive Revolution*. New York: Basic, 1987.

Gilbert, Daniel T. "How Mental Systems Believe." *American Psychologist* 46.2 (1991) 107–19.

Glaser, Robert. "Education and Thinking: The Role of Knowledge." *American Psychologist* 39.2 (1984) 93–104.

Goldenberg, Robert. "Talmud." In *Back to the Sources: Reading the Classic Jewish Texts*, edited by Barry W. Holtz, 128–75. New York: Summit, 1984.

Goldman, Alvin. *Epistemology and Cognition*. Cambridge: Harvard University Press, 1986.

———. "Epistemics: The Regulative Theory of Cognition." *Journal of Philosophy* 75 (1978) 509–23.

———. "The Relation between Epistemology and Psychology." *Synthese* 64, (1985) 29–68.

———. "Varieties of Cognitive Appraisal." *Nous* 13 (1979) 23–38.

Grovier, Trudy. "Critical Thinking as Argument Analysis." *Argumentation* 3, (1989) 115–26.

Haack, Susa. "The Relevance of Psychology to Epistemology." *Metaphilosophy* 6.2 (1975) 161–76.

Harman, Gilbert. *Change in View*. Cambridge: MIT Press, 1989.

Hart, David Bentley. *The Beauty of the Infinite: The Aesthetics of Christian Truth*. Grand Rapids: Eerdmanns, 2003.

Heidegger, Martin. *What Is Called Thinking?* New York: Harper & Row, 1968.

———. *What Is Philosophy?* Translated by Jean T. Wilde. New Haven, CT: Yale University Press, 1955.

Heschel, Abraham J. *God in Search of Man: A Philosophy Of Judaism*. New York: Farrar, Straus, and Giroux, 1955.

———. *The Insecurity of Man*. New York: Schocken, 1975.

———. *Man is Not Alone: A Philosophy of Religion*. New York: Farrar, Straus, and Giroux, 1951.

Irwin, Terence. *Plato's Ethics*. New York: Oxford University Press, 1995.

Kahane, Howard. *Logic and Contemporary Rhetoric*. Belmont, CA: Wadsworth, 1992.

Kahneman, Daniel, and Amos Tversky. "Availability: A Heuristic for Judging Frequency and Probability." In *Judgment under Uncertainty: Heuristics and Biases*, 163–78. Cambridge: Cambridge University Press, 1982.

Kornblith, Hilary. "Ever Since Descartes." *The Monist* 68.2 (1985) 264–76.

———. "Justified Belief and Epistemically Responsible Action." *The Philosophical Review* 92.1 (1983) 33–48.

———. "The Psychological Turn." *Australian Journal of Philosophy* 60.3 (1982) 238–53.

Lewis, C. I. *An Analysis of Knowledge and Valuation*. LaSalle, IL: Open Court, 1946.

Locke, John. *An Essay concerning Human Understanding*. Edited by A. D. Woozley. New York: Meridian, 1964.

Loftus, Elizabeth, and John Palmer. "Reconstruction of Automobile Destruction: An Example of the Interaction between Language and Memory." *Journal of Verbal Learning and Verbal Behavior* 13 (1973) 585–89.

Lord, C., L. Ross, and M. Lepper. "Biased Assimilation and Attitude Polarization: The Effect of Theories on Subsequently Considered Evidence." *Journal of Personality and Social Psychology* 37 (1979) 2098–2109.

Bibliography

Lukinsky, Joseph. "Law in Education: A Reminiscence with Some Footnotes to Robert Carver's Nomos and Narrative." *The Yale Law Journal* 96 (1987) 1836–59.
MacIntyre, Alasdair. *After Virtue*. Notre Dame, IN: University of Notre Dame Press, 1984.
Maxwell, Nicholas. *From Knowledge to Wisdom*. Oxford: Blackwell, 1987.
———. "Science: Reason, Knowledge and Wisdom: A Critique of Specialism." *Inquiry* 23 (1983) 19–81.
McPeck, John. *Critical Thinking and Education*. New York: St. Martin's, 1981.
———. *Teaching Critical Thinking*. London: Routledge, 1990.
Modrak, D. K. "Aristotle on Knowing First Principles." *Philosophical Inquiry* 3.2 (1981) 63–83.
Neusner, Jacob. *Invitation to the Talmud*. New York: Harper & Row, 1984.
Nisbett, Richard, and Lee Ross. *Human Interference: Strategies and Shortcomings of Social Judgement*. Englewood Cliffs, NJ: Prentice-Hall, 1980.
Palmer, Parker. *To Know as We Are Known*. New York: Harper & Row, 1983.
Paul, Richard. "Critical Thinking and the Challenge of Modern Education." In *Critical Thinking as a Philosophical Movement*, edited by Seale Doss, 15–42. Ripon, WI: Ripon College Press, 1989.
———. "Critical Thinking in North America: A New Theory of Knowledge Learning and Literacy." In *Argumentation* 3, (1989) 197–235.
———. *Critical Thinking: What Every Person Needs To Survive in a Rapidly Changing Word*. Edited by A. J. A. Binker. Rohnert Park, CA: Center for Critical Thinking and Moral Critique, 1990.
———. "The Critical Thinking Movement: A Historical Perspective." *National Forum*, 65 (1985) 2–3, 32.
———. "Dialogical Thinking: Critical Thought Essential to the Acquisition of Rational Knowledge and Passions." In *Critical Thinking: What Every Person Needs To Survive in a Rapidly Changing World*, edited by A. J. A. Binker, 204–23. Rohnert Park, CA: Center for Critical Thinking and Moral Critique, 1990.
Peirce, Charles S. *Philosophical Writings by Peirce*. Edited by Justus Buchler. New York: Dover, 1940.
Perkins, D. N. "Creativity and the Quest for Mechanism." In *The Psychology of Human Thought*, edited by Robert Sternberg and Edward Smith, 309–36. Cambridge: Cambridge University Press, 1988.
Philo of Alexandria. *Loeb Classical Library*, Vols. I–IX. Cambridge: Harvard University Press, 1929.
Pieper, Josef. *Leisure: The Basis of Culture*. San Francisco: Ignatius, 2009.
Plantinga, Alvin. "Epistemic Justification." *Nous* 20.1 (1986) 3–18.
———. "Justification in the Twentieth Century." *Philosophical and Phenomenological Research* Vol. 1, Supplement (1990) 45–71.
———. *Warrant: The Current Debate*. New York: Oxford University Press, 1993.
———. *Warrant and Proper Function*. New York: Oxford University Press, 1993.
Plato. *The Last Days of Socrates*. New York: Penguin, 2010.
———. *Protagoras and Meno*. New York: Penguin, 1980.
———. *The Republic*. Edited by Francis Cornford. London: Oxford University Press, 1945.
Polanyi, Michael. *Meaning*. Chicago: University of Chicago Press, 1975.
Pollock, John L. *Contemporary Theories of Knowledge*. Totowa, NJ: Rowman & Littlefield, 1986.

Quine, W. V., and J. S. Ullian. *The Web of Belief*. New York: Random House, 1978.
Reid, Thomas. *Inquiry and Essays*. Edited by Keith Lehrer and Ronald Beanblossom. Indianapolis, IN: The Library of Liberal Arts, 1975.
Rokeach, Milton. *The Open and Closed Mind*. New York: Basic, 1960.
Rorty, Richard. *Philosophy and the Mirror of Nature*. Princeton, NJ: Princeton University Press, 1979.
Ross, Lee, and Mark Lepper. "The Perseverance of Beliefs: Empirical and Normative Considerations." *New Directions for Methodology of Social and Behavioral Science* 4 (1980) 17–36.
Sayers, Dorothy. *The Mind of the Maker*. New York: Meridan, 1956.
Scheffler, Israel. *Conditions of Knowledge: An Introduction to Epistemology and Education*. Glenview, IL: Foresman, 1963.
———. "In Praise of Cognitive Emotions." *Teachers College Record* 79.2 (1977) 171–86.
———. "Philosophical Models of Teaching." *Harvard Educational Review* 35.2 (1965) 188–200.
———. *Reason and Teaching*. New York: Bobbs-Merrill, 1973.
Shuell, Thomas J. "Cognitive Conceptions of Learning." *Review of Educational Research* 56.4 (1986) 411–36.
Siegel, Harvey. *Educating Reason: Rationality, Critical Thinking and Education*. London: Routledge, 1988.
Solzenitsyn, Alexander. *The Solzenitsyn Reader*. Edited by Edward Ericson, Jr. and Daniel Mahoney. Wilmington, DE: ISI, 2009.
Sosa, Ernest. "Knowledge and Intellectual Virtue." *The Monist* 68 (1985) 224–45.
———. *Knowledge in Perspective: Selected Essays In Epistemology*. Cambridge: Cambridge University Press, 1991.
Sternberg, Robert J. "Teaching Critical Thinking: Are We Making Critical Mistakes?" *Phi Delta Kappan*, 67 (1985) 194–98.
Stich, Stephen P. "Could Man be an Irrational Animal? Some Notes on the Epistemology of Rationality." In *Naturalizing Epistemology*, edited by Hilary Kornblith, 249–67. Cambridge: MIT Press, 1985.
———. *The Fragmentation of Reason*. Cambridge: MIT Press, 1990.
Taylor, Charles. "Overcoming Epistemology." In *After Philosophy: End or Transformation?* edited by Kenneth Baynes et al., 464–88. Cambridge: MIT Press, 1987.
———. "Responsibility for Self." In *The Identity of Persons*, edited by Amelie Oksenberg Rorty, 281–99. Berkeley, CA: University of California Press, 1976.
Tversky, Amos, and Daniel Kahneman. "The Framing of Decisions and the Psychology of Choice." In *Rational Choice*, edited by Jon Elster, 123–41. New York: New York University Press, 1986.
Tversky, Amos, and George A Quattrone. "Self Deception and the Voters Illusion." In *The Multiple Self*, edited by Jon Elster, 35–58. Cambridge: Cambridge University Press, 1987.
Walzer, Michael. *Interpretation and Social Criticism*. Cambridge: Harvard University Press, 1987.
Wason, P. C "On the Failure to Eliminate Hypotheses in a Conceptual Task." *Quarterly Journal of Experimental Psychology* 12 (1960) 129–40.
West, Cornel. *The American Evasion of Philosophy: A Genealogy of Pragmatism*. Madison, Wi: University of Wisconsin press, 1989.

BIBLIOGRAPHY

Wolterstorff, Nicholas. "Can Belief in God Be Rational If It Has No Foundations?" In *Faith and Rationality*, edited by Alvin Plantinga and Nicholas Wolterstorff, 135–89. Notre Dame, IN: University of Notre Dame Press, 1983.
———. *Reason within the Bounds of Religion*. Grand Rapids: Eerdmans, 1984.

www.ingramcontent.com/pod-product-compliance
Lightning Source LLC
Chambersburg PA
CBHW070328230426
43663CB00011B/2255